# Sunspot Literary Journal

## 2021



Creativity is Power

Sunspot Literary Journal 2021
Volume 3 Issue 4
*Creativity is power*

Published by Sun Dogs Creations
*Changing the World One Book at a Time*
Print ISBN: 978-1-951389-13-0
eBook ISBN: 978-1-951389-26-0

Cover Image *Blind* by Taylor Moon, Geminga Runner-up
Cover Design by Angel Leya
Sunspot Logo by Timothy Boardman



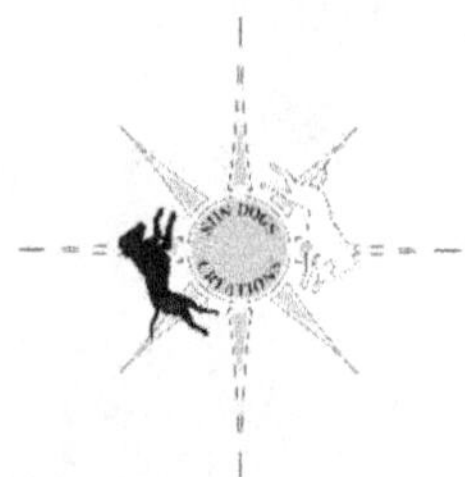

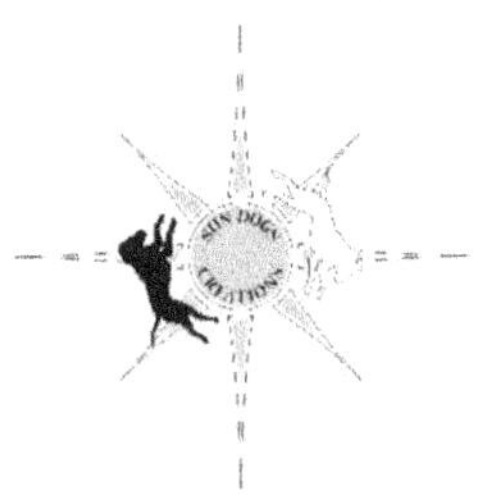

# Table of Contents

**Inception 2020**



**Culmination 2020**



**Geminga 2021**

**Rigel 2021**

# THE DOVES

SUSAN LANDGRAF

After "The White Dove,"
a photograph by Tracey Ranauro

The famous dove flew back
from the flooded land with a branch for Noah.

After the animals made up for lost time
mating among the grasses, on the sand, in the sea,
and air, Noah got drunk.

No mention about what Noah and his family
ate on board—maybe one less chicken or hare
at the end—or whether Noah had stocked
wine to last or this was the only bottle.

These days bigger boats and ample wineries—
no passenger pigeons, dodo birds or
Rabbs' fringe-limbed tree frogs—
just this dove in black and white on the page

in a forest of trunks
knifed with initials and hearts.

# Preparing to Eat the Forbidden Fruit

Susan Landgraf

Haloed at the kitchen sink by the ceiling light bulb,
I rap the pomegranate with a dinner knife's flat handle
to let the seeds know they're being
opened to the world.
I cut the thick red skin with a sharp knife.

My flesh wants the feel of my lover's hands, his lips
and loins, but he is not here, just me
in a trance-like state
with the pomegranate, knives, and bowl.
I look out the unblinded window, listen
to the translucent seeds fall louder than the rain
washing the glass.

I take my bowl to the table and to whomever
it was—Eve or a gardener
who first opened
this fruit—I give thanks.
I picture my lover in candlelight.
I eat.

# With Norma on the Reservation at Tahola

Susan Landgraf

*Your color is bright yellow but there's a dark spot.*
*Think about your lost child who needs a ceremony,*
        child lost when I didn't know my body,
        child no bigger than a raindrop.
She says I can find myself after I watch a thousand waves.

Norma hires a fishing boat to bury her adopted brother
at Shi Shi in the old people's way.
        She leans over the railing, lays a wreath
        on the blue-black waves. I spread carnations.
An eagle circles. A whale.
*They are witness.*

Before she felt the weight of her people's lost voices,
she remembers running in high grasses with the wind.
        She drapes the medicine shawl over her shoulders.
        Waves sage smoke. Sings the old songs.
Her legs black and withered, she runs her wheelchair
in a singular track. Says, *Heal thyself.*

Norma translates cedar talk. But of the screeching gulls,
she has no transcription. *They are either lonely or crazy.*
        Either way they will continue to shriek,
        though the wind always wins.

*It is a constant, like the moon's cycles.*
*Like the sacred cedars that talk to themselves underground.*

On my last visit, she is making wreaths with faux berries,
miniature totem poles and gulls for tourists,
        though few come north anymore. They stop
        at the casino in Ocean Shores.
*I can't see*, she tells me, *I can't see.*
She locks the healing shawl in a cupboard.

I go to the sea and watch the waves.
Sometimes eagles, sometimes whales.
        And once, dear Norma, I found a stone
        that looks like a half moon.

# DANDELION GIRLS

KATE KOENIG

Mama scooped my tongue out with a melon baller,
licked my tears away with the swipe of her worn thumb,
and told me that tongues were for ladies
with mouths that grew flowers.
And my mouth was full of weeds.

She added my tongue to a mixing bowl of skinned knees,
peeled off from last weekend after I wrestled the neighbor boy,
who lived in the house that smelled like honeysuckle
and who rained firefly light into my fists.

Mama warned me enough to mind my mouth,
pouring soil down my throat 'til I swallowed Midwest sun.
A lady speaks in perfume whispers
and blushes sweet cherry cheeks,
and I was old enough to bloom my garden.

Oh, I cried as she fed my tongue to the hounds.
They could holler all the words now lost to me,
and in turn, all the skinned knees I grew were devoured
until I forgot how it felt to plant my shin against earth.

In the quiet afternoon while Mama was inside,
I consumed dandelions by the fistful,
watered my mouth with tears that tasted like echoes
until my mouth sprouted a golden halo,
and feasted yellow until my head sprouted florets.

Dandelion girls don't need tongues to spread testimony.
They carry their stories in the veil of wind,
voices molting golden bursts to white wisps
that only know how to spread, to spread, to spread.

Watch me bloom, Mama.
Watch me bloom.

Ghost Rider / GJ Gillespie

# The Bird Room

Lyndsey Kelly Weiner

Our third pass
through the bird room at the zoo
trailing our boy with his fistful of seeds

acrid humidity clings
to our winter coats and hats
toes slick in the front of my boot

Luzon Bleeding-Hearts
white chests with a running wound-mark of red
the placard says not to worry

our boy points at his father's wool jacket
a brown and white smear by the zipper
drips onto his jeans and leather boot

lifting antibacterial wipes from my purse
I kneel
wadding the smeared ones in a pile on the water-beaded floor

it's been half our son's life since I've touched his father
Boobys and Birds of Paradise cock their heads and blink their beady eyes
*there* our son says

# Ragamala

Brian L. Jacobs

I never wanted a home
nor a *Lotus Sutra*
I am not a lotus eater

a home
is a place

to hang
history

floating
in etymological
*soundfacts*

a privilege
that is created

by language
illusions

orange heavily
hung my welcome'd neck

my funeral
sewn into scented *mala*
pollinated bead *mantras*

un god'd
in which I gallow

# I (On the Death of My Wife)

Paul Rousseau

1. I tread on paper-thin hope.
   She is sick.
2. I behave as though the days are routine.
3. I am in denial.
4. I am an asshole.
5. I hear the coughs and hard breaths, like stones cluttering her throat.
6. I slip behind closed doors to confess my fear.
7. I weep in darkened stairwells.
8. I lean on lavatory sinks and stare into mirrors.
9. I am lost.
10. I want to disappear.
11. I hear, "All organs have failed. It's just a matter of time."
12. I am regretful.
13. I am helpless.
14. I am alone.
15. I am grieving.
16. I know she is dying.
17. I know her dreams are as far away as forever.
18. I know the thump of her heart will cease.
19. I know the silence will be loud.
20. I know the silence will be death.

# The Epigrams Roam Free

Michael Brosnan

A line I read last night, waiting for dinner guests to arrive:
"What we understand and love understands and loves us also."

This was on page 67 of Robert Walser's strange and sad
and lonely novel, The Walk, which was published in 1957, when

I was 2½ and had enough language to beg my mother
for a small turtle, which died soon after I named it.

I read lines like Walser's on occasion. I underline them.
Write them down. But never fully fathom them.

I feel like the terrier staring down the garden gnome,
thinking, "Friend or foe?"

Later in The Walk, the protagonist says brightly,
before his psychic collapse,

"How beautiful is beauty, how charming is charm!"
I read this after the dinner guests left

and the peepers in the neighboring swamp
had reached the peak of their pressing chorus.

I know now not what they mean,
but why, in the web of nights, they must keen.

# Birthday Wish List

Sarah O. Oso

A porcelain pot for the geraniums at my window
who tilt their pink little faces toward what shines
I want three days in the life of a bluebird,
          a coffee-maker,
breath for my chest's ardent heart

One conversation with Ms. Gwendolyn Brooks
and a trip to Maine, up spiral stairs, to the top
of any lighthouse born to beam the savage sea

A way of lassoing back those words I don't mean

Bring me a sandalwood guitar with strings that sing,
two packs of cigarettes from Seville

I'll take a sweater that fits—in sophisticated rouge red,
and your remembering me as love outlasting a season,
          a few new dance moves,
the heavy of a grandad's hand on shoulder

Been dreaming of
knowing the difference between practical & pragmatic,
a sudden discovery of all lost socks,
one circle of incense from a place that's not here,
          the kind that, not too fast,
burns and burns through passing nights,
without ever turning to ash

# CONQUERED / MARY SENTER

# Dandelion Wine

Alan P. Marks

Driving into town he felt like a stranger. He hadn't been back at all since he'd cleaned out the old house when his father died five years back and, if he thought about it, he hadn't been there all that much in the five years before that. All those little changes, the things that you hardly even notice if you see them while they're happening, were suddenly all piled up, one on top of the other. A new house here and there. Some that he remembered—or at least thought he remembered—not there anymore. He couldn't quite say what was new and what was missing. There was just this sense that the landscape had shifted on him somehow.

It was less like coming home—odd that he still thought of it as "home," quotes and all—and more like going someplace you'd only read about. It seemed familiar but the details didn't quite fit with the picture you had in your head.

Worried that he might not make it in time, he'd ended up being too early, so he pulled over just down the street from the church and parked. Farther down, temporary *Funeral Parking Only* signs had been staked out along the side of the street. He couldn't actually read them from where he sat but that neat line of orange rectangles across the street from the church couldn't be anything else. Other than that, though, nothing said it was anything other than a normal Saturday morning. No hearse. No grieving family.

The idea had been to mix in with the crowd going in and sit in the back, then sneak out quietly at the end of the service. Not a great plan if you showed up almost an hour before everyone else.

From where he was parked, he could see all the way to the end of Main Street. Buggy's Market wasn't there anymore, but he'd known that already. Except in the back of his mind, Buggy's had always been there and that meant it would always be there, mean old Mrs. Wilson still behind the counter. But they'd knocked it down almost fifteen years ago, not long after Mrs. Wilson died. The way they told it, she'd been hollering at some kid she'd caught stealing and had dropped dead of a heart attack right there behind the register. Scared the hell out of the kid who'd dropped whatever it was he'd been trying sneak out with and had run screaming out of store. That was how they told it, anyway.

There was a bank there now.

A little farther down the street was a Rite Aid. That was new since his father died. He couldn't quite see it—the building was just a bit too far back from the road—but the sign for it was visible and he didn't really need anything more than that. One Rite Aid was pretty much the same as the next. You could see it even if you couldn't actually see it.

Most of the rest of Main Street was still familiar, though. Some new paint. A new sign here and there. But when he closed his eyes, he found that the picture in his head had at least the same basic outline.

It surprised him a bit, just how glad he was of that.

In his mind's eye, he could keep going down past the Rite Aid and around the bend right after. Just beyond that there was a flashing yellow light—still the town's only traffic light—marking the turn onto Miller's Road. A left there and he could go a couple miles along and be at the old house.

Somebody else lived there now, though, and they were welcome to it so, in his mind, he didn't go any farther than the bridge.

***She** was sitting on the rock wall just on the other side of the bridge, whoever she was.*

*He could see her there from his side of the stream but, until he was most of the way across, all she was to him was a pair of legs.*

*Bare legs.*

*Bare swinging feet.*

*They shimmered like a mirage in the late morning heat.*

*He slowed a little crossing the bridge, taking his time. She might know he was there. Could probably hear him. But if he couldn't see her face, then she couldn't see his. Couldn't see him looking at her.*

*They were thin, those legs, on the bony side maybe, but long and tanned dark even this early in the summer. In his sixteen-year-old's imagination, the rest of her might have worn just as little as those legs. For a moment, at least, she was nothing but possibilities.*

*The reality wasn't as good as the fantasy, of course—it never would be—but it wasn't all bad either. She was leaning back, resting on her hands, so she revealed herself to him a piece at a time the closer he got. Faded jean shorts, cut off so high he wasn't sure how they still held together at the bottom, high enough to show a line of white skin above the tan line. Exposed belly, as brown as the legs, maybe more so, and even from a distance he could see it slick with sweat and with the cheap coconut suntan oil he could smell the closer he got. A faded flannel work shirt, too heavy for a day like this, but with the arms torn off at the shoulders, and tied up tight under her breasts. From the shape of that shirt, it didn't look like there was anything else underneath. Maybe that was just more sixteen-year-old's imagination. Maybe not.*

*He was suddenly aware of the sweat dripping down the middle of his back.*

*She nodded to him and he leaned up against the wall next to her, saying hello as he did. He knew her a little, knew who she was, anyways—it'd be almost impossible not to in a town so small— though he'd never talked to her before. She'd be a senior in the fall, a year ahead of him, and she ran with a different crowd.*

*Her house was on the far other side of town but it turned out she had pretty much the same problem he did, the same reason for being outside on a day as unbearable as this one instead of inside where it might still be hot but would at least be out of the sun. She was hiding out from her mother instead of her father the way he was, but both their parents seemed to share the opinion that hanging around doing nothing wasn't the best way for a kid to spend the summer. It was dangerous to be too much in their line of sight unless you wanted something terrible to happen, like being made to get a job, or worse, being put to work unpaid around the house if there weren't any real jobs to be found. That she was all the way over on his side of town just meant that she had felt the need to get the heck outta Dodge earlier in the day than he had.*

*As if his showing up was what she'd been waiting for, she slid off her perch, into an old pair of sneakers, and started walking back towards town. There was something she needed to get, she said. She didn't wait for him but didn't seem to be in much of a hurry, either. It looked as if it was up to him whether he tagged along or not. He'd been headed that direction anyway, so he fell in beside her and, when she didn't look his way, he figured that she'd been pretty sure he would.*

*They didn't talk much while they walked. A little bit about their unfair treatment at the hands of their respective parents covered most of what seemed important, and it was too hot for much else. It was just over a mile back into town and it took almost half an hour to cover the distance. There was no reason to hurry, even if they wanted to.*

*Besides, killing the day was kind of the whole point.*

*They stopped at a rundown little store just at the end of Main Street. Buggy's, for some reason he never knew. He'd never heard of anyone called that and it had been old Mrs. Wilson who'd run the place as long as he could remember. Everyone who knew her thought that* Bitchy's *might have been a better name for the place.*

*Just before they went inside, she fished a couple of sweaty bills out her pocket (the struggle to do so making him aware all over again just how small those shorts were) and stuffed them into his hand, asking him to grab her a pack of cigarettes. It didn't matter what brand. Whatever was cheapest. Generics. Whatever. Before he could ask her why she couldn't get her own smokes, she disappeared into the back of the store leaving him to face Mrs. Wilson.*

*Either that or bail.*

*Did his father know he'd started smoking? Didn't he know that it was a filthy habit? Was he even old enough to buy cigarettes? No, Mrs. Wilson, he didn't. Yes, Mrs. Wilson, it was a filthy habit. Yes, Mrs. Wilson, sixteen and a half.*

*And then she took his money just like she was always going to. As she reached into the case behind the register, he caught a glimpse out of the corner of his eye of blonde hair and tanned skin heading out the door.*

*No, not that one Mrs. Wilson, drawing her attention to him as her head started to swing towards the door.*

*But you said . . .*

*Oh, you're right, Mrs. Wilson. Sorry. My mistake.*

*Outside again he couldn't find her until he went around behind the store out of sight from the street. Yes, Mrs. Wilson, no Mrs. Wilson, she mocked, but she was smiling and laughing and holding out one of the four bottles of Narragansett she'd lifted from the cooler in the back of the store, the top already popped. So, he didn't take it too personally.*

*Careful not to let the already sweating bottle slip out of his hand, he traded the smokes for it. He could see hers was already half empty but mostly he was wondering how she'd gotten them open and thinking there definitely wasn't any bottle opener hiding in those shorts.*

*She took the cigarettes from him but then, laughing still, flipped the pack into the dumpster beside her. Didn't he know that smoking was filthy habit, she said, and this time her impersonation was so dead on that he laughed along with her, taking a drink as he did.*

*It was piss, but at least it was icy piss and he finished half of his own bottle in one long swallow. Why, he wanted to know, hadn't she grabbed something good? She wasn't paying anyway, so why go for the cheap shit?*

*If he didn't like it, she smiled, he could always give it back, but he tipped the bottle back out of her reach and finished the rest. She did the same, and then both empties followed the pack of cigarettes.*

*They wandered aimlessly through town, each cradling one of the leftover bottles in a way that, as long as someone wasn't looking too closely, it could just as easily have been root beer. She wanted to save them for later. His had left a soapy taste in his mouth and he thought he'd probably let her have them both if she wanted.*

*The drink had loosened them up a bit, or maybe it was just that it had cooled them off, at least for a little while. Or maybe they were just easier with each other after their shared bit of larceny even if he hadn't known that was what it was at the time. They talked more now than they had before.*

*Nothing that really mattered much. He'd just gotten his license, for all the good it did him since he never got to take the truck. She might be spending some of the summer at her cousin's in the southern part of the state. He really hoped Mrs. Wilson didn't tell his father that he'd been buying cigarettes. Eventually they'd talked their way back out of town, by accident or design heading in the direction of her house a few miles away.*

*Every so often, she'd sneeze, a silly, squeaky little thing that hardly sounded real, but that made her whole body shake when she did. Allergies, she said. Pollen that he'd never have known was there if she hadn't told him.*

*The sun was at their backs, just starting down in the afternoon sky, and it burned the back of his neck in a way that didn't bother too much then but that he'd regret later on. It seemed even hotter now than before, if that was possible, and soon enough their talk dried back up.*

*His heart did a little jump when she took his hand, her fingers sliding in between his, but he tried not to let it show. Hers was quite a bit smaller, and damp, though not in a bad way. Warm in a way he didn't mind. He was hot and sticky and uncomfortable everywhere else, but this was nice.*

**A** *mile or so out from town, but still a ways from where she lived, they turned off down a small side road. The trees pulled up closer to the broken pavement down that way and, if the air was even more still because of it, at least there was shade.*

*If they kept on that way long enough—too far to walk even on a cool day—it would eventually take them to the next town over. Not that they would want to even if they could. If their town was small, that one was little more than a wide spot in the road, something most people would barely notice driving through on their way to someplace else. But it was a quiet place to walk if you didn't have anywhere in particular you needed to get to. There were no houses along that stretch, no cars coming either way to drive them out from the middle of the road, each of them swinging a now warm (and probably undrinkable) beer in one hand. The fingers of the others still laced together.*

*He wasn't sure if it meant anything or not. Probably not. But he didn't let go and neither did she.*

*At the bottom of one long hill he wondered aloud if maybe they ought to turn back. It was stifling, even in the shade of the trees, and he could see that those pulled back from the sides of the road towards the top of the hill and they'd be back out in the sun. Since they weren't really going anywhere, the hill didn't seem worth the effort. She didn't answer but just kept walking.*

*It was either let go of her hand or keep up, so he didn't argue the point.*

*The trees didn't just pull back a little near the top, he discovered. Instead, they disappeared completely and there were wide rolling fields on either side of the road. Overgrown with dandelions, they were more yellow than green and almost too bright to look at after having been so long in the shade.*

*As if on cue, she sneezed again, and even he could see the pollen floating in the sunlight now, could see it caked in yellow streaks in the dirt along the edge of the road where it had been washed the last time it rained. His own nose itched, but maybe more from the idea of it than anything.*

*Tugging at his hand, she drew him off the side of the road to the right. Two small trails like old tire tracks—which was probably what they were—just as overgrown as the rest but more green than yellow, wound across the field tracing a lazy arc towards the treeline off in the distance, disappearing behind a rise part of the way there. They followed along that track, winding as it did, keeping in between the two trails of green as if it were the obvious thing to do.*

*When they were out of sight of the road, she finally pried her fingers out of from his and sank down onto the ground into the bed of yellow, closing her eyes against the sun, the almost forgotten beer rolling away into the grass. His hand missed the feel of hers but seeing her stretched out in the sunlight made up for it, made him think of first seeing her next to the bridge.*

*She cocked one eye open, catching him staring. Embarrassed, but not sure he should be, he dropped down beside her. The ground felt cool underneath him, even more so in contrast with the sun beating down, but the grass scratched against the sunburned back of his neck in a way that made it hard for him to relax. When her hand slipped back into his, he stopped worrying about the grass or his sunburn, but it didn't do much to relax him. If anything, her hand was warmer than before. Or maybe that was just his imagination.*

*It wasn't his imagination when she squeezed his hand, though. He squeezed hers back.*

*She sighed and he could almost hear her shaking her head. While he was still trying to figure out if there had been some sort of signal he hadn't picked up on, she was suddenly leaning over him, her long hair hanging down in his face, her mouth pressed against his. She tasted faintly of Narragansett and something else he couldn't quite tell, but that wasn't unpleasant. The scent of coconut, faint and in the background all afternoon, now strong in his face.*

*All of a sudden, his shorts felt uncomfortably tight, but he tried to stay focused on the taste of her and the smell of her, and not on how much he wanted to reach down and adjust himself. He didn't want to look like he was reading more into things than she might mean. Didn't want to look like a dumb kid.*

*But then her leg swung over him and the tightness increased, painful now but also not as she pressed down on him, her lips never quite leaving his the whole time and that taste mixed in with the staleness of cheap beer growing stronger as he ran his tongue over the salt of her sweat. Afterwards he could never be sure how long they stayed like that, her face against his—the pleasure/pain of her on top of him—before she reached down to his waistband, shoving it down just far enough.*

*Somehow, she'd slid out of those shorts without him ever realizing. Maybe before she'd kissed him. Maybe during. He could feel her, warm and soft as she moved against him. And then a sudden shiver as she reached down to guide him into her. The same hand that had held his. The same feel of skin on skin. The same, but not the same. Not even close.*

*Her lips finally left his as she moved over him, her hair tenting his face, playing back and forth over it, making him keep his eyes closed even though she shaded him from the sun.*

*And the heat of her breath.*

*And the salt of sweat as it dripped off her face.*

*He reached up underneath her, fumbling at the knot of her shirt, wanting to find out if he was right about what wasn't underneath it, and she pushed herself up, sitting back on him, her weight pressing down wonderfully as she undid it herself showing him that he had been.*

*She stayed that way, her own eyes closed, hardly moving, the whiteness of her breasts stark against the brown of her shoulders, her neck, her stomach.*

*And then she sneezed.*

*One of those silly little sneezes that shook her whole body and she tightened around him and suddenly he was reaching down and grabbing her hips, pulling her harder to him and she was grabbing his shoulders and doing the same.*

*And then she was laughing in his ear and rolling breathlessly off him to lie again on the grass beside him.*

*When he'd finally caught his own breath and looked over at her, he was disappointed to discover that she'd already pulled her shorts back on again, just as quickly and as mysteriously as she had taken them off.*

*Her shirt still lay open, though, and after fixing his own shorts he propped himself on one elbow and let his eyes wander over her. He'd never forget how she looked lying there like that, watching him as he watched her, smiling as she did.*

*But he'd always wish he'd gotten a look before she'd put those shorts back on.*

*They sat in the shade of a half-fallen tree and drank the last two beers. She had tied her shirt back the way it had been before, only now there was a dandelion tucked down into the v of it. His eyes kept being drawn back to it, which was probably why she had done it.*

*The beer was warm, but it was wet and it didn't seem to taste so bad as it had before. It wasn't exactly fine wine, maybe, but maybe it wasn't piss after all.*

***W**hen they got back to the main road, she turned one way towards home, and he turned the other. He'd hoped she might slip her hand back into his while they had walked, but she never did.*

***H**e did end up getting a job that summer, one that actually paid, and he found out later that she had ended up at her cousin's place down south. By the time school started in the fall and he saw her again, she had a boyfriend, another senior. They stayed together all that year, though it didn't last much past graduation.*

*She was a year ahead of him and they hung with different crowds.*

*Every once in a while, though, when they were passing in the hallway, she would brush up against him, giving a funny little sneeze, a hint of a smile on her face as she did.*

**T**hey'd started showing up without his realizing it.

The hearse had pulled up out front and a lot of the spaces right across the street from the church were filled. He hadn't seen the casket go in, though. He was pretty sure he would have noticed that at least. It must have been inside already, in place long before the family got there.

Dark suits and dresses. A few sunglasses, even though it was cloudy. Your basic funeral uniform. But not a lot of familiar faces. A couple that he thought he might recognize but not enough to put names to. Not after so many years.

The husband he'd definitely never seen before, and he hadn't recognized the name in her obituary. He thought he'd heard that she'd married someone from away, so that made sense. He looked like a decent enough guy, at least from a distance. For whatever that was worth.

Seemed older than she had been.

He had his arms around the shoulders of two young girls, maybe nine and eleven. Maybe a little older. Their daughters.

Her daughters.

The younger of the two was already crying and the older one didn't look like she was far behind. The obituary had said she had "died suddenly," code that could mean anything from an unexpected heart attack to a car accident to swallowing a bottle of pills. Whatever it was, they had the shellshocked look of people who hadn't seen it coming.

They looked just like her. Even from a distance he could see it in their faces. Could see her face. This had been a mistake.

Starting the car, he pulled away from the curb and drove slowly past the gathering mourners and on up Main Street. These people were strangers to him, even the ones he might have known once upon a time.

She was a stranger. A dream he'd had a long time ago.

The funeral was for someone he'd never met.

**B**uggy's might not be there anymore, but he wasn't the least surprised to find that they carried Narragansett at the Rite Aid, even if he had to settle for cans. By the time he headed back the way he had come, a six pack on the seat beside him, the street in front of the church was empty. The mourners had all moved inside.

He kept his eyes on the road in front of him as he drove past.

**H**e shut the car off but left the keys in the ignition when he got out, bringing the beer with him. He wouldn't be there long.

There was that same 'there but not there' feeling that he'd had in town, everything only half-remembered. The basic details were there, but not quite the way they were supposed to be.

It should be sunny and hot, not cloudy. He shouldn't have to keep his suit jacket on to stay comfortable in the wind. And even if his eyes could almost see those long-gone tire tracks winding through the field, there were no dandelions. The season wasn't right for it. The field was all tall grass, brown instead of green, and the only yellow was in his memory.

The beer was the same, though. Still tasted like piss.

But no, that was wrong, too. It was too cold. That had been behind Buggy's, not up here. He should have grabbed some from off the shelf instead of out of the cooler, but he knew it wouldn't really have made a difference.

It hadn't been being warm that had made it taste good.

He finished it anyway, pitching the empty into the ditch when he was done and leaving the other five sitting on the edge of the road. He hoped maybe some high school kid would come along and find them. You had to be a certain age to appreciate that stuff.

Then he climbed back in the car and turned around towards home. This place wasn't that. Not home. Not anymore. Maybe it never had been. At least not the place he had in his mind.

That place might never have existed at all.

# CORRELATION IS CAUSATION

HEIKKI HUOTARI

To the horseless carriage I say get a horse. The naked eye sees two of everything but averages the brace of quail. Dear Liza, in this galaxy there's no black hole, dear Liza, with what should I fix it? As distracted, these contributors are mere participants. Their honorifics migrate night and day. They're oppositely gendered of their own volition. Innocently and or legally, their names have changed. One twin surrounds another in a glut of love. As my convergence is conditional, to sum to any number I'll be reconfigured. Stake your claim; I'll cry for me and mine. As fear is focused barely satiated taste buds blossom and as sunburn and consumption of ice cream are correlated correlation is causation.

# NEVER

AMANDA WOODARD

Ruben's always really nice to me. He's like my dad or like a dad could be, I think. He treats me like I'm his daughter. He drives me around and lets me play CDs in his car: *Hey, Mickey* and *Will the Real Slim Shady Please Stand Up*. He laughs when I sing along to *Hot in Herre* on the radio.

"Do you even know what that means?" he asks me, his eyes shining. Passing car lights show me he's watching me and wanting to laugh, his dark hands lazy on the steering wheel.

"Yeah," I tell him because I do know sort of. They're getting naked. He's hot for sex. I probably know more than he thinks I do.

He half smiles and just drives. We're at Braum's again. He loves taking me to get ice cream, and I love going to get ice cream with him. I either get mint chocolate chip – my best friend's favorite – or milk 'n' cookies. I know that's boring, but it tastes good. I always eat the ice cream really fast, so it doesn't melt all over the car seat.

Usually, it's just me and Ruben. Sometimes, my best friend comes with me, and we sing *Hey, Mickey* really loud, and Ruben doesn't get mad at us.

One time, he said we could draw on him. We were in the sitting room together, and he was on the floor watching TV with his shirt off. He likes to have his shirt off when he's at home. I get it, I think. I like to sleep in my underwear—but I don't do that now that Mom and I are sleeping on Barbara's couch and loveseat. I guess they're Ruben's couches too since he's Barbara's boyfriend, but we tell people we're staying at Barbara's since that's Mom's friend.

Jessi slept over with me one time, and Ruben said we could draw on him, but he fell asleep, so we thought it'd be really funny to get nail polish and paint him too. It was pretty funny, but I guess Ruben didn't think so. Barbara told me in the morning he was mad about it because it wouldn't wash off, but Ruben never told me that.

Mom told me something weird today. She's a light sleeper because of her sleep apnea, so she wakes up at least halfway when she hears something. She heard something in the living room with us, so she opened her eyes and saw Ruben sitting on the couch I sleep on, and he was looking at me, sleeping.

"What are you doing?" she said.

"I just wanted to tell her goodbye before I went to work," he said.

And she went, "So, tell her."

And he did apparently, but I don't remember that. I'm not a light sleeper.

It's summertime, so Ruben took me to work with him. He works at a gas station behind the counter. People don't ask me why I'm there when they come in and see me sitting in a chair beside him. It's just the two of us. He doesn't work with anybody.

There's no paper here, but there are envelopes. Ruben is really good at drawing on them. He's like me: he never uses pencil. I like to use pen and make the mistakes part of the drawing. It's easier to shade with pencil though, like my mom taught me. She's an artist, but people only know that because I tell them. Well, except once she came to do pencil portraits of kids in my class in the second grade, and it felt really cool to have my mom be there, being an artist, but a couple of the kids got mad 'cause their portraits didn't look like them that much. Mommy rolled her eyes to me in the car when we left. "Well, they kept *moving*," she said. "What did they expect?"

Ruben doesn't draw kids. He doesn't even try to draw things that he sees, like Mom tells me to do, to practice, but I guess I get that. The things around here aren't all that interesting: sticky counter, cigarette cartons behind glass, oil on the concrete through the door. He draws scary clowns, but they look really cool. He shows me how to shade using pen. I show him the heart I draw, with a dagger stabbing through it and a ribbon around it that says something different every time I draw it. It could be one of his tattoos or maybe mine one day.

"That looks really good, Famanda." He calls me that, and I don't know why. He thinks it's funny. It's his nickname for me.

I've never really had anybody spend money on me before. Ruben takes me to the store to get some clothes. One of them is a striped, purple, sparkly shirt like one Jessi has, so now we can be twins. People already think we look alike; we both have dark, kind of wavy hair that goes to our shoulders, and we both wear glasses. She has green eyes though, and I'm bigger than her, wider. I wish I looked more like her.

He buys me some pants too, some bell bottoms. Mom says they're coming back in style. She liked them a lot when she was a teenager, back when her cousin Donna was alive. I don't really care about being "in style." A girl at school tried to show me that one time: how to be pretty, like Sandra Bullock on *Miss Congeniality*, except I liked her better at the beginning of the movie anyway.

We don't stop at Braum's on the way to Barbara's house. We go straight there.

"When we get home, Famanda" he tells me, "I want you to give me a fashion show." Fashion's fun when it's just pretend, so I tell him OK.

When we get there, it's just us. He has to go to the bathroom, he says. I'm sitting on the couch with the shopping bags next to me, crinkling when I move, and I realize I've never been alone at the house with him before, and I feel weird. Scared. But Ruben's never hurt me. *He wouldn't do something like Wes did, right? I'd know if it was going to happen again?*

A few days earlier, Ruben and me were sitting on the couch, watching *Jimmy Neutron*. Ruben loves that movie even more than I do, and we were wrestling. Mom and Barbara were probably outside on what Barbara calls "the stoop," since she's from New York, smoking their cigarettes.

Ruben teaches me how to wrestle in case a boy tries something one day. He doesn't know that I *hope* boys try something one day. I hope the boy I like will kiss me. We almost held hands once.

Ruben pushes me down on the couch and tickles me. I get free and tickle him back—that's how it usually goes. But the other day, he pushed me down into the couch, face down, and he got on my back, and he told me I needed to be careful, that boys better not get me in that position. He bounced on me once then let me up. It was quick, and he laughed a lot, so I knew he was just messing around.

We're alone now. Ruben is in the bathroom, and the bags are beside me. *Where will I change? What will Ruben say when he looks at me?*

The front door opens, and Barbara walks in. She brings in the smell of outside heat and cigarettes, and it's like when my mom surprises me and picks me up from school: the smell, that feeling.

"What are you doing here all by yourself?" she says.

"Ruben's in the bathroom," I say.

She looks at the shopping bags, and her little eyes squint and give her more wrinkles, but she doesn't say anything.

I'm in the car with Barbara and Mom. I'm having to put up my hand like a car visor to block the sun. My glasses magnify my eyes really big, so I'm scared that if I look at the sun just right, it'll do that anthill thing to my eyes. I wish I had sunglasses I could see through.

Mom's asking me about pictures she found at a car shop Ruben has a second job at—no, police found them there. *Why are police looking at his stuff?*

"They found some pictures of you," she says, and I know which ones she means. Ruben took me to the car shop once. It was just the two of us again, and he told me to take my glasses off. He wanted to take a picture of me without my glasses, so I could see how pretty I looked, except I already knew what I looked like. I had Jessi take a picture of me without my glasses on one time with her digital camera, and you could see my lazy eye. I forgot my glasses correct my lazy eye. I didn't want to take my glasses off in front of Ruben.

But he really wanted me to take them off; he wouldn't stop asking. So, I did it, and he took the picture, but I wrote on the back of it, on the white bar at the bottom, "He made me do it!" in case someone saw the picture and thought I was trying to be pretty.

"What does that mean?" Mom wants to know. "'He made me do it!'?"

I tell her; it's nothing bad. "Why?" I ask.

Mom looks at Barbara who doesn't say anything or even move her head. Her thick, red hair whisps around a little. Her cigarette ash doesn't blow back at me this time because my window's rolled up. Neither of us can tell what she's thinking.

Mom turns her head toward me, in the middle seat, talking to me out of the corner of her eye. "A girl has accused him of abusing her," she says. Some people say "molest," but when Mom and I talk about what her boyfriend did to me, we always say "abuse."

"But Ruben wouldn't do that!" I say. I almost shout it.

"He never did anythin' to you? You'd tell me?" Mom asks.

"Yeah, of course I would!"

"You know what to look for? What's inappropriate touchin'?"

"Oh my god, Mom!" She doesn't tell me not to say the Lord's name in vain this time because Barbara curses a lot. I think she's her best friend. "He never *touched* me." It disgusts me to have to say that.

"Good," Barbara says for the first time. "Good."

It was some girl who went with him to work sometimes. I don't know her name. She's older than me, fourteen. She's skinny and has straight blonde hair; that's what Barbara tells me. She said she saw the tapes of Ruben at the gas station with her, and he never did anything to that girl.

"And if he was going to do something like that," she says, "he'd do it to you. Look at you! You're fucking built. Why would he want some flat-chested little kid?"

My boobs are "developing"—that's what Mom says—and I don't like having to wear a bra now, but I feel grown up when Barbara talks about me like that.

Barbara laughs in her raspy, high-pitched way. Her voice cracks at the edge of each *ha,* like a boy. "He never touched you," she says, only half a question.

"Never," I answer anyway.

We're at court. I don't remember ever coming this far with my mom's boyfriend. I remember being little and having to tell a whole group of people what happened, and I remember that I kind of didn't look at them when I was talking, but it wasn't like on *Law & Order* with a judge and all that. Wes said he was guilty before we ever had to come to court.

I'm here with Barbara, and we're watching the case. Everything goes really slowly, and people say a lot of things that aren't true. We're sitting behind Ruben, and his hair is different, I think, or maybe I've just never seen it from behind.

The girl is on the witness stand. She's just like Barbara told me she'd be: skinny and blonde. I guess she's pretty. She talks slow, and I hear someone say she has a learning disability, but I don't know if I believe that. I can barely hear what she says, and I can't hold onto anything I hear. It's too many lies.

But in the car I'm thinking, *How did he meet her?* and *Why did he bring her with him to work? Where was I when that happened?*

Barbara says there will be more court dates, but I can't go again; I can't miss that much school. In the passenger seat, I read my book about teenage girls who become witches and try not to get carsick.

**I** learned, from what my grandma calls "crime shows," that people are innocent until proven guilty, but I guess that's not really true because Ruben has been in jail for a long time. He sends letters to Barbara and draws on the envelopes in pen. Scary clowns. Sometimes Barbara lets me have them.

Ruben's been in jail for months and months when Mom says she has something to tell me in the car. It's dark outside. I don't know where we're going; I'm usually just happy to be going somewhere.

I can see the outline of her head turn toward me when she says, "They found Ruben guilty." She sounds sorry, or maybe just sad.

I'm crying before I know it. It's all just coming out. I haven't seen him in a long time, and I didn't miss him every single day, but I did miss him. I do. He's the closest thing I've ever had to a dad, next to my uncle RJ, who doesn't even like to hug me now that I'm "developing."

"Honey, we gotta know," Mom says, looking at Barbara, who is talking this time, but I can't make it out. She's always talking so loudly: it's "fucking" this and "youse guys" that. I practiced not saying "y'all" anymore because of her. I want to be tough too. "Did he ever touch you?"

I'm crying really hard when I say it, so they can't understand me at first. "He *did*?!" they say at the same time, scared and angry.

"NO!" I sob. "HE DID-N'T!"

They're quiet in the car after that, and they just let me cry. I play with the necklace Ruben gave me to calm me down a little, to make me feel like he's here. It has a black, cloth string with a piece of coily glass on the end, and inside, it has this tiny piece of rice with my name written on it — my real name, not "Famanda" like he calls me. Like he used to.

# Stay Where I Can See You

Jessica Ripka

There's a fifth-grade class doing presentations on their family trees in the Greencastle Elementary School auxiliary room. There are sneaker stains on the peach linoleum floor and a heavy smell of chilled milk gone sour. And there's a girl with pink aviator frames and Sunday School skirts speaking into a microphone while wearing her best lace blouse. The girl is ten and talks about how her mother loves blue flowers and Danny Kaye musicals but is allergic to cats. How her father gets cream vanilla candles every Christmas and wears a bright orange Hawaiian shirt from their favorite thrift store. How she has an older brother and sister both with very straight hair and every night they all sing a song called "Circle of Prayer" in pale cotton pajamas to ask Jesus to help them get to heaven. How they also sing as a family on stage at church every week and the father wears a tie with a white feather on it but changes right back into his orange shirt the moment they're all off stage. How every time he's in that shirt, everyone says they could see him even with their eyes closed or from a hundred miles away.

A hundred miles is a very great distance – the girl knows this now that she is no longer in fifth grade. Now she is forty and living 2,634 miles away from every member of her family as well as that Greencastle Elementary School auxiliary room. Now the mother sings in the audience of a megachurch surrounded by strangers and the sister homeschools her children with a house full of guns. Now the brother lives in a mental hospital with a locked metal cabinet full of bagged pills. Now the girl wouldn't set a single foot into heaven even if she believed in it and the father lives in a seedy motel in Alabama with insulin shots and cheap sneakers; a cell phone without service. Sometimes the girl closes her eyes and tries to picture the curves of her father's clean-shaven face or the laugh in his voice. Sometimes all she can see is the back of that bright orange shirt walking further and further away. Sometimes she still hears him singing.

# Aunt Ellen

Reg Taylor

My aunt Ellen was born around 1900 in a part of Adelaide that is almost unchanged. The original Georgian bluestone homes are nearly all still standing and the plane trees shading its broad streets then are just taller now. It's still quiet, too, though people might have to wait till very late at night to imagine the distant twitch of trams or the clop of horses heading into the East End market, or the unsteady steps of some reveler making his way home.

For many years my aunt taught at one of Adelaide's best-known schools, and for a time shared its faculty with someone who was to become a famous writer later on. He and my aunt must have met at school and since the writer dwelt on the College premises and Aunt Ellen lived close by, they might have crossed paths outside school hours as well; she modestly astride her bicycle, he marching bareheadedly along on the sort of blazing day he apparently enjoyed. In an incident on which one the writer's best-known stories is based she might even, in the longest of long shots, have witnessed the teacher and an Asian pupil who had attempted to bribe him with a bag of golf clubs, getting into a taxi at the school. But it would be pointless trying to otherwise connect them; they were separated by age and milieus–Aunt Ellen was a loyal Methodist while the writer seemed to have spent most of the time outside school hours in pubs with cronies–which meant their orbits would have barely registered on each other's consciousness, and if they intersected left no trace at all.

Publicly, she recalled only a flamboyance he brought to the school's annual Gilbert and Sullivan productions, which might not in any case have been to her taste. I can imagine the young browbeaten boys being swept along by the writer's energy and exasperation, but she would no more have given way to any spell they and their mentor and the medium were trying to cast than to the parlays of some showground hypnotist. She came from what used to be called a "musical family," and I can imagine her damning with faint praise Sullivan's music with some phrase like, "Oh, it's good *fun* ..." which, were he able to have heard it, might have been an infuriating reminder to the composer of light opera's–and his own–limitations.

Unfortunately, the encouragement of her parents could not extend to endorsing their gifted daughter's ambition to become an opera singer: the professional stage to them being, like medicine, an unsuitable female choice of career, they forbade it, and so inflicted the first disappointment of her life.

She was almost twenty when the First World War ended, and with the numbers of physically and psychologically sound young men so reduced, lucky perhaps to meet a returned soldier who was quite intact. The conflict had impaired neither the young man's health nor his equanimity and he became a welcome visitor to the home until Aunt Ellen's parents learned he was a Roman Catholic and all further invitations to afternoon tea were withdrawn.

It's sad and surely unfair, that love or its approximation seems to be handed out so inequitably in life, so that some become almost jaded from their enjoyment of affection while others live self-deluded and ultimately ruinous lives without it. Once Aunt Ellen's love, if she conceded her feelings that luxury, went unrequited, it was never to be granted another repository and for the rest of her working life her maternal feelings, at least, had to be spent on a new troop of small boys each year who, while their company might not stale, could never disappoint or please her as much as if they were her own.

Each Christmas she was rewarded with parent-wrapped chocolates and cakes and embroidered handkerchiefs from outgoing students, who most probably forgot her as fast as she did them, unless one of them rose to eminence in later life when her recollection of them in some phrase like "little *wretch*" could deprecate both their infant predisposition to impertinence or dirtiness or savagery, and any claim to adult distinction.

I was never quite sure what she thought of us, her sister's children. I can remember her restrained shows of amusement in our company which might have only veiled her disapproval. She *was* kind: apart from the five-

and ten-shilling postal notes she awarded us on birthdays she once sent up from Adelaide a package of football boots abandoned by their original owners, but otherwise she seemed most reluctant to stray far from her natural environs—until one year, while she was getting over an illness, and her employers, in a civilized example of the conservative ethos, had invited her to take extra time off on half-pay–she accepted an invitation to come and spend some time with us.

I don't know if, or how soon after her arrival, she missed home but she stayed on, perhaps out of loyalty, so she could attend rehearsals of the local Gilbert and Sullivan Society with her sister. They were performing *The Mikado* that year and my mother, thrust into a lead role by the resignation of one of the perennial principals, might have been glad of her elder sister's support. The resident diva who had assumed by right the lead soprano role for years had this year, in a gesture casting invidious reflections upon her maturity she contended, been invited to take the part of the ageing and vengeful Katisha, instead of her youthful and traditionally appealing rival Yum-Yum. High words were exchanged between her and the school teacher-director but in the end her protest was self-sacrificial and she went, leaving memories of her tendency to forget large chunks of dialogue under pressure and a way of negotiating high notes that reminded some listeners of a car changing gears.

On the very first evening, however, when the sisters attended rehearsals together the Company was in a state of crisis. A no-show from one of the principals was followed by an announcement from the director that the player in question would no longer be part of the production ... for unspecified reasons.

Which soon became specified: Owen Coates, mimesis of Ko-Ko and scout leader in some other part of real life, had been accused by one or some of the wolf-pack cub members under his charge of making indecent advances towards him–or them.

Under normal circumstances the scandal, disturbing as it was, would not have affected the Company greatly. Coates would not even have had a leading role. His singing voice (and my mother always drew the distinction) might have been borrowed from another, and spent sparingly on those grounds. Ejected from high in the nasal septum it had a strained "N-*yah*" quality to it, prompting more than one member of the Company to suggest its owner could do with a dose. He could not act–he could not even over-act–for years he had been planted where he could do least damage in the male chorus, but the indisposition of the Company's comic stalwart, whose "turns" had finally been stalled by arthritis, had thrust this pale shadow of the original into the limelight. The director's options had been limited; the glory days of the G&S Society were behind it, television's implicit home detention was already taking hold; a contemporized production from the previous year full of topical local references that would have had Gilbert fuming, while designed to breathe fresh life into *The Pirates of Penzance* had been played out in half-empty institute halls. The director had agonized over his selection of the scout leader: "I don't know, it could be the makings of him, it might bring him out of himself ..." he willed. But it didn't. Coates was very tall but drooped like a plant transplanted from warmer climes during rehearsals, chin lowered and spectacle-less so he didn't have to deal with the already intimidating space beyond the stage or even the proximity of his sometime partner, my mother, who was left like a pilot fish in her charge's wake.

His absence spared them both further embarrassment on stage but could not save Coates from something worse. It seemed incredible; his ineffectualness, extending to an incompetence in knot tying, tent erecting and navigation that had more than once led to cubs under his clueless charge spending the night shuddering under the stars, would have seemed to forensically exculpate him. But he was charged and a few days later he took his own life.

"Best thing he could have done," my bush-born father said, who probably saw the scout leader's demise as another kind of disposal of an unwanted or distorted life. But it left a gap in the Company's ranks much too close to the season's opening.

In this darkest hour though a savior appeared: if reluctantly. Kenneth ("Ken's the name") Brough was one of that rarest of breeds in the Riverland, a kind of gentleman farmer, which added to his enigmatic status; he'd also enjoyed youthful success on the stage in Adelaide, interrupted by the closing days of the Second World War when he enlisted and won a Military Cross in New Guinea, and then retired from all theatres of conflict to the large family fruit property. He was almost apologetic about its dimensions–"The old man did all the work, I'm afraid, God rest him"–while living alone in a Federation bungalow among an acre of roses. They might have been just for his enjoyment but he gave away masses to grieving and other deserving parties, brushing off thanks with signature asperity: *There they are, do what you want with them,* his manner seemed to suggest. He was tall, just greying, with a characteristic twitch to one corner of his lips suggesting that something, some memory or association, the person he was talking to even, having just been submitted to his scrutiny had provided him with momentary amusement. How he allowed himself to be drafted into the part remained a mystery–to others–he'd long made it clear to anyone who enquired what he thought of adding his presence to any public forum. Once he had given his assent though he slipped into the part the way the permanent man he employed on his property eased the top off his first bottle of beer for the day. After assuring my mother that he would give her all the room she wanted in their scenes together they struck up the most comfortable relationship while conceding each other all the space they might need. As a clown Brough performed his business with offhand nonchalance, as a singer he approached the score like a batsman with an appreciation of his limitations, utilizing the vocal equivalent of a firm low bottom hand grip. For some reason my aunt confessed–to her sister and no one else–that she was rather "taken" with Mr. Brough. She could hardly fail to be amused by him during rehearsals, of course, even if her appreciation was expressed in terms like *silly ass.* But perhaps there was something else in him that appealed to her, something other than his impeccable Old School background–"only St Peters"–as he actually joked with her–something in his appearance: a certain remediable neglect, a shirt crying out for a decent press ...

She stayed on for the run of the operetta anyway, an extended (seven night) season concluding with a cast party whose celebratory tone was only tempered in hindsight by a claim that the director, carried away with success and a Berri Estates sparkling wine, had fondled one of the prop-master's wife's breasts.

It was an indiscretion that proved minor in the larger scheme of things: a month or two later one of the Three Little Maids (Pitti-Sing), after first complaining of feeling unwell and reluctantly agreeing to see the family doctor, was bluntly diagnosed as being pregnant. Apart from being what used to be called "well-developed" for her age, the sixteen-year-old girl hadn't otherwise been very noticeable during the production. A member of the Lutheran church choir, she had also attended one of the local elocution classes designed to turn ten- or twelve-year-olds into excruciating prosodists, and had minced her way through her few lines of dialogue, but had otherwise performed her small role blamelessly enough.

Not long after this scandal broke, she disappeared from town altogether, though, and when she reappeared, babyless, and went shopping with her mother it was with cheeks red for the entire outing. Imagining that she was the cynosure of the town–which she was–anger and resentment must have added to her sense of betrayal as she realized she had got a very poor deal out of what so little time ago she thought would leave her forever poised on a pedestal of exclusiveness. She had long since given up the name of the putative father and some of the details of an affair which began when she had called at the predator's home as an emissary of the Lutheran choir seeking a floral donation and after that, having made no attempt to deny the accusations, there was no question other than for how long the offender, Brough, would spend in jail.

The original revelation had left people aghast or agog–the voyeuristic wondered how Brough could have short-circuited the normal resistance and misgivings of a sixteen-year-old: some might have wondered what extra mask he would have had to put on, what canniness–of the kind lacking in the scoutmaster's sad overtures, say–he would have had to employ, and whether the girl, if she had the wit and wasn't simply "sex-mad" or keen to impress her friends, was ever actually in love with him. She might have been and he, if he wasn't just trying to grasp at some scrap of his own youth, with her ... People could only speculate. Whatever their relationship, though, its legacy did no favors to either of them.

While he was in jail, Brough's property was sold off and he was never to come anywhere near the Riverland again, while years later the girl married a wool-classer with no knowledge of her history who was apparently at first shocked on their wedding night by his bride's complaint that he smelt of unwashed fleece, and then by her insistence on assuming a dominant role in their union's consummation.

Aunt Ellen seethed when she heard of the scandal, *And to think he invited me to have afternoon tea with him one day,* she wrote to my mother. *The pair of them want* whipping!

It was at least the third but not quite final disappointment of her life. Years later at what must have been the last musical get-together with her sisters she insisted on taking on something from her old repertoire and after failing to reach or cling onto a note broke down and retreated to a bedroom in tears.

She should have known better; while still managing to keep up the old family home in Kent Town, she was nearly eighty. As one by one her siblings exchanged the home for marriage outside of it, she had shared it (briefly) with both parents and then with just her father whose activity in his last years amounted largely to a scrutiny of the death notices in the morning paper, succeeded very often by the exhumation of a dark suit and tie from a handy recess and a measured stroll to the ex-acquaintance's place of committal. When even that activity was beyond him, he surrendered to the inevitable and the house became entirely and echoingly, I imagine, his daughter's own.

The day before she died, she was seen "pottering" in the garden by neighbors (and the day after obviously not). The house may have changed hands any number of times since, but from the outside it still looks much the same, and I sometimes wonder if any of the memories of the family still inhabit it. People may scoff but one of the reasons they buy old homes is surely in the expectation or hope that they will inherit some of their legacy. If any of Aunt Ellen's spirit does remain there, though, I can only think of her lying awake in the long pre-dawn hours–and listening; wondering if she can hear the step of a long banished and never actual lover now the coast is clear at last (not to be confused with the ghost of the once often-drunken milkman and his loyal steed who'd been known to stamp a hoof to recall its owner to his duties when he passed out holding the reins); or if it is just an echo of that unreliable chronicler and colleague-in-passing of my aunt, who having in a not unusually tipsy state himself slept past his tram stop, is now retracing his steps from the city fringes to the school ... where he will, of course, as Aunt Ellen crushes her handkerchief into a ball, make a clear eyed, bristling and guilt-free appearance before his adoring boys, as the bell sounds for morning prayers.

# BLUE

PAVLE RADONIC

Delectable enough to make you gasp going by drinking it in. Rarely was a stretch of water ever sighted as fulsome as that standing like an offering on a saucer. (In Singapore adults often slurped runny eggs from saucers.) Years ago an art teacher friend had memorably characterized blue as a cold color, when you had thought the beach, sky and even pictorial representation as warm and inviting. Baby blue. Egg shell. The soft pastels in the Derwent standup box. Certainly not cold. Further along grades of navy began. There was only light overcast. By the time the beach was reached a spattering of rain had begun to lash briefly, angled from clouds that stood away from the path. Further along again another couple of kilometres near the mangroves snot in the tone and all the lusciousness gone. After days of shirt-sleeves—or single layer thermal at least, with tee & sleeveless hoodie on top—the chill of the morning arrived with a wallop—sitting up in bed after brekkie the second doona had needed fetching. Five degrees it had been at departure midafternoon. Last week on two consecutive days blowies had buzzed through the window behind the bed, though certainly they had quickly disappeared. Last week a *YouTube* interview from the 80s had featured a novelist and writing teacher whose one and only rule for students had been no weather in the compositions. Understandably, especially in the US, that earlier generation had no call for that kind of thing. You had to take big salty gulps wheeling by, as usual recalling Knut Hamsun after his TB diagnosis on the train going back to Europe refusing to accept the fate the doctors had tried to hang on him. State of disaster officially declared. Last week Georgina in Darwin, originally a Melbourne gal, who had also cared for an aged parent to the end, remarked in a mail that the oldies in the homes would now confuse their periods with the presence of the fatigues. In the pic of the middle-aged blonde Greek wife of the nursing home mogul responsible for so many of the deaths the dame sat in her leathers on the bonnet of a *Lamborghini*, turned aside as the wind blew her hair.

# Back Roads

Summer Hammond

Our first truck.

I'd like to tell you it was badass.

That it was black, with two chrome smokestacks, curved like bull's horns, and a grill decked out in fangs.

But it was fuchsia.

I didn't know 18-wheelers came in fuchsia.

It was bright, the color of strawberry bubblegum, and glossy like nail polish.

We were in our late twenties, and so poor we couldn't keep the utilities on. We lived in a 125-year-old Victorian we'd inherited, or been left with, or, as it felt when the $600 utility bill arrived, were crushed beneath.

We were in our late twenties, both raised in extreme religion, Jehovah's Witness and Pentecostal-Charismatic respectively, taught well how to sublimate worldly desire and please God, live for Armageddon or the Rapture, and no clue how to live inside the real world.

We were in our late twenties and Aly's small carpet cleaning business, also inherited, had taken off during the summer, and nosedived during the winter, extinguished entirely after the cleaning equipment in the van froze and he didn't know how to fix it, and we couldn't afford repairs. He'd scrambled to find work, while I hung on to the fast-receding hope of finishing my teaching degree, while assistant teaching in a special ed elementary school classroom.

We were in our late twenties and our parents were gone, taken by death, or by mental illness so incapacitating they could barely function as humans, much less parents. After intense questioning, and a grueling soul search, we'd left our religions. We felt free and yet, no longer had a faith community to reach out to for help.

When the first snowstorm arrived, and we couldn't afford to heat the falling apart Victorian, our utilities were shut off. I didn't know toilet water could freeze, or olive oil, my breath taken by the gleaming golden statuette encased in a glass jar. In the mornings I leapt from bed, a frenzy of cold, teeth chattering, bundling into a winter coat to get ready for work, fogging up the mirror with my smoky breath, hands shaking so my eyeliner was all over the place, and I was ashamed. My coworkers went out to lunch and I stayed behind, claiming I'd brought mine. I didn't have a lunch. Famished, I once poured Ranch dressing from the workplace fridge straight into my mouth. I was ashamed.

At home, Aly and I stared down one bag of microwave popcorn, fallen over, all that was left in our cupboard besides an antique cobweb. We headed out, propping each other up along the icy sidewalk, and asked permission to use the microwave at the convenience store. We shared the last bag of popcorn for dinner, fingers greedy, warm with butter, and wondered what to do next. Huddled beneath blankets, we shivered in the dark and cold, staring out cracked windowpanes into another round of fast-falling snow, trying to figure out how to make it another day in the world.

The next morning, the teacher I assisted chastised me for being late.

She had no idea about the crumbling Victorian, the failed business, no family, no utilities, the golden olive oil statuette, the winter coat in the mornings, the last bag of microwave popcorn, and not a single dingy penny left in the couch cushions. She chastised me and I broke down, weeping into my hands. She looked at me with wide eyes, a little scared. I was ashamed.

This to say, neither of us cared that our first truck was fuschia. For us, it was nothing short of a gorgeous palace on eighteen wheels. It had a fridge and a microwave. It had bunk beds! An enormous steering wheel fit for Paul Bunyan. And an air horn. Best of all, most decadent, melting my heart with love and gratitude...it had heat.

A month into the trucking life, and I learned:

**P**igs shriek like demons in the trucks parked at Gwaltney Hotdog Factory in Smithfield, Virginia. The sound, and the smell, will keep you awake at night. Don't go out, don't try picking your way through the darkness to find a restroom. Do *not* go out. Pee in a cup. Otherwise, you might trip over the horror of an empty pig skin, laying there, deflated like an unzipped purse. Trucks pulling out of Gwaltney sometimes leak, slim red waterfalls jewelling the pavement. You will wince, turn away. One night at Gwaltney will teach you more about the real world, its barbarism, than all your years in college.

There's nothing, no magic in the world to rival Highway 71 through Colorado. Nothing to compare to the quiet elation of traveling alongside a rocky mountain stream mile after mile, watching it glint and glimmer in morning light, dazzle playful in the afternoon, then simmer in sunset, and at last, the full moon, a luminous wavy reflection, held gently in that ribbon of silver. You forget the road. That stream carries you. You can almost forget how far you are from a home that's stopped being home. You can almost forget your parents, dead or estranged. Forget how there's no one out there, in that big map somewhere, worrying about the two of you driving that big truck god knows where. No one out there, lovingly tracking your journey across the map, praying for you at the witching hour, 4 am to sunrise, praying your head stays up and your wheels stay steady. Your heart will splinter, when at last you must part ways with the faithful water. You'll blink back tears, flicking that turn signal, taking that exit, gazing in the rearview mirror. You didn't know a mountain stream could become beloved, a fellow vagabond, a friend.

Beware the shower rooms at truck stops. Much as you crave your *own* space, your *own* damn shower, at the Love's outside Nashville after an all-nighter. Nothing like being lost in an eighteen-wheeler, finding yourself on a road forbidden to trucks over a certain weight, running over a poor befuddled possum, before finally making it back onto the highway just in time for a weigh station that tickets you for being over, and you want to lose it, yell, *it's ice cream, dammit! We're bringing you people ice cream!* Nothing like that stress building in the cab, so flammable you should have the hazard tags out, finally exploding in egregious blaming, name-calling. At least, in the fiery heat of the brawl, the miles fly past. Now all you want is to be alone with your numb, weary heart and aching knees. Your baboon legs, and what you thought at first gasp was a beard, but is actually grease, and an accretion of sweat. But beware the shower rooms at truck stops. Even when you've locked the door and checked it once, twice, three times, pulling and twisting, just to be sure. You can't *ever* be sure. You didn't factor in the cleaning crew. Trust me, you didn't even think about the janitor's key ring, jangling with keys to every shower room, and the possibility of grave oversight. Your all-nighter sweat pants will be puddled around your ankles when the door swings open and swiveling in your undies, you will scream, he will scream, and truckers will bound from shower rooms, including your husband, wrapped up in a towel, and there will be an overwhelming flurry of apologies as you gather up your clothes and duffel bag and run, fast as your baboon legs will go, back to the truck, shaking, swearing, pummeling the Paul Bunyan wheel with your fist. You hate this life. You *hate* it.

Your first paycheck is deposited and you will always remember. After months of flinching against the computer-automated voice, whom you call Ms. Bank of America, informing you with what you swear is a small cluck of scorn, "Your balance is negative..." You listen to her tell you a new balance, an honest to God number, a number like nothing you've ever seen, or dreamed. You call again and again, just to hear her say that number. You and your husband trade the phone back and forth, listening, shaking your heads, laughing. The last time you listen, you're headed deep into rural Georgia, pine tree perfume thick inside the truck, and Ms. Bank of America's voice breaks up, then fades. You know why. It's because she knows how much this means to you. She knows better than anyone how far you've both traveled. You kiss your phone. You *kiss* it.

You might have to climb out at six in the morning in downtown Erie, PA, to midwife the truck through that tiny bridge. What is known, in industry lingo, as a *truck-eating* bridge. The bridge sign says 13' 4" and your truck is 13' 6". But this is the only route to the orchard where you are scheduled to pick up a load of apples in exactly twenty minutes. So, you hop out into the chill, stand on the side of the road and wave the truck forward, inch by agonizing inch, while early morning commuters crawl by. Their eyes pop at the eighteen-wheeler that's about to get its top scraped off like icing, and the wild-haired girl in the Wonder Woman pajamas whose fault it will be.

Well, you are giving the good people of Erie a story to start their day. And that's better than coffee.

At three a.m. don't expect to sleep. Instead you'll pull a trailer, packed to the gills with twenty tons of beer, up an endless mountainside in West Virginia, your truck heaving and straining, snorting bull-like, a fuschia bad ass. *Go, girl, go, you got this.* Glued at the hip, literally, you'll develop an intimacy with your truck, talk to her, coach her through these difficulties. You'll gaze into the side-view mirror, check on your lit-up trailer, hazard lights blinking, your new starry sky, the constellation that follows you down every interstate, through the night. You'll remember what it was like to be asleep at three a.m. The circles under your eyes will deepen, engraving into your skin the culmination of a lifestyle, twelve- to sixteen-hour days. Surging down the mountain, the Jake Brake will jolt you with its lioness roar. You'll lick your lips, inhale and exhale, eye the escape routes for runaway trucks, and you'll wonder, dear God you'll wonder, what are other twenty-somethings doing to survive, stay warm and fed, get the debt collectors to stop screaming at them. You'll wonder, the two of you, will you ever figure out this life. How long will it take.

Another thing you'll learn: highways are faster, smoother, safer than backroads by far.

Somewhere in Ohio, we're late to deliver because, yearning for countryside, I talked Aly into taking a back road. I feel bad, and even worse when we get behind an Amish buggy going roughly ten miles per hour. The buggy swerves a little. The horse's hooves kick up clouds of dust.

"Aly! Don't scare them," I screech. We're keeping a respectful distance but still, I can imagine how alarming it must be to have a fuchsia eighteen-wheeler trailing you on your normally peaceful clip-clop home.

Aly slows the truck even more.

The buggy veers, then turns onto a lane leading to a stately gray two-story farmhouse. Giant sunflowers droop in a lush country garden. A clothesline reaches from the house to the side of the big, red barn. Rows of dresses sway, long to short, along with a row of trouser pants, large to little.

Aly slows to a stop, and we wait as Bantam hens scurry, fluffy-headed, across the road. He grimaces, his hands a white-knuckled clench on the wheel. At this rate, we'll be at least an hour late. Walmart is strict about arrival, and punitive. An hour late, we won't get these frozen pizzas unloaded today. Out here, losing time means losing money. We can't afford that. It's taken us six months to pay off credit cards, past-due bills, and begin to crawl out of debt. Our last paycheck, we finally indulged, treating ourselves to a truck stop buffet. Thick ribs drenched in sauce and whipped mashed potatoes swimming in pools of butter and gravy, hot and gooey macaroni and cheese, warm peach cobbler, heaven, sheer heaven piling up on our plates. In a red vinyl corner booth with the stuffing poking out, we'd scooted in close, our knees pressed together, feasting like royals.

The cracked window panes, the swirl of snow and ruthless cold, one bag of microwave popcorn, we'll never forget. We're still fleeing.

We should've taken the highway.

If we want to get there on time, and be okay, we should *always* take the highway.

It's then that we see them. They've leapt from the buggy. They are running toward us across the big yard. The little girl holds her long dress above her lace-up boots. Her baby brother scrambles beside her, in suspenders, one hand planted atop his wide-brimmed hat. Before we know it, they've scrambled atop the split rail fence. As our engine thunders, they wave at us wildly, and then pull the air. A signal to trucks around the world. One we've been waiting for.

Our very first request.

My seatbelt is off in a flash. Aly and I take turns yanking the air horn. It bellows like a water buffalo across the countryside. The children leap from the fence, laughing and cheering. They are beside themselves. They jump up and down, clapping, then grabbing hands, dancing together beside the sunflowers, in the late golden light.

Clasping the air horn, Aly's hand finds mine, and our fingers twine. It's a pact.

We'll find our way, together.

And for the rest of our lives, we'll choose back roads.

They make you late. They cost you money.

And in return, they give you this.

# Eloping

Ayshe Dengtash

The time was approaching midnight. The plane he had boarded from Stanstead had probably already landed at North Cyprus's only airport—single-storeyed, the interior congested with pigeons desperate to escape the stifling summer heat. *He'll be here soon*, she thought to herself rummaging through the small cloth bag she'd found lying at the bottom of the kitchen cabinet earlier that day. She had packed a few t-shirts into it—he'd told her they'd be plenty for her to buy in London, more than she'd ever laid eyes on—along with a plaid skirt and a black tracksuit bottom, the only one that didn't bear stains of bleach or pomegranate juice or the heavy flow that paralyzed her for a few days every month. She had also dropped a few treats into her bag—three tubes of *Bonibons* and two packets of *Eti Cins*—certain she'd never again be able to taste the sweets she'd grown up with once she boarded the plane to London, to *his* family home, a few hours later.

This girl who sat on the edge of her bed, clutching the bag from which exuded the earthy smell of her mother's favorite food, *Molehiya*, was Fatima. She was fifteen years of age with long light-brown hair which curled in all the right places. Her almond-shaped eyes were the darkest brown and her lips were red and crusty from a constant bout of dehydration, which was nothing but her own fault. Close to midnight on the 17th of August 1987, her heart beat in her temples and her fingers twined and untwined her bag's strap. She had been waiting for this day since the summer of the previous year, thirteen months ago when she saw Hasan, aged twenty. This wasn't the first time she'd laid eyes on him of course. He'd visit once every year, only during the summers, a pasty boy who stood out amongst the other boys in the village who were by then ripened under the unforgiving Cyprus sun.

They'd play together: hopscotch and hide-and-seek, which involved hiding in every corner of the entire village. The summer of 1986 was the first summer they hadn't, preferring instead to stand around grand prickly pear trees, marveling at each other's beauty through the bloated thorny leaves.

Fatima pressed down on the rectangular button on her desk clock, and watched as a tiny green fluorescent light illuminated the numbers, the large clock hand pointing to the 10, while the small indicated the 11. The house was shrouded in an eerie silence and all she could hear were the noises of the outside: an owl calling out in a rhythmic hoot, and the rustling of the bushes as rats rushed back and forth, hiding from prey and preying themselves. She thought of the letter which had been given to her two days ago by Sumeyla, a woman in her thirties, overweight and unkempt, who everyone in the village assumed was slightly deranged. She spoke to herself sometimes or pulled out her eyebrows, replacing them with irregular clumps of orange henna. Yet Fatima confided in Sumeyla, who would listen and smile and nod when Fatima told her Hasan would be sending her a letter once a month and that she should bring it to her directly without showing it to anyone or opening it herself. The latest letter, which had arrived earlier that morning, wrote that he'd be coming for her on the 17$^{th}$ of August.

Fatima had spent the entirety of the day planning for that night. Her primary goal was to make sure her mother went to bed earlier than her usual 11 o'clock after watching two sets of soap operas whilst drinking cup after cup of Turkish coffee to keep herself awake. And since Fatima was the one who did most of the housework—washing the clothes, hanging them up and gathering them, shopping for the freshest fruit and veg at the market which came to the nearest town once a week, cooking the food, cleaning the dishes, ensuring her mother's clothes were ironed and of course that her coffee was always cooked to the perfect consistency, the perfect flavor—this was no hard task. Her mother had asked her about the whereabouts of her coffee all evening, and Fatima had claimed, quite rightfully so, that there was no gas left in the *tüp*. What she didn't tell her mother was she'd purposefully drained it over the course of the day, leaving the switch on, the hissing released from the *tüp* inaudible due to the countless tractors—piled high with fresh *tütün*—leaving the village and driving back. "I'll make sure we have a new one tomorrow," Fatima said to her mother. She added that it was better for her mother to drink *adaçayı* anyway, that it was good for the pains she complained she had in her knees and ankles. She made her mother two cups, filled to the brim. She was glad to see her mother's eyes closing like a broken shutter, even before the first soap opera had finished. "Mum, come on, let's go to bed," she said, wrapping her forearm around her mother's before she had the chance to protest.

Some minutes later Fatima heard her mother's soft snore and the silly vibration of her lips as she breathed in and out. *Everything's going to be okay*, Fatima assured herself as she listened to her mother sleep. *Mum will forgive me a few years down the line. Wasn't that what happened to most of the other girls' parents in the village who cried for months on end, especially the mothers, after their daughters left their rooms in the dark of the night? The girls were immediately disowned, then immediately forgiven when they returned years later, a small baby cradled in their arms,* she thought to herself.

Music seeped into her room from the road just outside her window—bubbly and energetic—a popular Turkish tune which didn't match her mood. She wiped her sweaty palms against her tracksuit bottom and walked toward her window, pulling down a section of the shutters. *Was it Hasan?* In his letter he'd written that he was to arrive at the village's *kahve* at around midnight in a navy-blue car. The car outside was scarlet, and as much as the streetlight allowed, she could see that four people sat inside. Two in the front, two in the back. As the car spun around, the driver's face was illuminated under the streetlight and Fatima saw that it was Berkan, a boy in his twenties with the largest, most crooked nose she had ever seen on anyone. He had been secretly seeing Fadime, the girl living next door, and sometimes when Fatima sat up late at night rereading Hasan's letters, she would hear her close the kitchen door. This was followed by a rustling, as she waded through the mulberry bushes to reach the street where Berkan was waiting for her. *Was she also going to leave her parent's home that night? What a morning it would be,* thought Fatima. *Would my mother blame Fadime's mother for her own daughter's disappearance? It would be so like her*, thought Fatima. She'd blamed Hatice for her low grades at school and accused Mahan of guiding her daughter onto a "wrong" path when they'd both bleached their hair a light shade of brown with a bunch of chamomiles they had brewed for several hours. When Fatima looked through the shutter again, the road was empty save from an owl which was pecking at something on the worn-out tarmac.

Fatima opened her bedroom door and made her way toward her mother's room. She pulled her mother's door ajar and glanced in. Her mother's head was buried beneath the pillow, something she did when she had a headache and wanted to squeeze the pain out. Her legs were sprawled across the bed, her feet hanging off its edges. She watched, hoping she moved. *Is she dead?* thought Fatima. *Had she perhaps sensed what I'm going to do? That her life would change with the awakening of the following day?* When she saw her mother's toes twiddle, Fatima pulled the door behind her, making sure it didn't shut completely, worried the noise would rouse her mother. Remembering the clock in the sitting room which her mother usually set to 4 a.m. for an early start to tend to the cows before the summer sun dispersed its scorching rays upon every section of the village, Fatima wondered into the sitting room to turn it off. Fatima contemplated what difference it would make if her mother woke at four or five or six to find her gone. She knew it would make no difference, that her mother would wail regardless, beating her thighs with her coarse hands, tugging at her dress, and slapping her face, desperate for her daughter to come back. *Falling in love is not a crime,* thought Fatima. *Mother did it too, leaving in the middle of the night and only returning two years later with me wrapped in a blanket, sheltered within her arms.*

It was 1972 when Menekse, Fatima's mother, fell in love with Lutfi, the *Muhtar*'s son, who lived on the other side of the village just behind the mosque which separated the village into two. Menekse would lay down on her bed all night, not sleeping, but looking up at the ceiling thinking of her lover's face, the sharpness of his chin and his golden-brown shoulder-length hair. She would do this every night, patiently waiting for the sun to rise at 5 a.m. before anybody from the village had awoken. Then she would rush out, her feet bare to prevent any noise emanating from the only pair of shoes she owned. She'd climb her father's ladder to the roof and look beyond the tall minaret of the mosque where she'd see Lutfi standing up straight gazing toward her. They'd wave at each other. Menekse couldn't see his face clearly, but she hoped that he was smiling as much as herself. After about half an hour, just before the older men of the village left their homes, mounting their donkeys to make their way to their fields situated on a steep hill visible from every point of the village, Menekse would climb down, slithering into her bed where she would sleep for an hour before her mother came in to wake up her, complaining that she was always sleeping when there was so much to do. One humid July night, she let herself out of the window and mounted the donkey waiting outside her home, Lutfi sitting high up, urging her to hurry. They welcomed Fatima nine months later.

It started raining. Fatima pressed down on the button of the clock again and saw that it was 23:40. Opening her sack and scouring through, making sure she had gotten the few things she needed, she hoped he'd hurry before her mother woke up. The rain pattered against the metal shutters and the wind whistled through the tiny gaps where the window frame met the stone wall. She sauntered to the window when she thought she heard the rhythmic drone of a car's engine and pulled open one of the shutters, laying eyes on a navy-blue car, its wheels dripping with a light-brown sludge. She draped her bag over her shoulder and gently pulled her bedroom door behind her. Tiptoeing along the hallway, she reached the front door, wrapped her palm around its cold metal handle, and opened it. She walked out into the quiet night, making her way toward the navy car in which Hasan awaited her. She glanced around at the jagged ancient walls of the *kahve* to her right and another to her left, each owned by members of rival families; the grandfather of the owner of the one on the right having eloped with the thirteen-year-old grandmother of the one on the left almost a century ago. The village legend told he'd abandoned her in the middle of field in which he'd tried to deflower her, only to notice that the deed had already been done. Fatima gazed up, realizing that two owls sat side by side on the electricity wires, unmoving and silent. *When will I ever see this place in which I've spent fifteen years of my life?* she asked herself. *When will I be able to help mother tend to the chickens and the vegetables again? When will I be able to dance on this road at weddings until the soles of my shoes are worn thin?* When she reached the car, Fatima hesitated before she took a step in, contemplating whether she was doing the right thing or whether she'd regret it in a few days, as had been the case with a hundred other girls in the village who'd left and been treated like maids by their husband's mothers. Her mother had told her countless stories. *But love*, she thought to herself, *where will I find it again?*

She pulled open the door and stepped in.

"Fatima you took long," said Hasan. Fatima looked into his eyes, their whites a faded pink from fatigue.

She glided over to him till her arm touched his. His arm warm against her own. "I didn't," she said, smiling. "It must have seemed that way to you."

"Hello, *yenge*," said the driver whom Fatima had never seen before. He was a young guy, a little older than Hasan, with black hair combed meticulously backwards.

"Hello," said Fatima. The young guy didn't say anything more, but pressed down on the accelerator and off they went, the engine revving a little too loudly for Fatima, who stared at her home through the back window, its white exterior getting smaller and smaller, and eventually fading from view.

Hasan placed his own palm onto her hand, and Fatima could feel that his fingers were clammy, his hand shaking. "I want to get to know you," he said to her.

Fatima faced him and was about to tell him they already knew each other, going all the way back fifteen years when she was forty days old placed into an empty pillow sack, as tradition would have it, and rolled around first vertically and then horizontally to scare away the demons hovering over her eager to take her fresh life for themselves. Hasan had been five then, in Cyprus for the second summer of his life, a child who stood out amongst all the others around him due to his smooth milky-white skin which the temperamental England sun had failed to darken. But Fatima didn't tell him any of this, realizing that seeing each other summer after summer, whilst playing with the other children in the village, or sitting for dinner with the other villagers did not necessarily mean she knew him—or they knew each other—at all.

As they drove along the dark roads devoid of any streetlights, Fatima stared out of the window at the black expanses on either side which she knew were fields sowed with all sorts of seasonal vegetables and fruits. The plump bright-yellow melons sitting on the damp soil wafted a sweet aroma into the air, conjuring in Fatima a restless hunger. She sat back and allowed her thoughts to overtake her, visions prying on her mind, the first causing her to wrap her fingers firmly around the seatbelt. She imagined herself with a belly larger than life, sitting outside on the porch of a small white house, sweat seeping down either side of her face whilst she breathed heavily.

"Fatima?" murmured Hasan. "Are you okay?" Her placed his hands on hers, and Fatima involuntarily placed her own against her abdomen, sighing with relief as she noticed that her palm touched a flat stomach.

"I'm okay," said Fatima, turning to face Hasan, his eyes shining under his bristly thick eyebrows. "I'm okay."

"It's just that you didn't say anything."

Fatima remembered what Hasan had asked her before the vision of a time that had not yet happened. "I want to get to know you, too," she said.

"We have a lot of time to do that," said Hasan.

"So, what's your home like in England?" asked Fatima.

"It's not a house," said Hasan. "There's no garden with fruit trees and vegetable patches as you have here." He did not speak for a few seconds, and Fatima stared at his face intently, trying to see if this was indeed the boy she'd fallen in love with. She traced the outline of his face, his forehead glistening with sweat, his lips round and flaky.

"What's it like, then?" asked Fatima. She turned her head away to look out of the window, glancing at the single-story houses shrouded in darkness, aligned one next to the other, small gardens separating each, endless fields behind them pregnant with food to eat and sell. "What do you eat there then?" she continued when Hasan did not answer.

"We go to big supermarkets," said Hasan. "Like Suleymanos in the village, but much, much bigger. They sell fruits from all over the world, things you've never seen and foods you've never eaten before."

"But is all that food they have there enough for everyone?" Fatima said. "Don't people need to grow their own food?" She felt a jab at her ankle and bent down to itch it, feeling her skin rising where a mosquito had just bitten her. "Suleymanos sells only some things," said Fatima. "But if we didn't grow our own things, we'd starve.... You know that."

"You will never starve there," said Hasan. "There's so much more than anyone can eat." Fatima looked at him, trying to decipher whether he was telling her the truth. *Where was this place he was taking her to which had such abundance of food?* Fatima tried to imagine portly aubergines piled on top of one another, from the ground all the way up to the ceiling, but she couldn't, they always came tumbling down.

"Is there a large stone sink outside where I can wash the clothes and clean the dishes?" she asked.

Hasan chuckled and wiped the sweat on his forehead with his sleeve.

"You'll like it, Fatima. Don't worry so much," he said.

*Don't worry,* thought Fatima. *Six hours away from home, past god knows how many seas and countries, how can I not worry?*

"But I want to know," said Fatima. "I need to know where I'm going to wash the clothes because I haven't brought enough with me. I need to know if I'll be able to wash them as soon as I get there."

"You won't be washing them by hand," said Hasan. Fatima watched him looking up at the shimmering stars. "There's this machine which will wash them for you."

The car roared and maneuvered around curved roads, plunging in and out of potholes, causing Fatima's head to loll up and down.

"But what will I be doing all day?" asked Fatima. "If others are going to grow my food and if something else is going to wash my clothes...." She hesitated, and contemplated herself sitting down all day, her bottom getting larger and her arms and legs getting fleshier as had happened to Gonul, a bride who'd come to the village three years ago from a few villages to the south. Fatima remembered how everyone was astonished by her beauty, by her large round black eyes which were now barely visible under folds of flesh, and by her slender body which now bulged out in all the wrong places, causing the villagers to gossip about her choice of clothing. Fatima felt a sudden fatigue settle over her, deeming her unable to move her arms, her hands bouncing up and down off the backseat as the car drove on.

"Fatosh?" Hasan asked. "What were you going to say?"

She gazed at the single streetlamp which lit up the road into which they had turned. Before them stood a tiny house, the garden at the front overgrown with tall scruffy weeds; beautiful white flowers fell from a stickly tree standing tall to the right. From inside came the shrill noise of a telephone ringing.

"Where are we?" she asked.

Hasan placed his hand over Fatima's, and she withdrew it as she saw a hunchbacked woman exit the house, walking toward them. *Three villages cannot stop me if I want to run*, she said to herself. *I can run faster than Emine's crazy donkey, Husnu. What's happening?* she asked herself. *Will they leave me here with this strange lady?* She remembered what her uncle had told them a few months back, when they'd gathered at Sumeyla's house forty days after her grandfather's passing to mourn his soul. Women with short legs and large hips, women with crooked backs are the friends of the devil, he'd said. Women listened to him, nodding, infused, believing every word he said. The wise words of the village imam.

"What time is it? We need to go we'll miss the plane," Fatima said as the woman reached the car.

"There's still time, don't worry about it," said Hasan.

The woman whose face was lit up by the streetlight ambled past the front of the car and stared in through the window on Fatima's side, her head craning left and right like a confused pigeon, her eyes narrowed to mere slits. "Is this the girl?" she asked.

Fatima looked back at Hasan. She watched the gentle rise and fall of his chest.

"Hello," said Hasan, looking over Fatima's head at the woman standing outside the car, her skin thin and almost see-through. "We're going," he said. "Please help make this journey easy for us."

"She needs to come out," said the woman. The air was pervaded by a dense mist as rain spitted down from above. "Ask her to come out."

"What is it?" said Fatima, grabbing Hasan's hand.

"She's going to pray for you," said Hasan. "We'll be cursed if she doesn't. You need to go, or we won't be able to leave. Every girl who leaves comes here," he said.

*Buyucu Kadriye*, thought Fatima. *It's her*. She was as ugly as every returning bride had described, her skin thick like plaster, embedded with dark lines which seemed to inhale her flesh. *What happened to her teeth?* thought Fatima. They were rotting and engraved with century-old plaque.

"Come on girl," the woman said to Fatima with great urgency. "Get out. I can't be getting wet just because you want to do god-knows-what with this boy."

"It's very simple," said Hasan to Fatima, leaning over her and opening the door. "Just do as she says."

Fatima stepped out and the women moved away, dashing toward the house. She turned around and motioned for Fatima to hurry. Fatima followed the woman along a brick path and around a bend which led into the front garden of the house that she had exited a few minutes prior. Hearing the squeak of the gate behind her Fatima glanced back hoping that Hasan was coming after her.

The inside of the woman's house was unremarkable, a sharp yellow lightbulb hung from the center of the ceiling lighting up the room, revealing a set of dirty beige sofas. Embroidered mats were thrown clumsily over the television and the rickety side tables.

"You sit here," said the woman, pointing at the sofa. "I need to get something from the kitchen. I'll be back."

Fatima did as she was told, seating herself on the edge of the armchair that creaked below her weight. Its metal frame pressed firmly against her bottom. She glanced around, observing the assortment of odd furniture filling the room. A large mahogany cupboard aligned one side of the room, its bottom shelf holding mismatched photo frames, some gold, some silver, each holding the image of a person resembling the older woman. Rain pelted against the windows, submerging the outside into a blur. The woman walked into the room, quietly carrying a tray on which sat a small clay jug. A thin wisp of smoke rose from the jug before dispersing into invisibility, engulfing the room with a bitter burnt smell.

"I'm going to circle this thing over your head a few times," said the woman. "You just sit there. It won't take long."

"But--"

"It's to make sure the evil forces stay away from you. You do something to betray your parents and these evil forces are always there," she said, placing the tray onto the table besides Fatima. She then scurried around her, carrying the jug, encircling it around her head. Fatima felt the urge to cough as she inhaled the smoke which wrapped itself around her throat, but she kept it in. After a few minutes, she put the jug on the table and dawdled toward the cupboard, from which she picked up a yellowed plastic bottle filled halfway with water. Twisting the cap, she poured some into her palm and sprinkled it over the jug. The smoke petered out with a hiss, releasing a grey swirl that gradually dissipated. Beside the bottle the woman had placed down onto the table, Fatima glimpsed something sparkly in a glass ashtray, in which also lay cigarettes smoked down to the filter. She leaned forward, eyeing the thing that had captured her attention. It was a bracelet made of a pink thread with two silver shells attached to it.

"You'll be okay now," said the woman. "You're all safe. Go."

Fatima tried to read the woman's expression. *Have I upset her?* she asked herself. *Why that tone?*

"Come on, now, go," said the woman. A clatter came from inside one of the rooms down the corridor and Fatima wondered if they were indeed not alone. The woman sauntered toward the sound; her hand tucked into her waist. When she was out of sight, Fatima grabbed the bracelet and rushed out of the open door. The streetlight that illuminated the road was now out, cloaking the road into a deadly darkness where field merged into road. She saw the car, its silver *Sahin* symbol glistening as it met the moonlight.

"What happened?" asked Hasan, as Fatima let herself in.

"She did something with some smoke," said Fatima. "She told me we'll be okay now."

His eyes glided across her face questioningly, then he sighed and stroked her cheek. "Who can stop love?" he said. "Who would want to?"

The driver, too, sighed in his seat as he cracked his neck, twisting it one way then the other. "Shall we go now, *gencler*?" he said. "There's still quite a while to drive. We'll try and get you in through the security before people notice that she's missing."

He reversed the car, looking over Fatima's head out of the rear window. They turned left onto the main road, light returning almost instantaneously as the streetlights illumined their path. Fatima glanced at the houses on either side of the road and wondered whether there were girls like herself sitting quietly on the other side of the shutters, peeking through waiting for boys to take them away to strange, unknown worlds.

They proceeded in silence and Fatima thought about this boy sitting beside her. She'd known him for a long time. *Why are we not talking? What is there to talk about?* she asked herself. *Was there really nothing to say?* She contemplated married couples she knew closely, *did they talk?* She remembered her own parents, always bickering over this and that: the way her mother had stitched his loose button too much to the left so it was always on the verge of bursting off again, how she never listened to him when he came home from the *kahve* eager to tell her about what he'd learnt from Sukru, the village gossip. She'd talk over him, arguing that what she had learnt from Kadriye, Sukru's wife, was of even more importance. Then, Fatima recalled them working side by side in the fields, planting courgettes, picking courgette flowers, digging up potatoes, as Fatima herself, five years old, sat under a tree watching them, a hot wind blowing across their faces to shake the brittle leaves of the olive trees surrounding them. She remembered how much she enjoyed watching her parents working with the soil, the whole world quiet as they toiled. She knew that had been peace.

Her heart grew cold as she realized that she had left her mother, in that house where her father had died, all by herself. She glanced at the rearview mirror at the driver's eyes, a severe expression creasing the surroundings of his eyes.

"How long left?" asked Fatima.

"Not long now," said the driver. "We'll be there in about twenty minutes."

*Is it too late?* asked Fatima to herself. *Is it too late to return home?*

About twenty minutes later, dazzling, yellow lights surrounded them as they neared a large, elongated building, brown with a navy sign that read ERCAN. Cars were parked in front of the building; to Fatima it seemed as if all the vehicles in the world had been dumped here.

Hasan sat forward and tapped the driver on the shoulder. "You don't need to park the car in the lot," he said. "Just leave us somewhere here, we'll go."

"Let me drive you around near the entrance at least," said the driver.

Fatima gazed out of the window breathlessly at people carrying suitcases, loading them onto metal structures that they wheeled away into the building, disappearing from sight. She realized that there was no one like her mother around, with her long flowing flowery dresses and the embroidered flowery kerchiefs she laced over her head to keep her hair away from her face so she could toil on the land, scrub the clothes, and sift through the rice one grain at a time, removing small pebbles that had somehow made themselves into the cloth sacks of grains her mother bought from the wholesaler who visited the village once every two months. Women wore trousers here, the cloth tight against their thighs and accentuating their figures as she had seen on celebrities on TV, and their jackets were made of the shiniest material, with buttons on their cuffs that served no purpose.

The traffic had started to build up outside the airport, cars beeping and drivers waving goodbye to people they'd just dropped off. Eager to see what was on the other side of the doors, Fatima swung around to see Hasan leaning into the back of the car. He pulled out a navy suitcase, pushed the trunk shut, and wandered over to Fatima. Fatima thought about whether she should have brought more, clutching the sack closer to her body, but she'd wanted to leave something for her mother to grieve over, as all the other mothers did in the village, pressing their faces into their long-gone daughters' clothes, inhaling the scent of those they'd given birth to, those who'd betrayed them.

"Are you ready?" he asked, extending a sheet of paper toward her, at the very top of which was written her name in navy ink, the letters scrawny and nervous. "You need to show this to the attendant we're going to see inside," he continued. "Do you have your passport?"

Fatima nodded, dipping her hand into her bag and pulling it out.

"Hold onto it," he said. He hesitated, then turned around to face the driver who was standing on the other side of the car.

"I'm going to go, cousin," he said. "You need anything?"

"No, cousin, you go," said Hasan. "Thank you for bringing us all this way. *Hakkini helal et.*"

The driver raised an uplifted thumb and bowed before entering his car. "Take care," he said before driving off.

"What was I saying?" said Hasan when they were alone.

"About the sheet," she said. She looked at where the car had been a few moments ago, traces of its tires embedded into the thin layer of mud gathered on the side of the shallow pavement.

"There's a girl inside I know," he said. "She knows about your age but she's okay with it. She's going to help us pass security."

Fatima glared at the tire marks, unable to believe what she'd just done. How had she allowed the only connection between herself and her mother to drive off like that, leaving her here with this boy who had told her he loved her once last summer?

"But you need to be calm," he said to her. He tapped her forearm. "Fatima? Did you hear me? You're my fiancée and that's all they need to know."

*A pair of tracksuit bottoms and six packets of Eti Cins*, thought Fatima to herself, *that's all I have*.

"Okay," said Fatima, nodding.

Hasan grabbed her hand and they sauntered toward the sliding glass doors, his smooth hands warm against her coarse cold ones. She'd never felt such a hand before, with a palm so soft one would never know it could belong to a human being. It reminded her of the bright-orange skin of the oval-shaped loquats she picked every May from the tree in her back garden or the purple skin of the aubergines her mother charred before scooping out their fleshes to mix with creamy yoghurt bestowed to them from the udders of a goat they owned, Fatima's favorite, she'd named her Feride, meaning *unique.*

They went in, Fatima's eyes fluttering under the bright lights. Sounds came from everywhere, culminating into a nonsensical chatter. She glanced around at the sea of heads, and the assortment of suitcases, pink and navy blue, some decorated, some plain.

Hasan detached his hand from hers and plunged his hands into his pockets, tiptoeing and looking ahead, his head moving swiftly left and right.

"Our check-in is over there," he said. He gripped her forearm and pulled her as Fatima looked at blurry faces, bodies releasing the ripe scent of sweat.

They joined a short queue, standing behind an old man who had dark brown freckles on his bald head. Fatima stood counting them.

"It's us next," said Hasan, as the man walked toward the counter, dragging along his suitcase. "Once we're finished here, we'll go in and eat something. I'm hungry,"

Fatima remained silent.

"Aren't you hungry?" he asked.

Fatima knew it was dark outside, late night-early morning, a time when she should have still been in bed, wishing the rooster, who would be crying out his morning prayer, to calm down so she could continue sleeping for a little while longer, before her mother would come barging in, hissing down at her. There were always a thousand chores to do. *It's not a time to be eating now*, thought Fatima to herself.

"I am a little," she said to Hasan, not knowing why she said it. She wasn't hungry, just tired. *But that's what wives did*, she thought. *Saying yes when they meant no. Always agreeing. Always saying yes.*

"Next," said the woman sitting behind the counter. She smiled when she saw them, her lips a bright red, a startling contrast with her pure-white teeth.

"Hasan. How are you?" she said.

"Can't wait to get going," he replied. "How's your mother?"

The girl turned to Fatima, her smile growing.

"She's fine," said the girl. Fatima glanced at the plastic nametag hanging over her breast. On it was written *Rahme.* "You know what she's like, always running around to please everyone, and now Fahriye's given birth again. Another mouth to feed, another child to look after."

"Must be tough," said Hasan.

"Where are your passports?" asked the girl. Hasan took his own out of his pocket and grabbed Fatima's from her grip.

The woman flicked them open and hovered her eyes over Fatima before doing the same with Hasan. An officer passed behind the counter then, bulky and armed, a ginger moustache sitting below his pockmarked nose. Hasan seized Fatima's hand which was dangling by her side and squeezed it, pulling her closer to himself. When the officer ambled away and out of sight he let go, placing his palm on the counter in front of them.

"You're all ready to go now," said Rahme, banging against the pages of their passports with a wooden block that left behind faded imprints of numbers and letters.

"Thank you so much, Rahme," said Hasan. He pursed his lips and forced a smile. "Really, truly, thank you."

"Don't worry so much about it," she said. "Just take care."

The woman put the passports back onto the counter and Hasan picked them up. "Bye," he said. She wished them goodbye, and Hasan intertwined his fingers with Fatima's as they walked further into the airport, past metal seats occupied by people who were either sleeping or staring idly ahead of them, their eyes heavy with sleep and their laps full of gorged backpacks.

"Which way do we go?" asked Fatima, pointing at the signs hanging high up on the walls. There were arrows pointing left, right and ahead.

"That way is arrivals," said Hasan. "We're leaving, so we're looking for departures." He stopped abruptly, and rotated on his hips, glaring around. "Look for the D," he said. Fatima wondered whether he was aware of her inability to read. She could identify letters, having learnt them at school in Year 1 and 2, the only years she'd attended. The teacher shouted at everything; at the students who sat at the back yawning with their mouths opened; at their inability to curve the swirl of the lowercase *g*. "Round and up" she would yell, "How many times do I have to repeat?" Fatima knew this wasn't the only reason she'd left, there were bigger things, bigger causes. She remembered those days vividly, sitting in the corner of the classroom on a yellowed cloth her mother had torn from a tattered bedsheet, wrapped to prevent the dark-red blood from running out and down her legs. She could still feel the knots pressing against her hips and the blood that seeped out little by little. She'd slightly lift her bottom every so often when her teacher swung around to write letters on the board, glimpsing at the blue fabric of the seat, hoping that the cloth had done its job. She'd done this month after month, walking to school slowly, her thighs numb with pain. One day she felt the knot on her right hip unravel as she watched her friends play hopscotch wishing she could take part. She held it as soon as she felt it, but the puddle of blood flooded out and down her thighs, forming streaks that ran all the way to her shoes. She ran back home where her mother was pulling out potatoes from the red soil in their garden. "I'm not going back to school," she said to her mother, holding the cloth within her grip, her hands a red mess. *Did he know that I can't read?* she asked herself as Hasan clasped his fingers around the strap of her bag and tugged for her to hurry.

"They're calling for us," he said. They ran toward a police officer who had his arm plunged into a bag, a young girl nodding before him as he looked up down at her, his glasses hanging off the tip of his nose.

Fatima felt Hasan's fingertips pinching at the skin of her forearm.

"You wait," said the police officer, pointing at the ground near their feet. After a few seconds, he passed the bag to the young girl, unzipped, its contents on the verge of spilling. He summoned them to walk over.

"You got anything you shouldn't be bringing in your bag?" he asked.

"No," they said.

"What do you have in your bag?"

"Just come clothes," said Fatima. She contemplated telling him about the snacks but decided against it, unsure of whether the police officer would take them away if he knew.

"Give me your bag," he said.

Fatima dropped its strap from her shoulder and shifted her position, moving closer to Hasan.

"Fatima," whispered Hasan. "Give the officer your bag. It's okay. It's just a routine check."

She extended the bag and the police officer picked it up with the tip of his finger, as if its very existence was an offense.

"You've never been on a plane before?" he asked, squinting.

"She hasn't," said Hasan. "She's going to England for the first time. We got engaged last night."

"What district do you live in?" said the police officer. "You're from Karpasia, I bet, they don't go anywhere over there. Marrying each other. Brother sister, everything." He plummeted his hand into the bag and scrabbled about, the *Bonibons* clattering in their tubes, the *Eti Cin* packet crinkling.

"What's this?" he said, pulling at the *Bonibons*. "You're bringing these with you? You've got one bag and that's what you choose to fill it with?"

Fatima thought about what to say, she knew exactly why she had brought them, but knew it was nonsensical, a packet of *Bonibons* that would go bad in a year.

"I can do with these myself right now," he said. "I'm a bit jittery you know, from all the standing, the noise in here. It's always so loud." He chuckled and placed the tube into his trouser pocket. "Off you go, then," he said, handing Fatima her bag.

She knew that there was no sense in it, that the police officer had done her a favor, relieving her from a remnant of home she'd have spent days holding within her palm, lamenting a life she'd already given up as soon as she'd stepped into the car that had driven her to the airport. *It's better to forget*, she said to herself. *Remembering is too much pain.*

They walked over to the only two seats that were empty, settling between a rustic-looking man who seemed as if he'd just left the fields, his long nails brown, filled with fresh soil, his boots holding clumps of earth, and a young man with ears that sat on either side of his head as if they were not his own but mere attachments.

Fatima hugged her bag and listened to a man behind them excitedly talking with someone about oranges and lemons. She gazed outside at the sun, which had started to make itself visible behind the shallow mountains in the distance, spreading its rays upwards towards the heavens. She thought about what her mother would be doing, whether she was awake, glimpsing at the clock on the bedside table before deciding to sleep a little more until the sun's rays penetrated through the curtains mercilessly, making it impossible to relax. *It's almost that time of the morning*, thought Fatima to herself, *maybe one hour or two hours away before mother discovers I've gone, before she blames herself for having done a bad job bringing me up.* "You should have remarried after Hulusi died," the neighbors would say to her. "A child needs a father in the house, someone she fears."

"It's cold in England," said Hasan, placing his hand on her thighs. Fatima winced, imagined her body moving further away, out of his grip, but when she looked down again his hand was still there, his fingers splayed like the spindly legs of a spider, caressing in rotating motions. "It's so cold you can't even imagine."

"Colder than early morning at the farm during winter?" she said. "It can't be colder than that. My ear lobes go numb when I'm at the farm. I get scared they'll fall off."

"Much colder," he said. "But there's clothes for it there."

They sat in silence. Fatima played with the strap of her bag, twirling and untwirling it around her index finger.

"It's Sunday today," said Hasan. "Everyone will be around to visit you. They're looking forward to it. Mum has been cooking for weeks." He itched at his cheek. "Then we'll have the engagement. Dad has already bought the ring. We were just waiting for you to come and then we'll get it done."

The man sitting beside Fatima lifted his right leg, propping it horizontally over his left, his shoe digging into her thigh. Fatima sat there staring ahead, looking down occasionally, trying to ignore the red mud that filled the dents under his shoes, some rock-solid, others threatening to crumble off.

A ring echoed through the airport, descending on them from above, a cacophony that startled them. Fatima sat up straight.

"This is an announcement to all who are boarding the two a.m. plane to London, Stanstead. Boarding will start in five minutes," bellowed the voice of a woman.

"That's us," said Hasan. "You take these. They'll ask for them when we reach the front of the line." He gave her the ticket and her passport. "You give this one," he said, tapping the ticket. "And sometimes they ask for this, too."

A woman strolled by, a plastic badge attached to her blazer like the one on Rahme. She was wearing a pencil skirt that wrapped her curves, a bright-red silk scarf was tied around her neck, her hair tied neatly into a bun. She'd seen women like her on TV before, smiling women with pure-white teeth, wearing heels, sitting behind desks. She wondered where those women came from, why there was none where she lived where women owned just two pairs of flat shoes, one for the field, one for when they travelled far—two villages down—at Eid twice a year to visit family. She thought about whether they were like herself when they were not dressed like this, when their faces were not concealed under a layer of paint that made them look glamorous. She stared at the woman's solemn expression, and noticed she was pulling a plastic box on wheels behind her.

"Come on, Fatima," said Hasan. "We should go, too. The line's getting longer."

He gripped her forearm and pulled her along. Fatima let him guide her to the end of an L-shaped queue which meandered around the seats. They moved little by little. Fatima glared down, making sure she didn't bump into the woman in front of her. Occasionally she lifted her head to look toward the glass door where people gave the attendants tickets and the attendants scrutinized them before handing them back. Out of the door they walked when the process was over.

1, 2, 3, 4, 5 ... 6 ... 7. Fatima counted the passengers ahead of her as they neared the doors.

When it was finally their turn, they were called over with an exhausted "Next." *Give the ticket*, Fatima kept repeating in her mind as she walked up to the woman. She extended the ticket and the woman snatched it out of her grip, tore half of it and gave the other half back to her. Fatima stood waiting for her to ask for her passport. The woman took a step back, glanced at Fatima and said, “Walk, go on that way.”

Hasan pushed her from behind. “We need to go out now,” he whispered. “The plane’s waiting for us.” She strolled toward the tinted glass doors and put her hands out, just in case they didn’t open, ready to pull them apart, but they parted as if they’d been waiting to take her all along. The sun had partially risen, painting the sky into a silky pink. Pointing at her was the airplane’s round snout, its wings outstretched on either side, suspended in midair, its body white, its tail a sharp red. It exuded a loud noise which caused her surroundings to recede, the mountains in the backdrop moved away, the sky rose, the sun a glowing sphere in the distance. She put her arm out to touch Hasan, but her arm was heavy in the wind that emanated from the hum of the plane. She craned her neck and saw he was right behind her, looking straight at her, a smile distorting his face, his eyes barely slits. *Were his eyes always this small?* she asked herself. *Who is he? How strange it is*, she said to herself, *that I was there just a few hours ago, surrounded by familiar structures, on a familiar road, the same owls hooting, the same rats scuffling about amongst the mulberry trees, and here I am now, walking on concrete I’ve never walked on before.*

Suddenly a strong wind swept around her, blowing her hair across her face, submerging the world into darkness. When she pushed her hair away, she noticed that it wasn’t the wind at all, but instead hot air bellowing from the plane’s vast body. She wondered if it would be this hot inside the airplane, how she would sustain herself in that heat for the entire journey, fearful it would be like the August heat in the village, so hot one could almost hear the sizzling of flesh.

Hasan held her hand and coughed, leaning in closer to her. She felt his sour breathe warm against her cheek. “We need to go up these stairs,” he said to her. Fatima stood at the foot of the stairs and looked up the metal stairs.

“There?” she asked, attempting to count them. Several times taller than the ones she climbed at home. They climbed up them one step at a time, Fatima timidly holding onto Hasan’s hand on one side and the cold metal rail on the other, not daring to look down. The stairs creaked and bounced below her as more people joined the line. She counted till twenty-four before she heard a voice.

"Welcome on board." She looked up and saw it was the woman with the red scarf and the pencil skirt she'd seen minutes earlier standing in front of her, lifting her arm and pointing at the interior of the plane.

Fatima turned left and walked into what appeared to her a rather narrow hall, seats neatly arranged side by side, aligned back further than her eyes could see. It reminded her of the weddings she'd attended with her mother all summer, maybe one, most times two a week, in enclosed outside areas where concrete had been poured over areas that once contained thousand-year-old olive trees. A concrete floor on which the bride and groom's family would arrange rows of plastic garden chairs that had been hosed down with water to cleanse the grime of the previous summer.

"When do I stop?" asked Fatima, speaking over her shoulder.

"The numbers are up here," said Hasan, tapping onto the plastic cabinets hanging high up on the walls of the plane. "We've still got a while to go," he said. "37A. That's all the way near the back."

People opened the cabinets, cramming in their suitcases, others had already seated themselves, resting their heads against their seats, their eyes gently shut, as if they'd done this a thousand times before. A baby was crying somewhere behind them, and to their right, a woman was picking at some grapes in a plastic tub. They strolled further down, and Fatima could finally see the back of the plane where women stood wearing the same red scarfs, the same navy pencil skirts.

"We're here," said Hasan.

Fatima slithered in, her chest rubbing against the seat in front of her. She sat, and rose when she felt a hard object digging into her bottom. Gliding her hands under her, she pulled out two short straps.

"You've got to fasten those in front of you," said Hasan, who was still standing. "Put the thin metal bit into the slot of the other."

Fatima did as she was told, letting the metal clasp fall into her lap when she heard a satisfying click. She glared at the back of the seat in front of her, reading letters and trying to remember the sounds they made when they came together. She listened to a conversation that a man and woman were having behind her about the contents of their suitcases, each listing the abundance of fruit and the likes that they'd brought with them, oranges and lemons, *molehiya*, *pastelli*, *sucuk*, *tarhana*, halloumi. Fatima stopped listening halfway, remembering her own tiny sack which she had placed on the floor between her feet. She was saddened by her lost opportunity, the plump citrus fruits that could have been placed into her luggage too, *cakistes* packed into plastic tubs which were once filled with sweet ice creams. She recalled her mother kneeling on the ground, bent over her various cousins' suitcases who were returning back to rich-old London, filling them with the remnants of a summer that was gradually dwindling.

"Are you ready for the journey?" said Hasan, placing his hand on her thigh. She winced and looked ahead at the same letters she had been unable to decipher. She nodded.

Before long a ring reverberated in the air, followed by the gruff voice of a man. "Ladies and gentlemen. Welcome on board. I'm Eser Baygin, your pilot. We will be flying very shortly. The weather is London is rainy and cold. Ten degrees."

Fatima thought about whether the human body could grow accustom to such a cold and what it would feel like. She remembered the coldest winter of a few years ago when the oranges hanging off the tree in their garden froze. Her mother had suggested they'd pick them before the ice melted away and transformed the fruits into a slushy pulp. They'd pulled them off their thin branches and placed them into the freezer for the summer, when they'd defrost them before squeezing them into the sweetest lickerish juice.

"Excuse me. That's my seat over there," said a voice to her left. Fatima gazed toward the voice; a tall man with a busy beard looked down at her. Fatima glimpsed to her right at the empty seat beside her. Hasan stood up and so did Fatima, allowing the man to pass by with his bulging backpack. They waited till the man had seated himself, dropping his bag onto the floor right in front of him, before they sat down too.

Fatima could smell that his breathe was tinged with wine, just like her father's, who would always go to the *kahve* to drink a few before he went home. The uniformed women walked by glaring into their laps. Another ring echoed in the air, the pilot's voice again: "Cabin crew ready for lift off."

The plane started moving, slowly at first before picking up speed, the outside a green and grey blur. Fatima rested her head against her seat and took a deep breathe, trying to ignore the vibration of the plane and the loud roar that drowned out any other sound. Within minutes the plane rose, and Fatima felt her back pressing firmly into her seat, her head being pushed back by an intangible force. The plane continued to vibrate and she lifted her arm eager to grab her armrest for support. Her hand settled on a warm hand, her palm ticked by a thin cluster of hairs, no doubt Hasan's. She wrapped her fingers around the hand, intertwining her own with his. The hand responded, enveloping her fingertips into its grip. A finger prodded her right shoulder, followed by a soft, "Fatima." She opened one eye and saw Hasan looking into her face and realized that the hand she had been caressing was not his, but belonged to the stranger she'd not even said a word to.

## ENGLISH TRANSLATIONS OF TURKISH WORDS

Bonibon: A round chocolate candy with a colorful sugar coating sold in Turkey and Cyprus, much like Smarties.

Eti Cin: An Orange Jelly Biscuit; another Turkish candy.

*Molehiya*: A traditional Cypriot dish made with the dried leaves of the Corchorus Olitorius plant. The leaves are picked, dried, then cooked in a tomato sauce with onions, garlic, and either chicken or lamb pieces.

*Tüp*: A gas cylinder which in Cyprus is used to provide gas to stoves and heaters.

*Tütün*: Fresh tobacco

*Adaçayı:* An herbal tea made with sage.

*Kahve:* A coffeehouse

*Muhtar:* A senior member in the government; one in charge of a village in Cyprus. Every village has its own *muhtar.*

*Yenge:* Auntie, generally used to refer to a close male relative's wife.

*Buyucu:* A necromancer and psychic of sorts. In Cyprus, they are believed to be able to predict the future and inhibit impending catastrophes by chanting prayers and providing people with rituals to undertake.

Sahin: A brand of a Turkish car.

*Gencler:* A word used by someone older to refer to youngsters.

*Hakkini helal et:* A common saying in Turkish which is uttered by one who is going to do an arduous, risky job and wants the other's blessing.

*Pasteli:* A nut and sesame seed brittle popular in Cyprus, and commonly sold at summer fairs.

*Sucuk:* A sausage-shaped sweet made of condensed grape juice. Not to be confused with the Turkish *sucuk,* which is an herbed processed meat much like salami.

*Tarhana:* A base for a soup made with buckwheat, black sesame, and soured yoghurt. Dried on the roof in summer and stored away for the winter.

*Cakistes:* A traditional Cypriot olive, cracked, preserved in salty water, and marinated in olive oil, lemon juice, and coriander seeds.

# DEAR DIARY,

MUHAMMAD SALEEM

Dear Diary,

2004: 7 years of age. A memory. A place: the school stage. A prince kissing a boy to wake him from eternal sleep. A taboo broken: fear, laughter, confusion. Embarrassment, humiliation. A closing, remorse, an exchange: the prince sleeps.

2007: 10 years of age. A page, then nothing. A rupture; of time, of self. Survival through forgetting. *The memory will come back when you are ready, don't crush your heart.* Sleep.

2010: 15 years of age. A line is a page. A boy's name: Areeb. A talking too much, too fondly. An accusation: gay. A denial, a justification: friendship, admiration, wonderment. A heartache. A forgetting. An oblivion, an obliteration.

2011: 16 years of age. A piling of fragmented words and thoughts; sex; desire; gay. A sin, a sin, a sin. Repent and abstain. An absence of explanation, comprehension. An abundance of fear of Hell fire: Everlasting Torture.

2012: 15 years of age, a correction. A farewell, a realization, a rejection: dissonance, disassociation. A dream, a desire; Areeb; skin; touch. An admission, a denial. A contradiction, a paradoxical existence practicing self-erasure: survival. A heartbreak. A forgetting. *The memory will come back when you are ready, don't crush your heart.*

2013: 16 years of age. A loneliness, a void, an estrangement. Inhabiting a liminal space, drowning in self-hate. A chance encounter, an unfurling, a new friend: Ahsan. A resurgence of joy, a fear of life. A story rewritten, a desire reexperienced: *Ishq ka Ain, Ahsan ka Alif.*

2014: 17 years of age. A joking confession. A silence, a withdrawal, a refusal to acknowledge. A spiral of self-doubt and hate. A desire for equilibrium, a loathing for being left on read. A void threatening to form, threatening to consume. A denial losing its hold. A truth breaking free. A dread of drinking from the well-spring of desire found within. An infatuation that persists through it all.

2015: 18 years of age. An introduction, a conversation, an acceptance. A community: a bond of flourishing. An impossibility of weeding shame and guilt, an assurance of its occurrence. A contradiction: a source of comfort, an opening of possibilities. A bubbling of memory, and then, a dam breaking; a flash flood of emotions and scorching self-rapprochements. A voice, a tender embrace, a soothing of a child's cries. A sharing of pain. An affirmation: your heart is a beautiful thing. *You are ready.*

20XX: A happily ever after: a community of queers.

# Untitled (from the series Facing It)

/ Jack Bordnick

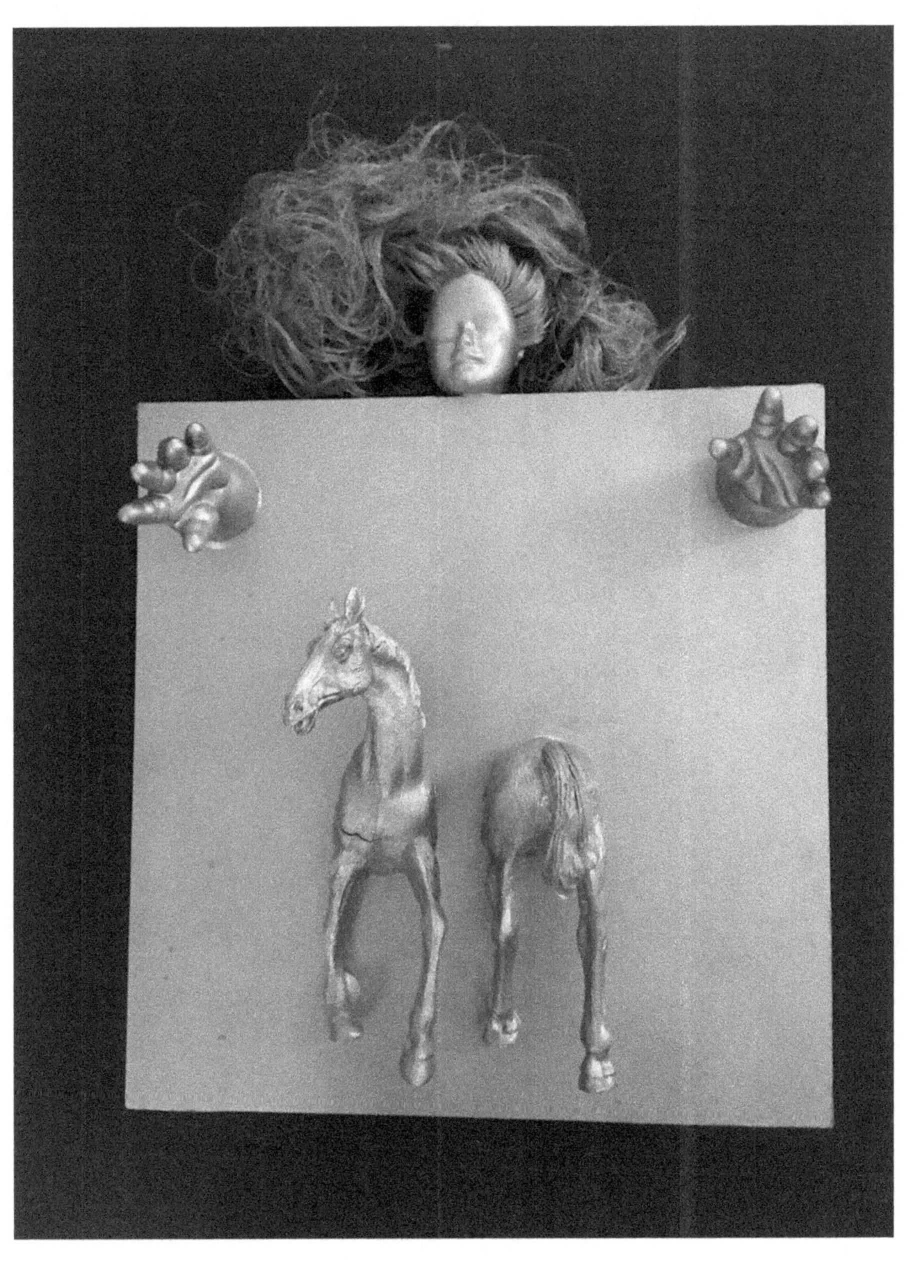

## Untitled (from the series Facing It)

/ Jack Bordnick

# PULALI

KC PEDERSEN

*"We live in a beautiful, sentient universe that yearns for you to tell the truth about it."*

—Carolyn See

*"You are going to feel like hell if you never write the stuff that is tugging on the sleeves in your heart—your stories, visions, memories, songs: your truth, your version of things in your voice. That is really all you have to offer us, and it's why you were born."*

—Anne Lamott

**Origins**

For a graduate workshop, I entitled this "Essay in Twelve Genres." Feedback: The word genre is phony, unnecessary, and insufficiently ironic, a pretension by someone fancying herself intellectual. I was, they suggested, using genre to seal myself up and be safe.

I too was concerned by the word, but it is the idea that disturbs me. When I try to write about Pulali, I grope for a form that captures my birthplace, my home. I attempt essay, dream, play, story. Word made manifest. Word made flesh.

A teenaged boyfriend's song, "Pulali Woman Made a Fish out of Me."

Shortly before said teenaged boyfriend went off to war where his head blew up, was patched back together, and he no longer makes songs.

But no matter how I attempt to capture Pulali, she's the doe that just swam past in the bay, driven off the cliff by a predator.

Pulali plunges out ahead, eluding my net of words.

Perhaps Pulali can't be captured. I grew up hearing my father say this thin slice of sea and land we call ours was appropriated from those who lived here for thousands of years. The original people, he said, did not believe land could be owned. We are, he said, Pulali's stewards, protecting her shoreline and uplands as best we can.

**Burial Grounds**

Pulali Point sits pretty much in the middle of the Olympic Peninsula and is itself a small peninsula jutting into Dabob Bay, Hood Canal, and Jackson Cove. The geological formation itself dates from the Eocene Era, and is about forty million years old.

For ten thousand of those years, The Klallam and other indigenous people frequented the area. According to David Brownell, Cultural Resources Specialist for Jamestown S'Klallam Tribe, "The nəxʷsƛ̓áy̓əm̓ or S'Klallam (Strong People) are today comprised of three Tribes, the Jamestown S'Klallam, Port Gamble S'Klallam, and Lower Elwha Klallam. At the time of European arrival around 1790, the S'Klallam were one people whose territory stretched across the northern Olympic Peninsula and across the Strait of Juan de Fuca to Vancouver Island. They continued to expand this range into the historic era, occupying Port Townsend and the lower (northern) reaches of Hood Canal and the new mill town of Port Gamble by the mid-1800s."

Other indigenous people who lived and still live along Washington State's Olympic Peninsula include the Hoh, Skokomish, Suquamish, Squaxin Island, Quileute, and Makah. The Tulalip people and others may also have visited from more far-flung parts of thc Salish Sea.

Around Pulali Point, the original people used the spit in front of what are now the unincorporated village of Brinnon and the coves of Pleasant Harbor, Seal Rock State Park, Jackson Cove, and other areas as summer camps for salmon and shellfish harvest and berry gathering. As with Pulali, some place names reflect the original Indian languages. These include the Anglicized Quilcene, Dabob, Duckabush, Dosewallips, Hamma Hamma, and Lilliwaup.

According to homesteader Ray Lindeke, Pulali Point, with its commanding view of waterways and Mount Rainier, was a location for ceremonies to send off the dead. In earlier times, he was told, bodies were placed in canoes with gifts to accompany the spirit onward, then set into the trees. Later, due to plunder of sacred places by early settlers and death from disease introduced by traders and settlers, the Indians adopted the European custom of burying their deceased.

**Family**

To me, Pulali was the commune I was born into, which the founders preferred to call a cooperative and what might now be called an intentional community. My parents, John Pedersen and Marilyn Sutherland, met at my mother's going-away party in Seattle. After completing a summer journalism internship, Marilyn was returning to Evanston, Illinois, to marry her long-time fiancé. My mother's photographer, Jack Keerl, knew John, my artist father, who lived in a longhouse in the Olympic wilds. Keerl suggested John attend the party.

According to family legend, John and Marilyn talked late into the night. "I want to show you Pulali before you leave," John told Marilyn. They took a ferry to the primitive site with the Olympic Mountains rising behind, Dabob Bay in front. For two years, John had lived on the land while he and the other communards cleared a one-lane driveway from the nearest county road, hand-dug a thirteen-foot well, put in deep earthen stairs to the beach, and planted organic gardens. They hauled stones and split logs and cedar shakes to build an eight hundred square foot cabin called the Big House.

Three days later, my father's Danish immigrant parents, Kirstine and Hans, and my mother's Irish mother Mary as witnesses, John and Marilyn were married in the Seattle Arboretum. They spent the first year of their marriage milling logs and splitting shakes for their own three hundred square foot log cabin a short distance through the forest from the Big House. A one-room affair, with bunks lining the walls and a pull-out bed for my parents, in ten years, they filled what we called the Little Cabin with six kids.

Legend also has it that when Mary Gilligan stepped off the plane, she took one look at my full-bearded long haired father, said, "He's an alcoholic," and fainted dead away on the tarmac.

**Intentional Community**

Prior to World War II, my father and his best friend Jack Anderson, recent graduates of Seattle's Cornish School, pursued commercial art in Manhattan. They snagged some big accounts and attended rent parties where world-class musicians played. When war was declared, an art school mentor told John about a special unit in the Aleutians. He and other artists and writers in his unit never saw combat, instead living in bunkers where they decoded enemy messages. Afterwards, John returned to New York, but commercial art no longer commanded his heart.

John and Jack decided to drive around Mexico to study the great muralists. They were drawn by the idea of the artists' belief that art should belong to the people. One afternoon, while sitting on a hillside near Patzcuaro, they watched peasants construct stone walls. That, they decided, was the real art. "We need to be on the land, Pete," Jack said.

They headed back to the north, where they met up with brothers, raised like them in West Seattle, Allen and Norman Jones, who were married to sisters Rosetta and Violet. As a union activist, Allen had been blacklisted. Allen always said they were all "parlor pinks," never carrying a Communist card but believing in Socialist ideals. Along with several other buddies who soon abandoned the rough rural lifestyle, the men pooled their savings to purchase a slice of undeveloped land bordering a wild rocky shoreline.

John built a longhouse based on the dwellings of the Klallams while Jack designed the eight hundred square foot Big House with its two closet-sized bedrooms on the ground level and a tiny room tucked into the eaves facing onto an open kitchen and living area with a floor to ceiling fireplace and stone chimney. A nearby Norwegian homesteader, Eivind Hjelvik, loaned the young men a portable mill and taught them how to split thick cedar shakes and line the inner walls with burlap. Jack and my father constructed the stone walls they'd admired in Mexico, topped by milled logs and fashioned the door from huge cedar slabs. They harvested clams and oysters from the beach and wild blackberries from the forest's edge.

Jack, a merchant seaman, periodically dried out by catching a ship. Back on land, his drinking would again spiral out of control. When I was six, Jack, drunk, walked into traffic in the middle of the night. John never got over Jack's death. "In dreams, he's always calling me to join him," John said. "He says, 'Come on over, Pete. The water's fine.'"

**Family Council**

In middle school, I sometimes attended John's night classes as he pursued a master's degree. I read the assigned books, and we discussed them during the hour-long drives. The professors acted as if it was perfectly natural that a child join a college class and treated me as if I were an equal.

Then, in an education course my parents took together, they learned about R. Dreikurs Family Council. Based on similar ideals as the Pulali Cooperative, Family Council supports respectful communication, equality of all, and consensus-based problem-solving. John placed a large bulletin board in the kitchen, and any of us, from then five-year Brynne to the teenagers and adults, could jot issues we wished to discuss. At scheduled weekly meetings, we gathered around the kitchen table. Visiting friends were included. The roles of chair and scribe revolved weekly. Over a ten-year period, the handwriting and styles of eight very different individuals filled three spiral-bound notebooks.

For their final project, my parents brought all six kids into class, and we held our regular meeting. In my father's elegant artist handwriting, the main item that happened to be on that week's agenda was that my eighth-grade friends and I had stolen my father's work truck and abandoned it a mile or two away. One of the Dreikurs' concepts is that behaviors have consequences. As everyone in Family Council had an equal vote, it was easy for me to propose that I had learned my lesson, would never do it again, and should have no consequences at all. After some discussion, mostly dominated by me, we voted. Results: Six in my favor. Two opposed.

The professor was appalled. "You'd better watch out for that eldest daughter of yours," he warned my parents. "She's headed for big trouble."

The professor, of course, was right. Reading diaries from the time, I see that overdosing on drugs and alcohol and arranging my body for my parents to find was my way to escape my high school crowd. My consequences were that I returned to Pulali's summer embrace. I slept in the Big House when the other owners weren't there, and in lieu of alcohol, binged on reading and writing. I forced my parents and siblings to assemble on the beach and listen to what became my first published story.

**Burning**

After they completed teaching certification in night school and taught for a few years, my parents gained some minimal financial security. Which for them meant they "splurged" on a polyester area rug and curtains for the cabin. On New Year's, we had gathered for our usual ritual of writing resolutions for ourselves and for our parents and siblings. We tucked these into a jar in the eaves to pull out and read the following year.

The weekend of the fire, though the elder kids were away at college, the younger three in the city with friends. John and Marilyn and their rescue dogs were on their own. John hung the new rug on a line rigged above the woodstove. It fell onto the burner of a hotplate where he was brewing coffee. In those pre-flameproof-mandated days, the rug went up like a torch and ignited the curtains and the tinder dry log cabin and shake roof.

John and Marilyn escaped in their pajamas and pushed the family van away from the flames. They flagged down a passing boat, but by the time the volunteer fire crew arrived, they could only keep the flames from spreading into the forest.

My sisters and I had taken some kind of workshop related to thought transmission. It's the kind of stuff we girls, as we called ourselves, believed in. Our parents never discouraged us, and Marilyn in particular simply assumed such communication was real. One sister was paged out of an art class. Your parents' cabin burned down, someone told her. They're okay.

From our far-flung locations, my sisters and I called each other. My parents, of course, had no phone. We weren't sure where they were, or if the van had burned along with the cabin. The only thing to do, we determined, was to pick a time and send our parents a thought message, some kind of dream or vision.

The following day, my phone rang. "We got your message," Marilyn said.

"What was it?"

"Last night, Daddy and I were curled up in bed in the Big House where we've been ever since the fire. We didn't know what to do. Then we heard a message."

We girls hadn't articulated a particular message. We just focused on some vague notion of healing energy.

"The words were really clear. 'Don't look back.' For the first time in three days we felt peace. We dressed in some old clothes of Allen and Rosetta's, drove into Quilcene and ate breakfast. Now I'm calling you from the phone booth!"

When they returned to the cabin's burnt core, the dogs ambled in from the forest.

My boyfriend and I drove and ferried and drove some more to meet my parents at the site. For days, we filled bags with debris and hauled it away. I was stunned by how much detritus a tiny cabin leaves behind, only the woodstove left standing. In the spirit of not looking back, Marilyn wanted a new location for rebuilding. She had never liked being so close to the Big House or tucked back into the trees without a water view. The four of us walked to the far end of the long strip of land, past where John's longhouse had stood and where the organic gardens still grew. We pounded in stakes for the corners.

Over the next three years, on weekends and summers, John and Marilyn camped in a tent on the new location. Using a kit, they constructed a cabin from the ground up.

We kids helped when we could. I learned how to wire a house and install outlets. We learned that Pulali was more than buildings constructed from wood.

**Dream**

In dreams, all paths lead to Pulali. Pulali forms my life's heart. In one recurring dream, my mother and I climb the tallest tree overlooking the bay. From there, we can see everything. Starting when I was three or four, I had another repeating dream. George the road man drives his huge grader down the mile-long dirt road etching through the forest to our cabin, as he often did to drink coffee with Marilyn on his breaks. He jokes he is going to steal me away. The grader is filled with gifts. I am terrified. The pulsing of the grader is my blood pulsing, the waves crashing against the cliffs.

**Memory**

My early memories are as clear as if etched in my skin. Someone places my crib outside the Big House kitchen so that Rosetta can watch me. Wrapped in towels, John and Marilyn descend the wide dirt stairs to the beach. As they vanish from sight, it is as if they vanish forever.

My grandfather and father helped build a dome-like auditorium to add to the four-room Brinnon schoolhouse. My elder brother's pre-school is there. As we still have no electricity in our cabin, I've never seen a television or film. Images flicker on the screen. Images flicker on the screen, but I don't know what they are.

The day my twenty-eight-year-old Aunt Lucille dies, I am eighteen months old. Someone knocks on the thick cedar slabs that form our cabin door. A tall stranger says something that makes the room contract in pain. Later, lying between John and Marilyn in their bed that folded down at night, my father sleeps with his mouth open, his eyes strangely soft without his glasses. "Is he dead?" I ask.

"Just sleeping," Marilyn says in her soft way.

She often walked my brother Hansi and me, with baby Lisa in the big buggy, up the driveway to visit the people we called Grandma and Grandpa Lindeke. Like Eivind Hjelvick, they were early white settlers who reached out to the young Pulali communards. The Lindekes lived in their own log house, always warm from the wood stove, smelling of cookies and Beauregard, their dachshund pup. As we walked the half mile from our cabin to theirs, Marilyn showed me tiny purple violets pushing up beside a stump blackened by a forest fire at the turn of the century.

"Those are Johny Jump Ups," she said. I imagined the little buds were my father pushing out of the earth.

We played in a sandbox just outside our cabin window, where Marilyn could see us as she washed dishes. Hansi wore sandals and Lisa a bright yellow sweater. I did not like the word sweater. Already, words produced a physical reaction: *dead, Johny, yellow.*

When I was four, John found temporary work as a carpenter in Home, Washington, a former Socialist commune. We lived in a house on stilts, and every day while John worked, Marilyn took Hansi, Lisa and me to visit an old man who fed us prunes. When John finished that project, we returned to Pulali. But although John tried to make a living through art, brush picking, logging, oystering, and other random jobs, and my mother wrote for *Sunset*, we could never quite make it. Grandma Pedersen found an old run-down farm south of the Seattle airport, and John started a concrete business, bidding on sidewalks, basements, stairs, and foundations for houses on the Alki cliffs.

The day we moved from Pulali, our tabby, Mother Cat, gave birth to four kittens at my feet. I watched each damp form emerge, and how the mother licked them dry.

## Theatre

John: "I walked to the doorway of the house where Keerl had told me her going-away party was being held. I was late. For the past two years, I'd lived in the woods. I hadn't seen many people. Suddenly, I felt very shy."

Marilyn: "He's wearing a black turtleneck. He smokes a wooden pipe. He has a full red beard, and his hair, bleached blond by the sun, grows down over his neck. He wears the turtleneck and long hair because for the years he's lived mostly alone in his longhouse in the forest, he's had poison-ivy. It's so bad his neck is deeply cracked with open wounds."

John: "I knock on the door of a mansion on Capitol Hill overlooking the University of Washington campus and ship canal. Marilyn rented the upstairs, and a wealthy Seattle family occupied the rest. But for her going-away party, the family let Marilyn use the entire house. She opens the door. She is the most beautiful woman I've ever seen. She wears a white blouse with full peasant sleeves and a full white skirt with Mexican embroidery on it. She has dark hair with auburn light in it. Her hair reaches past her shoulders in great thick waves. She tells me to come in. I am in a trance and must force myself to move up the steps and through the doorway. Inside, everyone is drunk. Most are passed out here and there around the huge house. One is lying on the stairway crying 'Lindy, Lindy.' That was her nickname in college because her stepfather's name was Lindenmeyer.

'Lindy, Lindy' he moans again and again throughout that long night. She is cooking dinner in the kitchen, though no one present is capable of eating it. That does not matter. I chop onions and celery. Lindy boils a pot of water for pasta, makes a huge green salad. Neither of us drinks. We talk. We talk until the light is rising and I need to go. I want to leave something with her. I give her my copy of *Portrait of the Artist as a Young Man*."

Marilyn: "He tells me this book will explain him to me." Marilyn and John are telling my siblings and me the story while we drive four hours from Pulali to Sol Duc Hot Springs and the trailhead for the High Divide and Seven Lakes Basin. The Courtship Story, we say. We love the story. Their telling takes us from Pulali to Sequim, from Sequim to Port Angeles, along the treacherous stretch of highway where logging trucks won't hesitate to rush at you headlong, and past Crescent Lake to the turnoff for Sol Duc. "Then he leaves. I write in my journal that I have just met a man like no one I have ever known. When I think that I will never see him again, I cannot imagine living. Yet Gene, my fiancé, is waiting for me. I am supposed to fly out that day to meet him. Friends in Lake Forest, where I grew up, and Evanston, where I graduated college, awaits the festivities postponed and promised for three years. Just as I finished writing these words, I heard a tap on my window. I climbed out of bed. There was John. Somehow, he had climbed the lattice and was tapping at my window. "I came back," he said. And I knew I would never let him out of my sight again."

We start the switchback climb from Sol Duc to Heart Lake. Brynne, the baby, carries her doll. "The high point of my life," my father said later of our three-day climb. "I ask nothing more than this."

Later, in Family Council, Brynne said, "I'm going to be the normal one in this family."

**History**

At around nineteen or twenty, I completed an independent study researching the communal movement in Washington State, including Socialist communes like Home. As part of the project, I attended a three-day writer's conference where I met a variety of Northwest poets and writers, including Duane McGinnis (*After the Death of an Elder Clallam*) and Carl Cary, (*Salish Songs and Other Rituals*.) I used old records, interviews and letters, lost when I was in graduate school and stored them in the basement of a professor's house. As, in graduate school, I too was lost. I was searching for my roots. I was searching for a Pulali of my own.

In the middle of a dark night, drunk in a college cafe, I confided in a waitress named Grace. "I need to find my home," I told her. Grace held a real estate license and offered to show my boyfriend and me places around the college town. "Your love nest," she crooned as she showed us properties completely unlike my dream.

**Submarines**

I grew up in the shadow of nuclear annihilation. In grade school, children huddled on our hands and knees in the hallway or beneath our desks, hands tucked over our heads. Or we were told to "walk awhile run awhile" to somehow arrive home before enveloped by radiation. My first paintings featured explosions. I created elaborate games to hide my younger siblings when airplanes flew low from the nearby airport.

To me, Pulali was safe, far from these drills. Then the U.S. Navy, long a nearby presence, commandeered the deep bay for Naval Undersea Warfare testing. World War II subs cruised and dove. Manned installations appeared on the cliffs, including the tip of Pulali Point. The Navy suggested the communards donate their land as patriotic service. If we strayed too far in our kayaks, patrol boats escorted us home.

The summer after ninth grade, I was on our beach reading *From Here to Eternity* by James Jones. Every day, Marilyn and my younger siblings would sprawl along the beach beside me. That day, though, they were still descending the broad dirt stairs when a torpedo emerged from the water, landed on the beach and split into two pieces, missing me by less than a foot.

"Sorry, Ladies," said the first of the hoards of enlisted men to arrive on our beach over the course of that day. "We misfired. You can go back to your sunbathing."

My mother's journalist friend Ruth took a picture of me in my spotted bikini with my book, and the local paper published it. On my first day of high school, the image was on the bulletin board of my home room.

**Word**

I asked Professor and linguist Timothy Montler, who created an alphabet and dictionary with Klallam elders who still spoke their original language, what Pulali might mean. "Pulali does not look like a Klallam word," Professor Montler emailed. "Klallam has L sounds in only a few words that come from English or French or another language. The word 'Klallam' comes from the Songees language. Pulali (like Dabob, Dosewallips, and Duckabush) may be a Twana or possibly Lushootseed word."

When I queried via the Tulalip Tribal website, educator Michele Balagot, Lushootseed Department Manager, responded, "Looking in our Lushootseed dictionary -ali actually means place where something is kept, place where something is typically located. The pulali was not in our Lushootseed dictionary, but we did find a similar word in the Chinook Jargon dictionary. The word we found was spelled polallie and it means powder, dust, or sand."

# The Sky Will Outlast Us

Tracy Mann

The dark tangos of Piazzolla are the soundtrack of my dreams. The young soldiers inspecting airport arrivals shift their weight under heavy machine guns. The square in front of Argentina's Pink House, La Casa Rosada, blooms with protesters. Some will disappear. On another night I am in Mississippi, where I have never been, facing off an armed militia of white boys, pushing my collarbone into the butt of a rifle. Yesterday, I ate a slice of pizza in Madison Square, my eyes reaching upward into the blue sky. A few clouds scattered. This sky will outlast us, I thought.

In an earlier dictatorship I developed a taste for Pasolini. I spoke no Italian and only knew *Porcile* by its Portuguese name, *Poçilga.* The pigsty. Outside the cinema, São Paulo's chorus line of skyscrapers flaunted headdresses of twisted antennae against the grey sky. My walk home, preoccupied with nihilist visions of Sicily's black sand and men devouring human flesh, led me past the basement prisons of the Department of Political and Social Order where naked college professors hung upside down, wrists and calves lashed against horizontal poles. Invisible to the street. I did not hear their screams.

You have to answer. You cannot change the subject to memories of a prior reign of terror that may or may not offer wisdom to the present. You must sit with the newspaper photos of the children murdered by a young man lost to his fanaticism. You must see your own daughter, grown now, and your own long-abandoned illusion of protecting her from the world. You must smell the aging dog, drying his wet fur by the fireplace, and brace for yet another loss. You turn, startled by your own misplaced saints who have returned to share the vigil.

# A Brutal Business

Jeanne Wilkinson

I called him Henry. I'm not sure why, but Henry he was, the last of my Holsteins. Black and white, but mostly black, with a white star on his forehead. I'd sold the rest of the herd to a farmer in the next county. To be with you.

No, that's not quite true. I would've sold them anyway, because it was all too much.

Illnesses, injuries, weather, weeds, breakdowns, bills, sweat, stings, fly strips, fieldwork, calf deaths, cat deaths, and the price of milk going nowhere but down. When you came along, I went with you. Left it all behind except for Henry. My last calf. A boy. Most of the calves born in my barn had been boys. Can't keep a herd going with boys. Useless boys. Cows are girls. You know. Milk?

Not even worth putting on the cattle truck, those adorable little ones with their wobbly legs walking up that tragic plank to a non-future, at best a cattle yard, food and drugs scientifically formulated to make them grow too fast: a terrible stink, squashed side by side, shit to their knees, rotting hooves, no room to roam. No. Some of the local farmers would bonk them in the head, the boy-babies, toss them into the woods to become a frothy maggot-wave squirming on the forest floor, a creamy carpet for deer to sniff and walk away from.

A brutal business, farming. I kept Henry, my last.

I backed him into a corner and slipped a rubber band around his balls with the stretching tool: snap. Better than cutting. Maybe. It seemed better. The band cut off the circulation; his bullish self withered and died; he became a steer. Magic. Not about to smash through fences to get to the source of that delicious cow-lady smell wafting in the wind, not about to run fierce and fast and bellowing to humpetty hump hump, humpetty hump

hump, hindquarters twitching, pounding, pumping. No, none of that. Instead those sweet and salty smells would drift right past his cold steer-nose, no more delicious than a diesel truck chugging down the road.

You and I picked each other up in the wind, across the room, down the road. We chased our sweet-and-salties smashed through fences fields forests humpetty hump hump ohmygod humpetty hump hump, shedding old lives with our clothes, rising up brand-new beasts from fragrant steamy soil. We had no rubber bands squeezing our randy souls, snap.

Oh, we were wild. We were delicious.

Your place had irregular fences. Or none at all. A swamp—we didn't call it wetlands then—and a sometimes corn or hayfield leading up into the woods, woods, woods all around that bled out deer, small herds and families nibbling corn and dappling themselves back into the woods again waiting for cold-snap hunters to take their corn-filled bellies home on top of cars, heads hanging slack over back windows, glazed and deadly glares knifing into the car at men in blaze-orange who should have been wolves. Couldn't see a house anywhere from your windows. A long driveway that flooded. Jesus, that driveway, with me always stuck on one side or the other in the track-grooved muck where the stream passed over, or parked by the road where everyone knew my car. Knew my story. Knew my past. Knew my gone-now herd. But better the smalltown scandal than my car sunk in a swamp-black slick of slurried ruts that filled with tiny fleeting fish during hard rains, fish who slid swimmingly into bird gullets or baked into mud-fried fish sticks in the subsequent sun.

We brought Henry there, to your place. We put him in a shed but he got out. It wasn't much of a shed. He wandered the abandoned fields and we found his shadowy self not far from the deer, herded him home, gave him corn. We'd ring the Henry bell; he'd saunter down to get his treat and sleep in the shed, and yes, he did that every night. We didn't fence him in; we didn't tie him up. We took chances with Henry. He ran wild, he did.

We took chances with each other. We cut our arms and bled each other's blood when the midsummer moon shone full on our shining blade. We were mother, father, sister, brother, cradled infant at our breasts: closer than words on paper; closer than lovers. Summer nights were star-pricked, candle-shadowed, floating in music, floating in flesh. Summer days were wind-songed, wildflowered. Roaming with our book we named those tender blossoms one by one: scorning the invasive aliens; breathing pistils and petals; leaving them be.

We ran wild, we did. We were pistil, petal, stamen and sepal. We did not leave each other be.

We wondered when we would eat him: Henry. Because Henry was not a pet. Henry was meat. Yet he *was* a pet, and happy, happy as a lone steer could be. And sleek. Furry black back smooth as oiled onyx. Henry and his good life. Then it was fall, with that snap in the air that hit you in the morning, that little slap of things going brown, shutting down, closing up, sleeping, rotting, dying. Hunting time. Butchering time. We wouldn't do it ourselves. We'd call the locals. It would be them, not us who shot him in the head, sliced him down the center, cut him into four pieces, and left us his heart in a pail on our doorstep, which I would give to neighbors. All too real, that heart. And the tongue, too, long and pink. Jesus. Then they would haul the quartered carcass to the cutting place of saws and knives where beasts become chops and steaks and burgers, letting him hang for a while to age and mellow, eventually returning Henry to us wrapped in clean white waxy paper. We would freeze and thaw him out piecemeal; he would sizzle in our pan permeated with that sweet-earth nutty rounded full and melting flavor common to right-living domesticated flora and fauna not stressed or poisoned, pushed or prodded. He would come back to us delicious.

This is the bargain we've long made with our food animals: we feed them; they feed us. Who gets the best of that bargain? After years of farming, I don't know. But the least we can do for our meat is to give it a good life, was my thinking.

A brutal business, farming.

**T**hen one day that fall, you had gone somewhere, probably to one of your jobs, the odd ones. It was one of those mist-rising season-turning days neither warm nor cold, where you could wear a jacket or not wear a jacket. I went outside to feel the still-warm sun and saw a strange thing, which was Henry lying on a pile of straw in front of the shed, rays of golden light striping through the fog onto his dark fur. Henry who was usually up and about and even gone by that time, leaving us to wonder once again if we should tie him up or fix the pen because would he really come back to us?

*Really?* we would wonder as his dark form disappeared into the trees, scratching our heads, doing nothing. But here he was this sun-buttered morning, our Henry, on his side, legs sticking straight out so I walked up to him lying in that strange way and saw that he was stiff and still as a stone, and I saw that he was dead.

I stared down while fog drifted in, a thick swamp mist that covered us like a blanket and tucked him in up to his eyes, Henry's eyes that lay wide open to the sky above, filmy and blank under long beautiful lashes. And I was alone. Alone in that sky-blotting mist with Henry, who was dead. Alone, alone, alone. I sat on the grass, wet like tears had fallen, yet my eyes stayed dry. How did it happen? Did he eat something bad? Did he swallow a piece of metal lying about? How did he die? Why did he die? Why why why? Still as stones we were that day, Henry and I. And when you got home, still as stones we were that night, you and I, sitting at the kitchen table, smoke from our cigarettes the only thing moving in the world.

We chewed on Henry's death like cud. He was too big to bury. We performed no ceremony. We called the locals who take dead animals, fresh dead animals. I didn't ask what they were used for. Mink food? Did they pay us? Did we pay them? I don't remember. I only know that a truck came and took Henry away, unceremoniously. He did not come back to us delicious.

We were still wild, that fall, you and I. We ran fiery-footed in frosted grass, me crazy frantic to warm myself at the fount of your hot soul and bathe in it naked like temple water, you cooling with winter winds that whistled through the cracks in Henry's empty falling-down shed. You with a gun chasing after deer in Henry's old stomping grounds; me curling up on the kitchen floor drinking a whole goddamned beer in the morning first thing, life slipping slithering into a slurried mess, ruts in the driveway freezing into mountains and valleys, no birds no fish just deer flying wild and wounded, just me flying wild and wounded, trails of cold thin winter blood dripping from our love skinned and sliced into pieces ...

... heart in an old tin bucket that I left behind that winter day. But I took my tongue with me, I did.

# ESTRANGED

MANDY CLARK

Sometimes I pretend I don't have enough memories to write a book about you. Everything I know wouldn't even fill up a short story. On days I'm very angry, I couldn't even sport a flash piece about you if I tried. That saying, "kill your darlings?" I try not to create them.

I've turned you into a superhero in some early pieces: Narcissist Man. And your only superpower is to squash insects. But then I remember you were almost an entomologist—and even if you tried to pretend you didn't care about insects—I'd know you were lying. Especially the way you crafted your own butterfly nets or showed your only daughter how to swoop swallowtails on the trails into the net to preserve their wings. How to paralyze them by gently pinching the midsection of their bodies. Keeping them beautiful, yet still.

You know that time you embarrassed mom about walnuts in cookies? I wasn't there. She told me you and her and Tim and Cindy were sitting on the back patio and Cindy brought cookies and when she said, "They have walnuts in them." Mom said, "Oh, Mike doesn't like walnuts." But you said, "Of course I do." You ate several and declared they were the best cookies you'd ever had. Even though in thirty years of marriage no one could pay you to touch a walnut.

I googled you last March, a Washington state phone number came up. It wasn't free. I logged on to PayPal and sent $9.99 to this WhitePages.com website. Now I get notifications about once a month, even though I didn't sign-up for continuous reminders of your absence. You've moved three times in the past six months and you got yourself a speeding ticket down towards Eugene, Oregon this past August. The website tells me I can find much more information if I pay a one-time sum or a monthly fee. But it won't tell me what I want to know. It won't tell me what that is, either.

# Will Be, Will Be

Garrett Candrea

**Part I**

It was one of those nights without much talking when Dan told him. He began by saying his name.

He said, "Nick."

Nick said, "Yeah." He said it distractedly. He was sitting in his room some five hundred miles away with his hands positioned keyboard and mouse and the 3-D world wheeling in his monitor. He moved his avatar from here to there. He purchased sundry items from a merchant. He killed a creature and looted its corpse and it was still a while longer before he realized that Dan hadn't said anything else. That was all right. He didn't mind the silence. He could hear Dan breathing in his headset and that was enough. After nine years it wasn't so much about the sound of their voices as it was the sound of each other, the body presence living in each other's headset. On their private voice server Dan had his mic set to be open all the time, always transmitting, and it was his breathing that Nick could always hear. It was more than a white noise. There was a warmth to it, or associated with it, a sensation the brain conjured up to perpetuate the subliminal hum of body heat. This is what was important to Nick, what he relied on at the end of the long day when all its thousand little pixelated disappointments resolved invariably into a composite weariness and dread. He worked in the regulatory reporting department of a mid-sized consulting firm, a stoop-shouldered guy nearing thirty who stared into a screen while phones trilled about him in a pitch of rote. There were the benchmark reports for companies X and Y. There was the sound his boss made when her mouth was moving. There was the subway ride home to his six-story walkup in Queens where he'd become faithfully committed to routine, microwaving day-old takeout before logging on to the Game to commiserate with Dan about this or that while their avatars embarked on some small adventure.

Dan said Nick's name again. He said it oddly, experimentally, as if it were a foreign word he'd just learned.

"Yeah," Nick said.

But there was nothing else save Dan's breathing. Then Dan made the pterodactyl screech. It was a noise they made sometimes after a long period of silence to let the other know he was still there.

Nick echoed the screech, smiling briefly, and went on playing the Game in the dark.

Then Dan said he had cancer.

Nick was not sitting in the dark by choice, like this is what lonely people do, come home from their ten-hour workday in a grayscale cubicle to sit in the dark. He was sitting in the dark because the bulb had blown out the week before and he'd yet to go for a new one and he very much wished he had. His first reaction was to turn in his chair, to swivel around halfway and stare at the light switch on the far wall because he wanted to turn it on. As if that would have changed something. As if it were too dark to have heard him correctly.

He'd met Dan on the Game almost a decade ago. Dan had only been an avatar then by the name of Flophouse, a panoplied paladin standing in a clearing among the bloodless corpses of several polygonal pumas. From across the virtual slaughter they had at first simply waved to each other, a robotic gesture as rendered by their humanoid avatars. Then Dan had sent him a private whisper: *You doing this quest?*

Now Dan said in his ears, "Nick. Did you hear me?"

"Yeah," Nick said. But he kept his mic closed, on push to-talk, and he'd not pressed the button and so this word drifted off unheard into the semidarkness.

Then he pressed the hotkey. "Yeah," he said. He couldn't think of anything else to say beyond this perfunctory remark. The words were careening back through his brain. *Cancer. I have cancer.* Or looming outsized, the silhouetted meanings and unmeanings. In truth the first thing they had done was target each other. They had dragged their cursors over their screens and targeted each other's avatar and hit Enter and typed out /wave and hit Enter again. You wave at Flophouse. Flophouse waves at you. This was the system-generated text that had appeared on Nick's screen nine years ago. On Dan's screen it would have said Pandiculate. For the first year of their friendship they called each other only by their pseudonyms: Pandiculate, Flophouse. Or Pan, Flop, Floppy, Flap, Dickle, any number of corrupted nicknames. Then one day Flapjack had asked Pandle what his real name was.

Dan said, "I probably won't be coming on much anymore."

Whatever will be, will be. He would sing that now and again, Dan would, que será será, in a lilting mock-baritone. It was a kind of rueful mantra belted out following some unfavorable event within the Game. Or *obladi oblada.* Or *dippity-doo-da.*

"Nick," Dan said.

"Yeah," Nick said. He said this to himself. There was a stupid little *blup* sound that played whenever the hotkey was pressed and he didn't want to hear that right now.

Then Dan burped. It sounded stifled but it was a burp and it made Nick think of Dan's rants and musings, the occasional booze-garbled sermon yammered out among warped burps and how he button-mashed with piston frenzy. Nick could always picture Dan sweating when he was drunk, could hear him sweating, the mannerisms and quirks alluded to by sound alone. It was all there in the lumbering sentences and slurred renditions of old songs or viral songs or singing muddled lyrics of his own composition. Sometimes Nick would hold down the button patinated with finger gunk to sing along, improvise a measure or two. There was no one else who could draw him out of introversion like that.

"Nick," Dan said. On the screen Dan's avatar was jumping around Nick's where it stood dumbly on a cobbled road. Nick could hear Dan pressing his spacebar. Then he heard Dan burp again and he realized that stifled was the wrong word. It sounded painful. He wondered if they caught it early. Did he say they caught it early? Or he just found out? Did he say terminal? He rose from his chair and stepped to the window and opened it, he didn't know why, the answers to these questions were nowhere out there. He held his hand against the screen to feel the breeze, warm summer's breeze with a slight dampness to it.

Serendipity. This had been one of Dan's drunken tangents, asking who the hell came up with the word and how ridiculous it sounded.

Serendipity. Dipity. It has the cadence of a children's singalong, he'd said, because you'd need to be a child to believe in it, some magical *dipity-doo-da* whatever going on in the background that brings everything together.

Dan said, "Hello? Are you there?"

Nick sat down. "Yeah," he said. When he took his finger off the hotkey it made a sound like bloop.

It was a long while after they'd first met before Nick finally allowed himself to see a picture of Dan. He didn't want to put a face to the voice. He was afraid it'd be like going to see the movie adaptation of a book you liked where the lead actor cast for the role is so at odds with the mental image you've already constructed that it irks you to watch the thing and the book is ruined forever. But he thought the face matched the voice quite nicely.

"Well," Dan said. The voice was deep and rounded, ballasted with a slight gravelly texture. This was Dan. "I guess that's it," he said.

Nick wanted to know when his last day on the Game would be. Dan said he didn't know how to answer that question. He said he would be on tomorrow. He said he would be on at the usual time or try to. He told Nick he would text him when he left work. Nick wanted to ask why he was still going to work but didn't. He wanted to ask how much time he had left but didn't.

Dan said, "I'll try to tell you when my last day online will be. I will tell you. I don't want that day to come out of nowhere."

Then Nick did ask. He said, "How long?"

"How long what?"

Nick didn't answer. He knew Dan understood.

Dan said, "Six months. Give or take."

Their private voice server was named The American Puma Society, a designation made in tribute to that long-ago moment when they'd first bumped into each other while sitting some five hundred miles apart. Upon its creation the server had a single default voice channel labelled General. This was later renamed to The Great Loin Cloth Tour following a drunken gaming session during which they had stripped their avatars down to their pixelated undergarments and run from one end of the Game's continent to the other. There was a lot of dying at the hands of high-level creatures and the odd enemy player and they'd gone through a six-pack each by the end of it.

Nick said, "You want me to come?"

"To come," Dan said. "You mean here? To Maine?"

"Yeah."

**Part II**

This was all new to Nick. He'd seen Dan smiling before in photographs but he'd never seen Dan make a smile, the way the mouth corners curled up, the way the ears shifted back ever so slightly, the way the cheeks went plump and the eyes how they went narrow, the noticeable change of light in them, grading the shades of excitement. The face was still pudgy, still bearded, a thickset guy in faded jeans and wrinkled field jacket standing beside a car rental ad among the flurrying bodies in this dimly lit baggage claim.

And there were words formed in real-time: Hey, bud, you made it. And the arm extending outward, the hand opening to accept his own, clasp and embrace, two strong pats thumped out against his back.

They exhausted the stock conversation about airports and travel during the short walk to the lot where Dan had parked his car and there was little talk during the hour's drive over to Kineo. An old blues tune fringed with static played on the radio while Nick looked out the window, watching the trees and meadows go scrolling by, the outskirt homes with rotted screen doors and scrap-metal chimes. Nick didn't ask about the cancer directly but questions that edged the topic of it. When do you think you'll put in your two weeks'? You have anything planned for after? Any trips? Dan said he hadn't really thought about it. He said he mainly wanted to hang out, relax, maybe play the Game.

"Maybe," Nick said. He smiled at the mountains in the distance.

The car was a silver Corolla from the early nineties time-buffed down to a faded gray, nylon upholstery and a tape deck, peg locks, window cranks. Dan told Nick he was free to roll down his window but Nick told him he was fine. Dan leaned and rolled down his own, wind sputtering in the gap. He drummed his fingers on the steering wheel, hummed along to the radio. They passed a lumberyard, a cemetery, a large hangar with its corrugated flanks painted bright cherry red and the words Big Red Barracks bolted over its lancet door.

"Dance hall there," Dan said.

"Yeah?"

"Always wondered what it's like. Like what kind of people really go there? Used to be a tire depot."

Nick made a small sound to communicate interest. He tried to think of something to say to stave off the droning quiet. He understood that Dan's comments were nudges at conversation but he was still struggling to acclimate himself to this, sitting here next to Dan, who now began scatting to himself, beatboxing, breathy bilabials together with a few hissing sounds strained through his teeth.

But then Nick thought this was normal. Forget this two-lane state road flanked by woods and overgrowth. They were two guys sharing a silence and saying nothing much. Dan turned onto a narrow road marked by a canted sign and Nick watched mailboxes on wooden posts flick past in the window. A car for sale. A basketball hoop. No, there was nothing strange about this at all. It was Nick watching scenes within a frame while he listened to the Dan noises in the background.

Finally Dan pulled into a weedy drive and cut the engine. "Here we are," he said. A modest rambler of vinyl siding streaked with mildew, branches jutting from the gutters.

Inside Dan told Nick to put his stuff down wherever. "You'll be there on the couch," he said. "It's a pullout."

Nick had set his duffel down near the door and was standing beside it, watching Dan go around the room pulling on the blind cords, pale daylight fanning out to efface the gloom. There was a couch and coffee table and a small flatscreen TV on a crude media unit composed of cinderblocks and a raw plank. The air had that vague odor of someone else's habits, somewhere between musty and sour. For some reason he found himself looking for a fish tank even though Dan had never once mentioned owning a fish. The couch had a floral print cover that he could not imagine Dan sitting on. He thought it was something Dan had perhaps claimed from the estate of a dead family member. And who had helped him bring it in? These were matters so far outside the context of the Game that they took on in his mind the charm of folklore.

Dan yanked down on a final cord and stood there by a Formica table in the kitchen. He asked Nick what he wanted to do.

Nick wasn't sure. He made a sound analogous to a shrug and stood looking at the floor. It was hardwood and then it was linoleum.

"What do you have planned?" he said.

"I don't have anything planned."

They ended up in Dan's room. It was a template room with stock furniture and white walls. But there was something a little off-kilter here, a kind of visceral disorientation, and it took Nick a moment to understand what he was doing, standing there at the threshold of the room and trying to reconcile the configuration of the furniture with the image he'd been carrying around in his mind for so many years, a kind of presumption pieced together out of all the conjectural details gleaned from the open mic. How the room was smaller than he'd imagined and how the bed was there and not here and how the light came in from that way, not this way, slatted light from the aluminum blinds.

"You'll be on the potato," Dan said. By potato he meant his old crappy PC. He'd crossed the room to a closet and disappeared behind the open door and his voice came out among several things shifting and crinkling within. "Just looking for the ethernet cable," he called out. "Took my old rig out last-minute thinking I'd get you set up before I got you."

Nick said, "My life is potato." He gave a stunted laugh and stood there by the doorway grinning dumbly, waiting for Dan to register the joke. It was from an old meme Dan had posted in the voice server long ago and it was a second before Dan paused his rummaging just long enough to deliver an onomatopoeic acknowledgment.

"Hah," he said.

But Nick couldn't quite read the tone, whether it indicated impatience or preoccupation. There was a little more depth or breadth to Dan's voice here in the starkness of his room, uncut by all the technical protocols that had always ferried his voice the five hundred miles into Nick's ears. He stepped into the room and listened to Dan rifle through the closet. There were DVD and CD cases arrayed on a shelf. These were largely documentaries and blues albums and a few steelbook cases of certain games. He didn't need to verify this. Dan had talked about them before, his collection. He'd even mentioned the shelf, which was not a plank of splintery wood hanging from the ceiling by two lengths of chain as Nick had always imagined but a standard prefinished shelf supported by standard brackets.

There was a last shove of something from within the closet followed by an object or several tumbling to the floor among a muttered curse. Then Dan stepped out holding a tangled skein of orange cable.

"Let's get you set up," he said.

They played the Game largely in silence, sitting at the same desk and listening to each other mash their keys, drag their cursors. They drummed out impatient ditties during loading screens. What speaking they did was all laconic phrases delivered with neutral inflections that took on the form of litany. You get that quest? Yeah. You loot that corpse? Yeah. You coming? Yeah.

This was normal. Nick sat there comfortably behind the twenty-seven-inch flatscreen monitor and followed Dan's avatar through a variegated hinterland. The trick was to keep his eyes on the screen. The desk was a large one of wood vinyl on caster wheels and they were seated diagonally to each other with Flophouse moving in the screen and Dan on the other side of it and it was the immediate duality of this that was still too surreal for Nick. He found it easier to look at Flophouse, talk to Flophouse. When Nick made the pterodactyl screech, it was the virtual Dan who screeched back.

I have to hand this quest in. Okay. I'm on the flightpath. Okay. I'm selling my junk. Okay.

Then Flophouse stopped moving and Dan rose from his chair and left the room without comment. He came back a moment later with a glass of water and went over to the nightstand where he opened a drawer and rattled out a pill from a prescription bottle. He didn't say what the pill was for and Nick never asked.

They went on playing the Game all through the evening and into the twilight hours. It was Dan who wanted to go out, get some food, and he had to make it clear to Nick that, no, he was not going to have chips for dinner.

They went to a roadside tavern on the other side of town and sat at a booth. The bartender came over with a pad and jotted down their orders and walked away. Nick looked around. The dim lighting of this place, the stained-glass lamps branded with beer logos and the neon signs hanging on the walls among framed portraits staring out from monochrome pasts. What else was there? There was the idle drumming upon the table and the blank thoughts huffed out in raspy spurts because out with Dan was uncharted territory and Nick didn't know how to behave.

Eventually there came the staccato talk about plans for the weekend, maybe hiking, sure, or something else, whatever, trite comments to fill the gap of time before their beers were set down before them, brown ale in nonic pints.

They ordered a second round before the burgers were brought out. Then a third. Nick made a derisive comment about the service. Dan told him to relax, that he wasn't in New York anymore, using a stereotypical Brooklyn accent. Nick grinned and called him a certified dumbass. They were looking at each other now, talking louder than was necessary. Nick could feel his teeth going numb between cold swigs of country mud juice, he was calling it, and bringing up old inside jokes and heeling with laughter, the two of them, clapping, pounding on the table, Dan leaning in low and making some hybrid pterodactyl-puma squawk. It wasn't too much longer before he was slurring on about some metaphysical posit, making dumb marionette poetry with his hands and beating out his argument upon the table in anaphoric cadence—there is no this, there is no that, there is no other thing. Nick had heard this tone before, earnest, dogmatic, the foundered sentences and flotsam thoughts that wash up soon or late. It all aligned nicely with the ruddy face before him, groggy-eyed and sweat beading on the forehead, telling Nick to think about it, to imagine, rigging up improbable or paradoxical scenarios between mouthfuls of his burger, which had at some point appeared on the table.

Then there were just the fries left and then those too were gone. Another beer, a shot of whiskey, and how silly Nick felt to have needed liquor to open him up to the person he'd known as his best friend for so many years.

Dan rose and fed a dollar to the jukebox and came grooving back to the table, smacking his knee in time to a shuffling rhumba blues tune. He fell back into his seat laughing and they talked loudly between verses they felt compelled to sing aloud. They chucked back a few more shots. They had their run of the jukebox, tottering up the bar floor and back again and finally out along the dark roadway singing rude verses of their own composition, *old fuck barkeep gone took my keys tonight*, in a lumbering twelve-bar blues. A car lurched by with the horn going doppler in their ears and they cursed at the receding taillights through improvised bullhorns fashioned up out of their cupped hands. The car stopped. They cut through a field. They staggered through an overgrown trail using their phones as flashlights, through a backyard, more of them, trampling flowers in garden beds, straining their bodies through scratchy hedges. Dan roared like a puma. Nick joined in. A windowlight snapped on in an upper floor. They ran, the night heaving, hurtling past.

They made it back to Dan's house where he wrenched at the knob and told it to fuck off and tried again. The door gave way, they stumbled through.

They sat on the couch in the dark and stared at the blank TV screen. They burped each in turn. Then Dan farted. Nick said nothing, staring on with a bovine stoicism as a rancid stench filled his nostrils.

"You ever take solace," Dan said, "that in one universe, you're successful."

Nick turned his head and peered out his bleary eyes at Dan's profile. There he was. He hiccupped.

"I want the one," Nick said, "where I'm not about to vomit."

Their laughter guttered out and there was just the refrigerator thrumming softly in the kitchen.

"There's also one," Nick said, "universe. Where we never met."

Dan looked at him. He raised a hand and let it plop onto Nick's back. *Pat pat.* He said these words, and patty pat. Then his hand slid off and fell to the cushion.

"*Que será será,*" he said.

Come morning Nick was standing outside Dan's bedroom feeling sluggish and a little woozy. He could hear Dan stirring drowsily about in his room and he rapped the door and asked if there was any Advil. Dan told him to check the bathroom.

It was a normal bathroom with normal bathroom things. He found the Advil in the medicine cabinet among some antacid chews and a depleted tube of prescription acne cream. He stood looking at that. Then he reached in and took it. The name on the tube said Daniel Kaplan. He didn't care about the last name. He was wondering who Daniel was. He stood staring at it, the

Daniel, with a dull pain pressing up against the back of his eyes. Did Daniel know about the Great Loin Cloth Tour? Did Daniel know how to make the pterodactyl squawk?

Dan was Flophouse. Dan was the person in the other room, asking Nick if he found the Advil.

Nick didn't answer. He said, slowly, beneath his breath, "Daniel."

Dan was born in Maine, went to college in Maine, dropped out of college. Dan hauled boxes around a distribution center two hours away by car. Dan had bought his car at a seized vehicle auction. Daniel probably owned a luxury German driving machine that he waxed weekly in his perfectly paved driveway. Daniel was the stranger. Daniel had acne. Dan had cancer.

He heard Dan's bedroom door open and he put the tube away and closed the medicine cabinet. He stepped out into the hall and asked Dan if he wanted to play the Game, maybe do some dungeon runs. But Dan wanted to get his car. Nick told him his car wasn't going anywhere and they should get in some dungeon runs before the weekly reset. But all Dan said was that the Game's not going anywhere either.

It was about a twenty-minute walk to the tavern, slogging along the dusty roadside with the sun harassing them between blots of shade and the way before them heaving slightly inside swells of vertigo. They stopped beside a road sign where Nick watched Dan stoop over hands on knees to make strange hiccup sounds at the asphalt. He wondered if this was the cancer at work or just the hangover but didn't ask.

They reached the car before noon with his head still throbbing and their shirts clinging damply to their skin. Dan reached under the driver-side wheel arch and took the keys off the tire where the old barkeep had said he'd leave them. He unlocked the driver door and sat in the car with one foot in the gravel lot. Nick said they should hurry back and try to get a few raids in as well. He reminded Dan that he needed that shield. Dan said he wanted to get breakfast. Nick said he'd be fine with some cereal if Dan had any back at his place. He told Dan that the shield and the breastplate were the last pieces he needed to complete his armor set. Dan reached over the console and unlocked the passenger door and told Nick to get in. He told him there was a diner not far from here. Nick told Dan that once he completed the set he could finally drop enchanting. He said he might pick up weaponsmithing and get in on the dagger trade. Then Dan told him to stop talking about the fucking Game.

Nick stood there. He wondered if mood swings might be a side effect of the pain medication. He wondered if this was Daniel speaking. There was the numb whirring of insects in the field and the warm wind blowing through the trees and Nick wanted to ask Dan what the hell was his problem but instead just stood there sweating in the sun. Then he got in the car. It was all stifling heat in there and Dan was still sitting with his left foot hanging out the open door. He put the key in the ignition but didn't turn it.

"You were the first person I told," he said. "I told you before I told my parents."

He'd yet to look at Nick and seemed unable to do so. He shifted his head slightly but could not manage even a glance and it all seemed so false to Nick, so untrue to Dan's character that it scared him a little. He didn't know what to say. He didn't know if he should say anything at all. He waited for Dan to continue.

Then Dan said, "Let's just head back."

That night Nick woke to an awful sound. He lay on the pullout listening. It was Dan retching long and hard behind the bathroom door. It sounded raw and painful and Nick raised up on an elbow but that was as far as he got, holding there like a piece of fallen statuary. In one of the windows an old air conditioner rattled and throbbed and just below this sound he could hear Dan gag and hiccup and spit. The spitting sounded a desperate thing all its own, something dire about it. It sounded as if he were trying to spit the cancer right out of him.

Nick didn't get up and he wasn't going to. He could not bring himself to confront this Other-dan retching into a toilet or a sink. He eased back down against the pillow. He listened to the awful sounds straining out from his friend's mouth. He tried to convince himself that it was just a perversion of the pterodactyl screech. He wondered might these be the sounds hidden away in the AFK channel, the Orb of Immutable Loneliness, where mics go mute by default.

After a while the toilet flushed and the door opened. A deep silence settled as the pipes stopped hissing in the walls. Nick lay on his side with his back facing the hall, feigning sleep. He could sense that Dan was standing there in the hallway contemplating some action. It was all there in the humming tension of the modulated air and the light from the bathroom doorway how it cast faint shadows in the room. Then Dan turned off the light and walked away.

They were sitting at the kitchen table the next morning when Dan looked up from his cereal and told Nick that he deleted Nick's character. Nick stopped chewing briefly, then smiled and spooned up some more cereal. Dan told him he wasn't kidding. Apparently Nick hadn't bothered to actually log off when he'd finally gone to bed at one in the morning. Dan told him to go check for himself. Nick sat there with the spoon halfway to his mouth. He sat there waiting for Dan to smile. Then he put the spoon back in the bowl and got up and hurried off toward Dan's room. He came back a moment later and stood glaring from the edge of the kitchen.

Dan told him to calm down. He told him he could call customer service to have his character restored. He told him to look on the bright side. "Now we can actually hang out," he said.

Nick didn't understand what he was talking about. He called Dan an asshole. He told him he was out of his mind. He asked him what the hell have they been doing the last two days if not hanging out.

Dan laughed at that but there was no humor in it. He said, "Why did you even come here?" The question was blunt in a way that might have been intended to knock some perspective into Nick's head. But Nick just stood there staring at Dan as if he were something far away.

"I go to work," Dan said. "I come home. Go to work, come home. Play the fucking Game. For nine years I do three things. Make it two things. Work and the Game. And now." He stopped there, letting the thought float away toward the ceiling.

"And now, what?" Nick said. "And now you're dying." He felt mean as ever to put it out there so bluntly but there was no helping it. "We both wasted nine years on the Game," he said, "So what? I don't regret any of that." There was a pause here, a moment where things left unsaid drifted through the space between them. It wasn't simply an avatar Dan had deleted.

It was all the private anecdotes and inside jokes and the drunken rants and screeches and the breaths rustling into his ears.

"You could've done whatever," Nick said. "But you didn't. One day you could've just not logged on, ever again. And that would've been it. You could've been off doing whatever it is you apparently wish you'd done."

Dan sat there listening to all this and in the end he looked away and shook his head. He shook it slowly and sadly as if to say Nick would not understand. Then Nick walked over to where Dan was sitting and punched him in the face. Dan lurched back in his chair and settled and sat looking up at Nick with the last few seconds gathering into his stunned eyes.

Nick stood watching. He himself looked startled. In truth he didn't think he was going over there to punch Dan but to sit and talk this thing through. His hand was throbbing slightly but the pain was still back there with the strike. He asked Dan if he was okay. Dan lunged at him. He knocked the table cockeyed and tackled Nick to the floor where they writhed against each other all stunted words and strained breath. They knocked over one of the chairs. Milk was spilling onto the linoleum and pooling in the cracks. Through gritted teeth Dan kept asking why he fucking came here. One of his flailing fists caught Nick in the ear. Nick kept saying variants of the word fuck. Fucking. Fucker. He was trying to grab hold and restrain Dan's arms. Instead his knee lurched up into Dan's stomach and Dan shoved himself away and clambered off a short distance where he gagged and retched on his hands and knees. Nick watched him from where he lay. He asked Dan if he was all right. Dan didn't answer. He rolled over and they lay there together panting on their backs.

Eventually Dan called Nick a dipshit. He told him he didn't even delete his character but just changed the server he logged in to so it looked like it.

Nick's ear was still ringing. He touched it and opened his mouth in a faux yawn. He called Dan a certified jackass.

Dan grinned. Even amid his panting he had a laugh that was all goofy horseplay, a quality of cartoon scuffledust, and Nick couldn't help but to join in.

It was quiet again once their laughter died out. Nick lay there listening to Dan breathe while he traced a crack in the ceiling with his eyes. It ran through the plaster from one corner to the other and when he reached the end he hauled himself up. He held out his hand and helped Dan to his feet and asked him if he'd meant all that stuff he'd said.

Dan righted the overturned chair and sat. He seemed to be thinking it over. There was a kind of shadow movement at the corner of his mouth, an inward smile.

"I think you don't want anything to change," Dan said. "But it's going to." He'd been contemplating the soggy bits of cereal on the tabletop and now he looked up, glanced up, a slight tight-lipped smile that Nick chose not to interpret.

He pulled out the seat adjacent and they sat there together for a long time, each staring at an arbitrary spot in the room while milk dripped off the table.

Then Nick looked at Dan and said, "Daniel."

That night they drove back to the airport without much talking. Nick wished he could stay longer. He didn't want the last few stilted hours to be the coda of his time with Dan, but a three-day weekend was the best he could do on short notice. Someone from his team was already out on vacation. He'd told Dan that he could take a full two weeks in a couple of months but Dan had said that there was no way to tell how he'd be feeling by then. There were no streetlamps along the road and the headlights bored through the darkness. The needle on the speedometer was creeping toward sixty. Radio music rattled in the speakers and the wind was flapping loudly in Dan's open window and he said something but Nick couldn't hear him. Before he could ask Dan cut the wheel and they were off the road and in a dusty lot among cars and pickups and a corrugated hangar painted red. Music was throbbing from within. The words Big Red Barracks burned above the door, the brightest lights for miles.

Nick wanted to know what they were doing here. He reminded Dan about his flight.

"There'll be another," Dan told him. Then he parked the car and got out.

Nick watched him go. He thought he could call Dan's bluff by sitting here in the car amid the engine clacks and dashboard dust. But there was no bluff.

Inside it was loud and hot and dimly lit. The air smelled of sweat and spilled liquor and Nick stood at the edge of the dance floor watching all that untamed movement, the people spinning freestyle over the scuffed boards amid yips and cries and the band how they rocked the platform, the basskick thumping beneath plosive mouth harp whoops and the fiddle notes skittering crazed in triple time.

Then Nick saw him there amid the stomping feet and whirling bodies, Dan, one of them, doing some strange country rhumba and shouting, hollering, scrawling out in the air a helical slang with his big hands, clapping and sweating and how he shuffled his way through the crowd with his big grin stretched taut across his face and the music pulsing underfoot.

He came and hooked arms with his friend and it was Nick and Dan out there wheeling amid the body heat, howling, roaring together in the heaving crush.

**Part III**

*Obladi oblada.*

He barely played the Game anymore, logging on now and then to stand in a city square and watch polygonal strangers drift past in the screen. He'd get bored quickly and log off. In his friends list the name Flophouse was grayed out, with a system-generated note attached: *Last online 3 months ago.*

Then one day after work he booted up the Game and did a few circuits around the capital city and logged off and canceled his subscription. He did it without ceremony and then sat there for a while starting at his monitor trying to figure out whether he wanted to masturbate or take a shower. The voice server was minimized and he clicked it up from the taskbar as if seeking its counsel on the matter. It was late February and the days were cold and brittle and Flophouse was still there in the AFK channel. Nick would not disconnect from the server for as long as he remained there. He checked every day after work, turning on the bedroom light he'd finally replaced and crossing to the desk to wake the monitor. Pandiculate, Flophouse, together in the Orb of Immutable Loneliness.

It was Dan's sister who had eventually delivered the news. He didn't even know Dan had a sister. The number had come up in his phone's screen as an unknown contact, ten digits from Greensburg, PA. Her name was

Courtney and he'd learned about his best friend's death in the voicemail she'd left for him. He was invited to the funeral, up in Maine, but he didn't go. It was a week after the call when Flophouse at last disconnected from the voice server, only Nick knew it wasn't Flophouse but his sister or whoever turning off his computer, or the electricity had been cut, or the internet had gone out.

Then the mementos came. They came in a box. Dan's documentaries and steelbooks and blues albums. The question of how or why never fully crossed Nick's mind, perhaps an executor fulfilling some notarized wish. There was no note, just the items crammed together in a box branded with the logo of a popular paper towel company. A few days had gone by before he decided to sort through them, dragging the box out from beneath the desk where he'd stowed it and lifting out the items one by one.

He had not thought about it then, that the last time he would see Dan would be in the car outside the airport, a clumsy embrace over the gear shift followed by some parting words, something generic, he couldn't remember.

Eventually Dan's sister called again, asking if he'd received the package, Dan's things, he wanted you to have them, she'd told him. And how she'd heard a lot about him, how Dan had talked about Nick all the time whenever he'd call her, now and then, just to check in.

What he did remember was Dan's grin, the goofy look of it, not in the car but on the dance floor, grinning like a fool amid the heaving bodies and hard-driving music and the two of them hooking arms and wheeling in that shapeless freestyle crowd, roaring like idiots.

The documentaries were on war and crime, economics, generational ethe. He inserted one of the blues CDs into his computer's ROM drive but the disk was too scratched to be read, almost all of them were. Some of the cases had no disk at all or had the wrong disk. He found a country album and a top forty compilation album hidden away like guilty secrets in a Sonny Boy Williamson II discography set.

In the end the day did come out of nowhere. It happened under the pretense of routine. They were talking and then they weren't and after a long interval of silence that was not so irregular Dan entered the AFK channel and never left. Nick didn't think it was Dan's intention to leave him in limbo like that but that he'd entered some stage in the horrible process of dying against which a person's will is no match.

I didn't even know he had a sister. This is what Nick had told her, the second time she called, when she was checking to confirm receipt of the box. He never mentioned you, he'd said.

Eventually he came across a blues CD that was still readable. The first track struck up in the speakers, distant voices suspended in a staticky prelude, breathing, warm-up chords softly stroked.

There had been a deep silence on the other end of the line. Then she said, Well, that's Dan for you.

The blues track was an old thing or sounded old, grainy and a little sloppy, a sense of improvisation, of musicians gathered in a room by coincidence alone, with mouth harp roars to startle them, voices galvanized out of the backdrop static along with laughter and handclaps.

He'd apologized for not attending the funeral and offered a boilerplate condolence to which she reciprocated, neither becoming undone by this, just the perforated phrases uttered into a mouthpiece.

He'd uploaded the blues tune to his phone and had taken to listening to it on repeat. Folding laundry, eating leftovers, standing in fusty railcars among the snuffling Gore-Tex throngs on his way to work and back. Consider now all your frottaged notions of those around you. This sounded like something Dan would say. There was something in the raw sound of the piece, in the dusty niches of the meter, that was oddly reminiscent of some crude Danism. At work he began to repeat some of the stuff Dan had said over the years, swiveling away from his keyboard and scooting back over the monochrome carpet to whisper amid the whirring stress some tchotchke phrase to the back of his cubemate's head. None of it changed anything and after a time he reverted to his introverted self. It was the moments between the notes that he liked, the rests. In the rests he could hear coughing, he could hear a throat being cleared, garbled banter. In the rests he could hear breathing.

It was a quiet evening on the cusp of spring when she called again, left a voicemail that said, Hey, it's Courtney, Dan's sister.

Nick sat on the edge of his bed staring out the window, watching a bird preen on the fire escape while he listened to her voice. It sounded like she might have been driving at the time. There was a low thrumming. There was a metronomic clicking. She would be in New York next week, in Manhattan, on business, and was wondering if, maybe, would he want to meet up. We can grab some lunch, she'd said. I could go for a New York slice. And she laughed dumbly to herself and there was the measured clicking of a blinker in the background. Let me know. The bird stopped and looked at him and flew away.

He called her back the next day between meetings and they arranged a time and a place, a little pizza joint in midtown.

He knew who she was even before she pushed in through the creaky glass door. It was her profile that gave her away, walking along the facade window. Nick could see the resemblance. The parlor reeked of garlic and sweat and when she entered he rose from the booth and raised his hand, gave a small wave.

# South Road

Claudia Putnam

I was on Ranger mountain the night Rusty Chappell killed his wife's prized mare. They tell it like Rusty was this Paul Bunyan figure, able to throw a crazed horse to the ground and strangle it with his bare hands. Just last night I heard another of those tales, pinstriped John Buckley yucking it up while grilling brats next door at the lake. It was hilarious. The horse practically sprouted wings. She was frothing at the mouth. Rusty saved the world, but not before bumbling around like Yogi Bear. My sons and his were wide-eyed, our wives rolling their eyes. The story gets crazier with each retelling, Rusty drunker, his antics more manic, his wife screechier, even though you wouldn't believe it to look at her today. To look at either one of them today, or at this town today. It's like Ireland around here now, practically suburban, practically Connecticut, a round of remodelings now sliding back into decay. Home sidings starting to chip again, SUVs bought new at the end of the Clinton administration rusting. A whole generation sent off to college where their parents never graduated from high school now wandering back jobless.

There are no horses in the Chappell pastures anymore; I heard they were looking at growing Christmas trees. Rusty's joined AA, along with half of the state of New Hampshire, according to Facebook. He's got himself three or four working dump trucks with fading logos; he has exclusive access to the sandpit at the end of the South Road. The Chappell foundation has been jacked up, skylights went in about ten years ago. I don't know what happened to Rusty's daughters. I never ask.

I'm not from here. In 1978, when Rusty killed the mare, I was staying up on Perkins Ridge. After a few postcollege years hitching around in the wake of the Grateful Dead, it had dawned on me that I might have to grow up like every other preppie burnout I knew. I temporized by going to business school first. Partly because my college roommate, John Perkins, lived nearby, I'd picked Dartmouth. It was still possible to choose, yourself, a school like that then, if you had the scores and the grades. We didn't quite grasp that it was privilege then, especially those of us on the edge of it, the ones who really did have the scores and the grades, and not quite as much money. My buddy John and his wife, Anna Halloran, had taken me in.

Every morning on my way to class, I'd drive out on 107, passing the lower pastures on Ranger where Rusty's wife kept her horses. She crossed Connemaras—a breed I knew from childhood books about a pony named Blaze—with Thoroughbreds. She'd be out there even in the bitter cold, mucking shit, busting hay bales, riding her showy mare at a fence. For my entrepreneurship class, I had a professor who liked to talk about pluck, and I'd think of Suzy Chappell, a woman six feet tall and nearly as burly as her husband, astride that fourteen-hand mare. I wasn't sure which half of that image most captured my imagination: the woman or the horse.

John Perkins would stare down his long nose at it all. White trash dealing in steeplechase horses. But Anna had an artist's eye, drawn to paradox. I'd find her with expedition binoculars trained on the Chappell pastures, then she'd disappear into the converted sheep barn she used as a studio. Shut out, I'd squint across the valley, unable to distinguish much.

Coming home around 3 a.m. at the end of spring semester, I had Zeppelin cranked on my eight-track, the Saab's windows rolled down so I could breathe the night trees. The eastern forest was awesome to me, its rustlings and moistnesses, its varieties of barks and leaves, its peepers and crickets, all of which were absent on my uncle's ranchland in Colorado where I'd grown up.

I turned off 107 onto South Road, thinking I'd circle around to Perkins Ridge the back way. I slowed my car, sucking the humid air. As I rounded the first curve, I realized I was gripping the steering wheel. Through the windows crept what I can only describe as a Bad Vibe. I remembered hearing Anna talk about this place, how she avoided walking or bicycling through it. I slowed more, wanting to roll up all the windows, not wanting to stop the car to do it.

There were no houses along this stretch of the South Road. I pushed through the dark till I crested a hill and nearly ran over Rusty Chappell. He was standing on the yellow line, shouting. I couldn't swerve; the road's shoulder was blocked by a great orange dump truck. I shrieked to a halt just a few feet from Rusty. He reared over my hood like a troll, his shadow stretching far down the pavement behind him. My headlights brought flame to his carroty hair, bleached the freckles from his skin. He continued to yell, waving at his truck. Though I was tempted to jam into reverse, I climbed out of my sedan instead. I drove a foreign car everyone recognized. There was no way around helping him out.

Rusty went on screaming in a voice strangely high-pitched for such a huge being. "Cocksucka, cocksucka, mothafuckin cocksucka!"

"What happened, man?" I said, when he finally paused for breath. I saw he'd driven the truck into the ditch. The two tires that remained on the road were flat. Scorched oil hung in the air.

He reared around. "Fuckin *beast!*" he said, then fell silent.

I introduced myself, though I was sure he knew who I was. "Ethan Codding." He shook my hand and then dropped it. Disquiet crawled over us like fog.

"Damned spot for a flat," I said.

"Ain't just flats." He tugged the shoulders of his t-shirt, as if trying to turn up an invisible collar. "I'd a driven out them. Oil pressah's gone. I can't afford to lose the whole rig, drivin' with the gauge flat as a heart attack."

"Leave it till day," I advised. "I'll drive you back to Ranger."

"Decent of yuh." He shook my hand. I felt puny and pigeon-toed beside him.

"You need anything from the truck?"

"Nah. T'morrow."

I drove him back to 107, turning almost immediately onto the rutted trail that wound up a third of Ranger Mountain to the Chappell spread. Named for Rogers' Rangers, who camped nearby during the French and Indian War, the mountain rose straight across the valley from Perkins Ridge. It stood steeper and taller than the surrounding hills, its Kojak crown begging for a fight. In winter it was sheeted with sleet; in summer hammered by lightning. In the forest along its flanks, the atmosphere was sweet with horses and centuries of maple sugaring.

Rusty turned and nodded at me. "Better come in for a beer, then."

*Beah.* I trudged after him, counting as I went. One front-end loader. Another dump truck, this one small and red and loaded with manure. A flatbed truck with one of its wheels jacked up, a thin layer of hay strewn across its bed. A tractor that looked like it hadn't moved in a while. A looming bulldozer. Three Buick station wagons up on blocks. A rust-spotted horse trailer, a shiny red Ford for pulling it.

The kitchen was lit by a pale and flickering florescent light in the center of the ceiling. The room was spotless, or as clean as anyone could make it, given the bad light, the wood counters that had lost their varnish, the linoleum worn down to plywood. Blue tarp covered a fresh-looking hole in the ceiling, possibly cut for a skylight. Suzy Chappell sat tall at a big oak table.

"Where you been?" She looked at her watch before getting up and marching to the fridge to get our beers.

"Bogwater," Rusty said, raising his can at me instead of answering her. He dragged out two chairs and we sat beneath the bleaching light. With an air of resignation, Suzy packed a small pipe. As we drew our hits, Rusty told Suzy how he'd been stranded, turning to me for corroboration when he got to how I'd come roaring over the hill and almost knocked him down.

"That's not a spot I'd want to be stuck in," Suzy said. Her accent was much softer than her husband's.

"What's wrong with that place, exactly?" I asked. "Is it haunted?"

Suzy shook her head. "Polluted?" she suggested. "Always been that way."

"Yeah," Rusty put in. "Seems like every house around here's haunted, anyways. Ghosts ain't nothin."

"Really? You ever see a ghost?" I took another hit, looked over my shoulder.

"Sure," said Suzy. They traded off stories for over an hour. I didn't believe any of them, despite what I'd felt on the South Road. If ghosts were that common, everyone in Europe would have white hair. You'd never see an *Unsolved Mysteries* show, because we'd take it all for granted.

Suzy got to her feet, thundered to the fridge again. Six feet of muscle was what she was. She wore a halter top that exposed ripples in her upper back. Her jeans cut her hips and squeezed her thighs, not because she was fat but because her pants were small. Brown hair curled down to the points of her shoulder blades. John and Anna had sometimes cracked jokes about the fights that landed these two in the hospital. Rusty was bigger, but if he were drunker, she might have the advantage.

She took out more beers, looked at the man's watch at her wrist again, sighed. "No sleep again tonight." She slapped a frying pan down on the stove, started cracking eggs into it. Rummaging in one of the plywood cabinets, she pulled down a box of brownie mix and dumped its contents into a bowl. By the time the eggs were scrambled, she'd slipped a pan into the oven.

She plopped steaming brownies down on the table, clearing away our plates, emptied of eggs. Striding to the door, she pulled a pair of Wellingtons over her bare feet.

"Want a hand?" I asked.

"Sure, if you're offering."

We left Rusty nursing on another beer at the table. "I thought you were going to chop off our heads when we came in," I said, as we walked toward the barn. The vehicles and equipment we passed seemed dull in the brightening light.

Suzy didn't seem quite as large. "I was pissed because I figured he'd been to the Rooster Tail. Then he makes such a racket when he does come home. I don't want him waking our girls so they can see him all wasted like that."

I was surprised to hear they had children. I thought if they did, the kids had probably already seen all there was to see.

Inside the barn, early light streamed through the high windows, setting off gleaming brass hinges and door latches. Dark, oiled beams began to glow, cobweb-free. The floor boards were swept. The only smell came from fresh straw and sawdust, from horses fed on sweet grass and good corn. My Colorado uncle mostly kept his Quarter Horses outside, letting them grow coats as nature intended.

Suzy clucked her tongue. Four heads appeared over the stall doors. "Morning, hons," she cooed to them. "These are the ones I keep aside. For breeding, but in the end they're really for my daughters."

"Do they ride?"

"They don't want to," she said. "But that's not the point."

She gestured back through the doorway toward her husband's disabled fleet. For a split second I could almost envision it all becoming, if not a bluegrassed horse farm, at least one of the more prosperous estates you passed on I-89 closer to Hanover.

"Which is the famous horse?" I asked.

Suzy picked up a grain shovel and moved toward the first stall, the only one that didn't have a horse head sticking out of it. When she approached, I heard a stifled giggle.

"Mice!" she cried.

The giggles turned to shrieks. She stomped toward the stall.

"No!" came a voice. "We ain't mice!"

"What are you then? Rats?" She growled.

"No, not rats either!"

"Oh, it sounds like children. My favorite! Fi-fie-fo-fum!"

Two heads, one orange like her father's, the other darker than her mother's, popped up over the stall door, grinning. The darker was older; she had a baby tooth missing. The redhead couldn't have been more than four. She looked a little scared.

"What are you two doing up so early? What if you got stepped on?"

I didn't think the anxiety in Suzy's voice came from fear for the girls' safety. We'd just been talking about the things she didn't want to her children to see, and it had turned out that the kids had been awake for quite some time.

"Lady would never step on us!" said the darker girl.

"We were surprisin' yuh!" said the younger. She backed out of the stall, dragging a shovel loaded with manure.

"And we wanted to say good mornin' to Lady," her sister added.

I looked into the stall. The bay mare gazed after the children. I am not an expert on Connemaras, but even pregnant, this mare exuded grace. She was smaller than any Quarter Horse—more the size of a small Arabian. But her legs were strong and long for the rest of her. There was no question that she was bred to jump.

"Say hello to Daddy's new friend, Mr. Codding," Suzy said to the girls.

The older girl, called Amber, came to shake my hand. "Look what I got for my birthday!" she exclaimed. "That was yesterday!" She reached with her left hand to pull a pendant from beneath the collar of her t-shirt.

I stepped back.

"Don't you like it?" she asked. "It's just an old nugget. I have it because of my name."

My unease faded like déjà vu. The pendant was the kind of thing you could buy at any tourist trap up north, small and cheap. Sometimes they sold them with bugs inside, though I had never understood the appeal of that. This one might even have been plastic.

Suzy ushered the girls out of the barn, murmuring something about swimming lessons at the lake. Amber called out, "See yuh, Lady!" blowing a kiss.

I felt a bit let down by the banality of the mare's name, until Suzy returned and explained that it was short for Lough Conn Lady, which meant, roughly, Lady of the Lake. I could get into the mythological overtones, not to mention the reference to the heart of the local geography, Big Shire Lake. I looked at Suzy anew, wondering if she'd read Mallory, or Scott.

"When's she due?" I asked.

Suzy clipped the horse to the cross ties in the middle of the aisle. "She's still got a little more than a month left."

When we hiked back up to the house, we found Rusty dozing on the couch while his daughters sprawled and rolled on the rug, manipulating Barbie dolls on Tonka trucks. In sleep he looked smaller, more vulnerable, a freckle-faced boy perhaps too restless for learning well in school, but earnest and striving all the same. Suzy bent to kiss him.

His daughters began climbing over him. I expected him to toss them aside as an awakened giant would, but instead he gathered them into his chest, resting his chin first on one head and then the other. "Squeezin' us!" the darker girl, the one with the necklace, cried.

He stood them on the floor, his hands trailing through their hair. "Daddy's got work." He looked at me. "Time to check on that truck."

I hesitated. I'd been planning to go home and sleep for several hours. But I found myself repeating the offer I'd made to his wife. "Want a hand?"

"Appreciate it. Know anythin' bout engines?"

"Maybe a bit. Let's go take a look." I did know a little, from my uncle's ranch.

I followed Rusty out into the yard, waited for him to select a vehicle. To my surprise, he chose the front-end loader. As we wobbled and bounced down the driveway, Rusty handed me a plastic bag and a packet of papers. "Roll a doob," he said. "Needs cleanin'."

I spent about five minutes picking oily seeds out of the crumbly Columbian Gold or Panama Red or whatever throat-scraping weed we smoked back then. He took the sloppy joint from me with a skeptical grunt, pinching it between thick fingers. "Thirsty? There's Bud in that cooler."

I found two sandwiches, more brownies, a twelve of Bud. "Seems early," I said.

He shrugged. "We'll get to it one way or another."

So I cracked one. It calmed my scorched throat. When we hit the pavement, he accelerated. The jouncing grew more pronounced. I grabbed the door handle. It didn't help. We turned up the South Road. Normally I took these turns at warp speed in my Saab, so now I had a chance to stare around me at the landscape. Accustomed to the grandiosity of the Rocky Mountains, I had never fully absorbed the local beauty. Perkins Ridge rose to our right, a grassy hillside with a blue smear of duck pond at its bottom and John and Anna's wide-porched house at the top. Through the trees I could glimpse bus-sized boulders dropped by the last glacier. All the history—geology, woodland Indians, Rogers' Rangers—felt beckoning, mysterious.

Until we pulled in behind the dump truck. The vibe settled around us again.

Rusty got out and circled the behemoth three times counterclockwise. I dropped out of the loader, went around to the hood of the truck, wishing I were wearing long sleeves. "How do you get it open?"

"From the side."

I climbed up on the wheel and groped for the catch, heaving and grunting until the fender swung open. Rusty bent at the rear of the vehicle, examining one of the flats. "I can't see what caused 'em," he said. There was a whine in his voice.

"Maybe there's nails or glass under the wheels," I suggested.

"Helluva nail," he replied, standing.

While I stared into the engine, he strode back to the loader and yanked out a red toolbox. Veins stood out along his freckled arm. "See anythin' yet?"

"Not sure what I'm looking for."

He climbed up on the running board beside me, reeking of grease and sweat. “I’d guess the gasket’s blown. Hope that’s it, anyhow. Top half’s cheaper to fix than the bottom.” *Cheapa t’fix.*

“Can’t you call a tow truck?” I wondered where you’d find a tow around here that could haul a rig like this one.

“Nah! All’s we got to do is take this head right off, get her back to my shop. I ain’t takin her to no garage. Highway robb’ry.”

Later he added that a boy from down in the village of East Enshaw, Billy Tanner, would come to Ranger to fix the engine head. I nodded. I had already heard of Billy Tanner’s ability with motors.

When I wasn’t fetching tools or beers, or rolling joints, I worked elbow-to-elbow with Rusty. There was something satisfying in the sweaty labor; I couldn’t help respecting his knowledge and his strength. I enjoyed the movements of my muscles, the rhythm we fell into despite the thickening humidity and the uneasiness that seemed to permeate this section of woods. Rusty breathed hard through his nose. He twice dropped tools. The socket wrench didn’t go far, but the smaller one clattered all the way through the engine cavity. I had to crawl underneath to get it. I felt as if I were pulling myself out of something sticky as I climbed back up beside Rusty. I wondered what it did to people, to live for generations along the South Road.

“Ha!” Rusty pushed off the truck as if it were a boat. He hurried over to the loader, where he rigged up a mess of chains that enabled him to winch the engine head from the truck and hang it off the teeth of the shovel. Practically next I knew, we were rocking down the South Road with the engine penduluming a few feet from the windshield.

I rolled another joint. “So the truck’s all right sitting there till you get the engine fixed?”

“If I say so. Who’s gonna tow it away?”

“The load doesn’t matter?”

“Nah. Was just takin some gravel over to Blake’s. Fill in that old well before someone else gets hurt.”

I nodded. Charlie Blake, aged five, had fallen in the well the previous week. Luckily it was a dry well, and somehow he’d come out with only a broken leg. This was another side to Rusty that Anna had mentioned. He was prone to dropping off free gravel, or a load of firewood, in the yards of people who needed help. Though ... why at 3 a.m.? I never did figure that out.

After he got back on 107, Rusty drove straight past the turnoff to his house, keeping his foot nailed to the floor, his eyes straight ahead. The engine head swung on its chain, adding to the lurching of the vehicle. I just accepted the situation.

After a mile or so I praised his wife's horses. Rusty stiffened, as if I'd mentioned something embarrassing. "Lotta work."

"Do you like the horses?" I ventured.

Massive shrug, followed by a sigh. "Kinda scared of 'em," he admitted. We sat in shocked silence over that. "And I can't see it getting us anywheres," he added after a while.

I thought about the fine condition of the barn. I'd figured that despite her excessive care for the mares—my uncle would say that was a waste of money—Suzy had to be making some kind of profit from the operation. I didn't want to ask: the one thing you never mentioned in northern New England in those days was money. "Seems like Suzy has a big dream."

"I got one of my own," he said. "But she don't like it a'tall."

He didn't elaborate. I supposed it had to do with all his equipment. And gravel.

He pulled into the Rooster Tail's parking lot. Suzy's complaint about bars seemed distant. As we trudged through the dust toward the front door, a faded black Ford truck came skidding into the lot. "Now you get to meet Billy," Rusty said.

Billy Tanner was about ten years younger than I was, muscular but short, with an imitation of Rusty's swaggering walk. His dark eyes were quiet. He took my hand firmly.

"Billy's working for me this summer," Rusty said. He turned to me, doing an exaggerated double take. Perhaps carried away with the camaraderie of the afternoon, Rusty asked me if I wanted a *real* job. "Could use more goddamned help runnin' the skidder up to the woodlot. Above my house. Fifteen bucks an hou-ah," he said, sticking out a filthy hand as if we'd just met. Rusty leaned into my face to see if I were man enough to take it.

It astonished me to know it, but I wanted to be. He'd made me feel small, the way my uncle did, summers on the ranch. At any rate, saying no never occurred to me. I already had a summer job teaching sailing at the lake. But sleep-deprived, hungover, stoned, also fascinated, I clasped Rusty's gnarled fist. I imagined that that once I finished business school, I'd be stuck inside offices for the rest of my life. I suppose I saw Rusty's offer as my last hurrah.

The painter known as Anna Halloran, then my landlady, did some of her finest early work during the month I spent with the Chappells. When I had a break from the blitz of blind-sweating labor, beer, and doobs, I'd go home to shower. I'd reverently bring Anna coffee in her glass-walled shed. In contrast to my relationship with Suzy, this would be all the access I would get to Anna's inner space. John would be off at the real estate office in nearby Kensington, where he transformed bits of his family's Colonial land grant holdings into retirement properties. I didn't quite allow myself to lust after his wife—John and Anna, as a pair, were too holy in my imagination. I don't remember much lust from that summer at all, for the record. Probably the pot.

Anna's studio was not an analogue of Suzy's barn. While the stable was churchlike, Anna painted in a mess of heaped rags and knocked-over jars. Yet the same light that gilded the interior of Suzy's barn filled Anna's canvasses. A pitchfork shadowing a dappled mare's fetlock. A freckled bicep bulging over the dark well of an engine. I brought stories home the way a cat delivers songbirds. From beneath her brown fringe of bangs, Anna's eyes lasered onto that canvas what I hadn't known I'd seen. Even now, when I come across one of those paintings in an art magazine or a *New Yorker* review, I'm disturbed by how little I saw.

The morning everything changed, I hadn't been home to shower or speak to Anna in two days. It started, as so many mornings did, in the barn. After a couple of weeks, I'd groggily realized what Rusty was doing—using me as a shield against his wife. We'd go to the Rooster Tail, then stagger into his kitchen at one or two in the morning. Suzy would be waiting up, she'd douse her angry fire when she saw me, lighting our bowls, cracking our beers, serving up our late snacks, sometimes sullenly, sometimes cheerfully.

As the nights flicked by, I began to sense a sadness beneath her heat, as if all her feelings toward her husband boiled down to disappointment. I'd occasionally catch her gazing at Rusty before she left for the barn. I began to think that I was a second choice, that she wished it were he, rather than I, who would take up the pitchfork alongside her. Then she'd look away from him as she snorted up her line of black beauties and pulled on her mucking boots.

Even though it left me feeling inexplicably hollow, I kept accompanying her to the barn. I realized what she was doing, too—using me as a way of keeping her husband relatively tethered.

"You want to ride?" Suzy asked, after about a month had gone by.

"Sure," I said, stoned as usual.

She pulled a saddle off the wall. As she tacked up, she mentioned that later in the day she'd need me and Rusty to help her bring Lady down from a higher pasture. "I'm concerned she'll foal soon. I want her kept nearby, barn and paddock only, till then."

We saddled the ponies, led them outside. I mounted tentatively, expecting the small English saddle to spin upside down on its flimsy girth. I took the reins, doubting also the lightweight bit.

"This way," Suzy called, pointing Skylark toward the top of the pasture. Suzy's long legs were so far doubled up that I half expected them to hit her chin. I began composing descriptions for Anna. It occurred to me that Suzy was something of an artist herself, trying to forge something beautiful out of her life. In the process, raising up a host of paradoxes for Anna to harvest in her own art. Whoa, that's intense, I thought. I had a moment of panic, as if I were trapped like an insect or a bird in Suzy's barn.

I had work boots on, the wrong kind of jeans for riding. The inner seam chafed my knees. The horse's small size had led me expect a choppy gait, but the animal moved smoothly. When the ground leveled out, Suzy sprang off to open a gate, then we were following an old two-track into the forest. "Cow path," she said. "There used to be a big pasture up ahead. Now it's all trees and stone walls."

We cantered beneath the web of branches. Stone lined both sides of the path. I got off on watching all the different kinds of leaves—raggedy oaks, broad maples, flickering elms—flutter and bow in the breezes that seemed to come from all around. Then we turned a bend and came into a small meadow. Suzy's girls strolled ahead of us, holding hands and carrying plastic sandbox pails. I blinked at the bright colors.

With a whoop, Suzy was off her horse. "What're you two doing here?"

"Surprisin' yuh!" They both held up their pails. The redhead offered her blue bucket to her mother, who took out small, red berries.

"Delicious," said Mother Suzy. "Wonder if you could surprise me getting up early for swimming lessons one of these mornings." She gave the older girl a light shove. "Give some to Mr. Codding."

Amber lifted her red pail. I carefully removed a handful. They were much smaller than any strawberry I'd seen. I put one in my mouth and sat in rapture. Sunshine and sugar and Jerry Garcia tunes wrapped around my tongue, sank down through my body.

"Never had wild strawberries before?" Amber asked, watching me.

I shook my head.

The girl bent to pick more berries at her feet.

Suzy said, "You two go home and get ready for swimming, okay? Put the berries up on the counter and I'll stew them for shortcake."

"Shortcake! All right!"

I turned in the saddle to watch them as they darted back down the path with their Rockwellian burdens. Kids. I shook my head. A part of Suzy's life, like the mares, but alien to me. I was always pretending to myself that the Chappells had no children inhabiting the margins of our inebriated lives.

"Come on," Suzy said to me. "It's just a little ways up the path." She gestured toward the meadow. "We're not using this for pasture. Rusty wants to grow Christmas trees. I figure, why not?"

I gave a thought to the regularity, to rows and rows of perfectly round trees for Massachusetts and Manhattan weekenders. I couldn't suppress a shudder. Something there is that does not love a row. But why not? Perhaps it was the kind of blight along the South Road that conspired against rows and walls, and Frost's neighbor was right to struggle against that.

Ahead, the air glimmered like rain. As we drew closer, I realized that the trail ended on the side of Ranger Mountain, an outcropping known as Eagle's Nest. We came out into the sun. Big Shire Lake stretched beneath us, flecked with white from the wind that also tore our hair. All that water. I hadn't seen it from above before. I thought of the berries in the meadow. No matter what had driven the original colonists west—winters, stones in the earth, blights like the South Road—this land had its abundances, too.

There were hikers out already, staring at Suzy as if she'd emerged from a parallel dimension. Ignoring them, she sat her pony and gazed past the granite cliff. Her dark eyes shone with the wet of the lake. I thought I would bring that image, along with the tiny red berries in their sky-blue pail, back to Anna. These secrets of the land delivered to the one other person I knew who would see them.

Eventually Suzy pulled Skylark around. We galloped back down the path and through the strawberry meadow, slowing only to let the horses calm themselves in the last stretch before the barn. In the yard, Rusty had the girls up in the loader. The younger one sat in his lap, beaming, pretending with both hands and all her might to work the enormous shifter. Her father grinned and waved at us as we dismounted.

Suzy scowled, looking up at him. I felt, in that way you feel sure of the thoughts of those around you when you're stoned, her grief that her daughters were in the truck and not riding at her side, in place of me.

Billy came spinning up the driveway in his Ford, and the three of us went up the mountain to log, after Suzy reminded Rusty that she'd need help later. As we worked, Rusty outperformed us all. He truly was Bunyan-like in his strength, no matter how stoned or drunk he might have been. And all day as I skidded logs to the truck that would carry them to LaValley's lumberyard, the lake lay there before me, as if framed in my third eye.

I had a headache when we quit for the day, just a few minutes before eight. Rusty beckoned me up into the cab of the truck. Around the scalped clearing, blue diesel smoke hung. Why the hell had I given up a summer of sailing for this?

The three of us piled into the logger. The right-side mirror lay on the floor in front of the passenger seat, because we routinely used it for snorting "cocaine." Raunchy stuff, mostly speed, but I'd been drinking Rusty's beer and smoking his hooch all summer. I wasn't getting picky now. A cassette tape hung out of the deck like a tongue. Billy punched it in. Aerosmith, local summer kids made good; there was a lot of pride about that. Our hearts were racing as Rusty barreled down the rough road until we reached 107. We were about to turn toward the Rooster Tail—it was too late for LaValley's after all—when Suzy came flying up the highway in the shiny red pickup.

"Shit," said Rusty.

"She wants help with the horse," I remembered.

She got out of her truck, leaving the driver's door open. Rusty got out, too. They stood on the roadside, nose to chin. I thought Rusty might strike her. I thought she might strike him. Rusty suddenly slumped, hands in his pockets, looking down. Then he climbed back in with us. "Could use a hand, guys," he said.

Rusty turned the music down, maneuvered the logger to the side of the road. We piled our sorry asses into Suzy's truck. When she got to the house, she pulled a hard right, heading down a rough two-track that I hadn't seen used before. Driving was mainly a formality, I think, because I doubt we'd gone two hundred yards before she pulled over at a gate and Rusty got out. Suzy stalked up behind her husband. Invisible punches whistled, Rusty wanting her to leave him alone so he could go the bar with us, and her wanting him to do what she'd asked without her ever having had to ask it.

"Where's the horse?" I said.

Suzy struck out across the field. The rest of us followed, the lowering sun splashing our boots.

"How come Suzy didn't just bring Lady down herself?" I asked Billy.

"Bitchuva pony goes nuts sometimes. Unpredictable. But we four can handle it, by Marg'ret."

I recalled Suzy's anxiety when she found the girls in Lady's stall my first morning at the Chappells'. But she came as easy to us this time as she had then. We practically walked into her. Or she walked into us. I had a hard time believing she would resist the lead, especially when she thrust her head forward for the halter, nuzzling Suzy as she secured the buckle. I swear that mare kissed the woman's face.

"How's Mama's best hope?" Suzy murmured.

Suzy caught a loop of the rope. I took its very end. The two of us led the horse, graceful despite her broad belly, past the truck, down the road, toward the paddock.

Rusty went ahead of us to hang a trouble light off a pole in the paddock. I hadn't noticed it was getting dark, but somehow the artificial light bled out the day.

Then I tripped. I nearly went down on my knee.

Lady reared back. Suzy instantly dropped the rope, yelling for me to do the same, but my reflex was the opposite. I jerked back as hard as I could. The rope seared through my palms. It must have been the alleged coke combined with the roar of pain: I suddenly wanted to break that horse's neck. Her eyes whitened the trouble light as she reared again, jerking me to the ground. Billy ran forward, only to take a hard kick in the ribs. Suzy tried to drag him free. "Let her go, let her go," she said to me.

It was then that Rusty did what killed the horse. Despite the way people tell it, it was a small thing. It's not supposed to be possible by hand, or with a horse that's rearing out of control, but the act itself, it was small.

Rusty shoved Suzy out of the way, rushed that horse like a berserker, coming in under her hooves. He got hold of Lady on the front of her face, where the nasal bone ended. He pinched her airway shut. A man just a fraction less strong, a more ordinary man, a man you wouldn't tell a story about, it would have been nothing.

Lady threw her head, half-rearing, but Rusty held on. Suzy got to her feet, grabbed at Rusty's shoulder. He threw her back. I clung to the rope.

Lady sagged. Rusty sagged with her.

Rusty and I half dragged the stumbling horse to the paddock before she collapsed. The trouble light shone dimly in the blood beneath the mare's lowered nose. Suzy punched us both to the ground. Rusty's head cracked against mine. I turned, punched his shoulder. It's a reflex when my head gets hit. I've punched car roofs, door frames, tree limbs. Rusty didn't notice my fist.

Lady's eye clouded, her breath racketed. Billy stopped moaning about his own pain. Suzy kicked at Rusty where he lay, in the balls, again and again in the face.

"You did it on purpose. Motherfucker. Motherfucker. Motherfucker."

There was only one horse vet this side of the lake; by the time he arrived, Lady and Suzy had long gone quiet. He ran gentle hands along the mare's neck, listening through his stethoscope to her chest.

"I'm sorry," he said, after a long silence. She had hemorrhaged into her lungs. Apparently there was no way to reverse the damage. He said an artery in her airway had ruptured. A small one, but "that's all it took."

Applying his scope along her swollen belly, he again shook his long narrow head. The foal too was dead.

Suzy knelt by the horse. Rusty stumbled to her side, his face swollen and hideous, and laid a hand on her shoulder. She didn't shake it off.

No one paid any attention to me. I shuffled over to where Billy slumped against the barn's wall.

"I can drive you to the hospital," I offered. "Or just to your house. We can take your truck. I'll walk up Perkins Ridge from there." I was anxious for the whole adventure to be over—not just the night's, but the whole month's worth. I wanted Lady's last struggles and everything else about these people's lives to fade into nightmare and be gone. I didn't have to live with this forever. Whatever part I might have played, I told myself it was still their drama. Let John Perkins smirk over my association with white trash. Anna could find herself a new source for her painting subjects. I put my arm out to support Billy.

But it wasn't over yet.

"Hey!" said Rusty. "I got to clean this up before the kids wake up." I looked up at the attic windows, astonished at his delusion that the children might still be asleep.

Rusty shook the vet's hand and sent the skinny man off. Then he began marshaling his fleet. The loader, which kept stalling. The dump truck, its engine now repaired by Billy, but its tires still flat. And a bulldozer with a whirling orange light on top.

Rusty directed me to the cab of the 'dozer. I figured out what he wanted. I laid my palm, oozing with rope burn, against the knob of the shifter, jammed it in gear. Pushed Lady into the shovel of his loader. Her head dangled free when Rusty lifted her into the air. Her coat still shone. I rubbed my eyes as his stuttering machine swung around and crawled up to the dump truck. Maybe it was the exhaust smoke and the weird orange light, or maybe Rusty forgot to account for the truck's list. But when he lifted the loader as high as it could go and eased back on the lever to flip the shovel downwards, he missed.

I climbed out of my cab; Rusty leapt out of his. Even Billy lurched forward to have a look. Blood oozed onto the gravel, and one small hoof stuck out of the belly.

We all heard Suzy say it: "You've done it now, Rusty, you've really done it." Until I turned around, I thought she was talking about the horse.

Her daughters stood behind us. The older, dark-haired girl came to peer at the mare. Her solemnity swallowed the engine noise, our breathing, even the pace of our hearts. She dropped to her knees, one hand going to the necklace at her throat. She pulled the gold chain over her head and draped it onto Lady's. It only reached around the mashed ears, forming a halo in the whirling lights.

It called to me, that shiny bit of resin. It wanted me to be the fly, it was begging me to climb inside. Any number of summer people do that, get jobs with the locals, start drinking, start shooting cocaine, never come back out. I kept staring at the horse, at that little hoof sticking out, at that pendant. I was already polishing it. I was letting it harden. It was my cheap little souvenir. It's the reason I'm here, sitting on the porch of my summer camp, listening to the mosquitoes whine on the other side of the screen, watching the red and green of the port and starboard lights on the motorboats far out on Big Shire. It's reason I'm telling you this. You can't really tell a story unless you were passing through it.

The girl stroked the mare's twisted neck, her eyes moving across us all, grave and sad in their wells of broken sleep. Under that gaze the harshness fled from her parents' faces, leaving only ruin behind.

# Hide and Seek

Charisse J. Tubianosa

Please remember our kiss, a big fat kiss while we are huddled under the dining room table laden with *lumpia* fried chicken spaghetti *pancit* and barbecue, hidden by my Mama's favorite mantle for when guests come where we are waiting to be found by cousins who didn't want us to play hide-and-seek with them in the first place because they said: *You're too little*—we are six—but you took my hand and whispered: *Let's hide anyway*, as they started to count down. I protest, again, that nobody would ever come looking for us because we're not part of the game and you, so calm so confident, shrug and tell me: *It's alright the important thing is that we're still playing*, then you beam me a big happy smile I smile back and I look at the mole on the left side of your upper lip, that's when you kiss me; now I don't want to be found I just want to stay here with you where it feels safe, still, someone looks under the table and finds us but then we don't want to hide-and-seek anymore we go to play with my doll house to invent our own family instead.

We are eight when Mama says I can't play with you anymore when I press her for answers she says it's because your mother is not a good woman: *She does bad things with men for money*, what things she won't tell me but neighbors talk about the fancy jewelry, the expensive bags, the trail of cloying cologne your mother leaves behind, the parade of much older men coming by your house and how these relate to you or me isn't quite as clear until Mama tells me: *Kung ano ang puno, sya ang bunga*, which is something about knowing a fruit by its tree and how such laws of nature are too powerful, so powerful that I imagine your mother as a tree with all her bracelets and bags on her branches and all those old, *very* old, men struggling to mount her, I want to ask more but Mama looks like she's done explaining. I hide from you when you ring the doorbell I find I'm really quite good at hiding and the day comes when you finally stop trying which makes me cry which makes me angry at how quickly you let me go, I spy on you from the window to see what you're doing without me I listen to your laughter as you play with the other kids in the street, then we are thirteen and I don't hear your voice anymore and I overhear Mama telling Papa that maybe your mother has finally done right by you has taken you to your grandmother, some other responsible adult who can care for you properly—or so she hopes—because my Mama fears your mother might have sold you to the perversities of some dirty old man and my father scoffs at that: *But she's only thirteen*, Mama counters with the case of that congressman who went to jail for soliciting sex from a minor (in his blubbering defense: *I thought she was eighteen!*) and Mama adds: *I wouldn't put anything past that woman*, she crosses herself which signals that the subject is closed.

We are twenty-three when news breaks out that an adult-movie actress about our age hiding behind a ridiculous stage name is accusing a trio of local comedians of drugging her of kidnapping of rape, the case drags on for months and overnight everyone is an expert tossing unsolicited ideas about: she had it coming she was hallucinating she just wants to be famous; but suddenly the charges are dropped and the tabloids say the matter has been settled out of court, the actress receives a huge sum of money and a condo unit way up on the twenty-fifth floor so she stops making movies and we no longer think about her and we laugh again at the antics of these three comedians, until one day she leaps from her balcony on an express journey to arrive at the poolside of the building that was designed so lovely with coconut trees and trellises and her blood splattering on the immaculate whiteness of the plastic deck chairs. I look out from the wide window of the hotel room overlooking streets office buildings shopping malls after my lover who is married who is also my boss has fallen asleep, I find myself speculating if that actress had been you and I see you sitting in that condo alone in the dark remembering the un-funny things those comedians did to you what people said about you, I wonder as you jumped if you had spared a thought for me for how things were so much simpler when we were under that dining table, I pore over news articles video footages with images of the dead actress checking every grainy photo for that telltale mole just above the lip and I don't know if I am relieved or disappointed she doesn't carry your mole.

We are twenty-eight when the papers go crazy again about the chop-chopped body parts of a woman which had been found inside large garbage bags under the Guadalupe bridge a woman without identification without anyone to claim her, I let your name idle in my tongue to see how it would fit this poor broken-up woman wondering whether she was someone's wife someone's whore, was she someone's mother was there a child waiting for her to come home was she missed at all? But I'm also thinking if I should change jobs as my boss-lover explains about not being able to come over because there is a dinner with the in-laws but promises to take me on the business trip to Hong Kong—I don't really care but care enough to lie to my Mama about the people I see and some of the things I do—if only we can be six again be safe again, this time I find myself praying she's not you this quartered unnamed woman and though I haven't heard mass haven't prayed in quite a long time I cross myself.

Now we are thirty-four and I am sipping on a piña colada much too sweet on an island off-Palawan that's only accessible by chartered plane because my ex-boss-on-again-off-again-lover would like to make amends, I am thinking of you and in my thoughts we run away together to live in some other city some other country, somewhere where we are so regular that nobody double-takes to see two women kissing, where you're a teacher just like you told me you wanted to be and I am a celebrated but reclusive painter hiding from the limelight—instead of someone trudging day in and day out in a bank in a crowded joyless loveless city with too much heat traffic pollution—some weekends you let me paint you my deft brushstrokes translating your long brown-black hair on canvas, I always tell you: *Sit still for a moment! Please!* Stop twitching that lovely mouth so that I can place that mole perfectly but it's not possible because our Labrador our Pit Bull our Chihuahua all three come bouncing around demanding total attention wanting to play hide-and-seek. Or, I am a naturalist an explorer and you a photographer we travel endlessly from Borneo to Madagascar to Ecuador never staying in one place for too long publishing articles and photographs in top magazines, I give lectures at universities at conferences and wink at you from across the room. We adopt a baby girl a baby boy or we just have a terrarium, we settle in a country where we can marry where we decide not to marry, whatever we do we laugh ridiculously way too much over many years—and we kiss we always kiss—then we are old and when you die it is a peaceful death while you sleep, I follow you a few weeks later because what point would there be to stay on without you and I too die easy knowing you have been safe with me.

We are forty and I am sitting in a café along L. P. Leviste Street in Makati near where I work where I am ignoring a phone call because I want to be alone because I don't want to be alone, I look up my breathing comes to a full stop because there you are—right there really there—two tables across from me sipping on a large cup long hair pulled back in a ponytail, I search I see the mole right above your lip, you wear glasses now you have on a plain white T-shirt tucked in faded blue jeans your face free of makeup so clean; you sense me you also look up and I'm not sure how much you see because the sun is behind me, I am uneasy of this sun that shines on the bracelets on my arm on the latest designer bag that sits smug on the extra chair beside me—would I remind you of someone else? That I look at you doesn't unnerve you in any way, still calm still confident, you return my look so I wait I hope for you to remember until you are distracted by a little girl who comes suddenly who wraps her small arms around you, I hazard a guess she is five or six this little girl looking so much like the one I hid with under the table looking like it was someone else's life a long time ago, but behind her is a man, a man who looks solid strong stable a man with his smile that warms his smile that protects who plants a soft kiss on your lips as the floor beneath me crumbles, then oh then you turn to look at me again you smile but it is a vague smile the kind given to some strangers the kind where the lips spread to a thin line and reluctantly turn up at the edges; finally and finally I look away I don't smile back—*I* don't give smiles to strangers.

# American Silhouette

Garrett Candrea

It's a slip of paper about the size of his finger and it perhaps saves his life. It comes to him in a complimentary fortune cookie tossed in among a #7 combo platter and a can of cola and he's sitting in his cubicle reading it, somewhere near nine p.m., the fluorescents dimmed and a vacuum going in a corner of the office. The floor is otherwise empty. Perhaps someone from Sys Ops or some other backend team but he hasn't seen him or her or them. The AC has been turned off and the day's stresses are seeping out of him in a faint and sour reek and it's just three words printed on the fortune slip. He reads them over and again. He thinks maybe he's missed something. A janitor wanders over and flashes a perfunctory smile while music blares away in her earbuds all handclaps and antic wailing and without a word he rolls away from his desk so she can access the small waste bin beneath. She upends it, rattling out candy wrappers and chip bags, crumpled soda cans, food scraps, cryptic notes, the wadded dates of days gone by and their useless bits of trivia, on this day in history, all falling away into a large trash bin on wheels while he sits there staring at the slip between his thumb and forefinger.

It reads:

*Don't stop now.*

It's seventeen months ago:

Here he sees the silhouette of life. It is grainy and striate and there is a clear form to it that he can recognize, such a little thing huddled in a cavity, the image rendered from soundwaves.

The doctor says, I'll give you two some privacy.

It is the profile of life. Perhaps this sounds better. A fetus framed within a shape that makes him think of the symbol that means Wi-Fi, only upended. Perhaps the symbol for Wi-Fi was modeled after this, meaning connectivity, a thing connected. He can see the cord. But no, he can't. Or he thinks he does, the thing that tethers it. That is not a penis. But it might be. Only there's no way.

This is the shape of life, what he is seeing there on the sonogram screen, the outline of it. It makes him wonder how such a thing is possible, it makes him marvel at the science of it. It makes him wonder how he could be capable of such a thing. Because he is just himself. He sits in a template cubicle for ten hours a day breathing stale office air while he types out some simple code and stares numbly at a screen, keyboard patinated with fingergunk and a stack of business cards in a drawer somewhere with his name printed on them along with the words *Senior Data Analyst* but what he really is is a cliché.

Do you see it? he says, and points it out to her with one hand on her shoulder in this room that smells of plastic and disinfectants and the fluorescents in the tegular ceiling are humming a cold flat light. He's hunched down so that their faces are side by side, nearly touching, smiling, and he tells her, whispers, That's ours.

**H**e will see it soon. He sees it every time, twice a day. He makes sure to find a window seat facing the Hudson River so he won't miss it. These are the palindrome times, from Cold Spring to Grand Central and back, the syncopated clunk of the wheeltrucks that pace the commute and the onboard air whirring numbly. Five days a week. Sometimes more, those crunch times before some deliverable or new build is to be shipped and he's sitting in the stifling must of his cubicle on a Saturday sweating in gym shorts and a plain tee because the AC isn't running.

He will see it today for the second time, it is coming. The canted rust-scabbed sign that flicks past in the window tells him to perk up, get ready, only he's limp weight in his seat with his forehead propped against the fingersmudged glass and his worn satchel in his lap, the work phone buzzing dully in a side compartment to inform him of afterhours tasks as monotonous as this commute, somewhere between Cold Spring and Garrison.

And here, there it is, way out to the south, the river meandering off into the folds of the flanking mountains and there's something in the image that seems not to belong. It's a steel structure sprouting out from a point where the mountains east and west of the Hudson seem by some trick of perception to fuse together, this is what he's looking at, what he makes sure never to miss, and maybe jutting is a better word. The east tower of the Bear Mountain Bridge that erupts from the landscape.

It's ten months ago:

He wakes at some anonymous hour and again finds himself alone. The empty spot beside him and the hint of downstairs light in the hall, he checks for the first and then the other. He knows the first guarantees the other. A cold wind is grinding against the window and the walls shift and settle and he can hear her down there through all of this, stirring numbly about in the kitchen with a cup of tea gone lukewarm in her hand while the other holds the nothing in her stomach, he's seen it too many times to doubt this very image roused up from the groggy ache in his mind.

Tonight he won't go down there, won't descend the creaking steps to stand in the kitchen entranceway and offer stock words of solace to the woman pacing in a nightgown, the dark hair frayed and matted and the face so haggard in the sallow light and those dark eyes, pupil and iris one black hole holding no reflection or else this is what such deep sense of guilt looks like, standing now remote among the shadows cast on the floor and a wall clock tracking the silence all tick and tick and tick.

Instead he reaches down beneath the covers, closes his eyes, thinking of the cam girl he'd earlier that day chatted with, flirted with, spent a portion of his paycheck to wad her up among her sheets from half a world away while his wife sat in her therapist's office in the town over. Because there is a threshold. There are only so many times you can say a thing before even the thought of it raises a taste like bile to the back of your throat.

You couldn't have done anything. You didn't do anything wrong.

It's not your fault.

Or you say it so often you begin to wonder who are you truly trying to convince here?

Because didn't you fucking tell her?

**H**e raises his hand over the water, a father showing something to his son. Think of a father sitting beside his son on the rocky bank of the Hudson with the rail tracks behind them and the sleepy country homes obscured by trees and he is pointing something out to his boy. Can you see it? he says. I want you to see it.

The green mountains across the way, the escarpment there and the sheerness of it with its parapet of ancient trees you can't imagine anything on the other side.

It is yours.

This is what he tells the boy, what he wants to tell the boy, staring off over the water with a mossy smell wafting up from the shallows and a commuter train clattering by at their backs. He points up now, over there, in the east. He likes to see the moon like this, already high among the clouds with the sun not yet down and it looks like another world indeed.

It is yours.

There is a thing you can do: you take the ashes of a loved one and use them as fertilizer. You watch how her remains give birth to a flower in a ceramic pot that sits on your windowsill. Or the pot is plastic. Or it is unfired clay because your days and thoughts have become just as malleable and it sits on the kitchen table. Let's put it in the garden.

Let's watch the freight train go.

There. Do you see it? Across the river there.

It's a great chain of rusted bars sliding slowly along the hazy bight, mute and toysized and now its whistle the lonesome bawl of it.

All of this is yours.

Now imagine these words are handwritten. Imagine you are reading this out of a notebook, dogeared pages and the cover peeling back at a corner. Imagine the words are in blue ink, black ink, sometimes red, and they carry in their curves and slants all the idiosyncrasies belonging to a person. The scuttering shorthand and spastic flourishes and pay attention to the stroke patterns that make the *I* between faded blue lines—I love you, I love you—the slight variations that betray the nuances of your mood. And imagine there is another line that swings up into the margin, handmade among the dirty thumbprints, it meanders through scrawled annotations and doodled reveries to terminate in a slapdash arrow that points to the beginning of all of this, and a note:

None of this real. This is fiction.

Imagine these words are crossed out, the frantic strokes that make you think somehow of the boarded windows of an abandoned home. These are dreams that are dogeared, not pages.

This is a wish. This is a fantasy. You have no son. You are no father. The boy is dead and has been, was so before you ever met him, before you could even tell him his name.

**He** sees it first on his walk from Grand Central to the Bank of America Tower, the shape of something unfamiliar through the park trees, a glass structure, it looks like, flickering out now and again from behind the busses and trucks groaning along West 42nd.

At the corner he crosses the street and ascends the broad granite steps at the end of the park and he's staring at it now, wondering first how they managed to get it there, then what the hell is it exactly? It's an enormous glass sphere centered on the lawn of Bryant Park. But that's not what it is. It's a new public art installation. Or what the hell is it? Someone walks past him, a woman with a small white dog, talking to it in a goo-goo voice as she steps onto the lawn and toward the thing, *look at that, what is that?*

It looks to be two, three stories tall and just as wide. There are some boom lifts scattered about it. At its center floats a smaller sphere, also glass or appears to be, and branded with block text going around its center. From where he stands he can read the words AN AMER, or rather just one word and a fragment of another.

There are some people gathered about it as well, the backs of their skulls tucked into their napes, staring up in awe, with more on the way, approaching the thing with steps that seem wary. They touch it experimentally, as if to make sure it's real. It is real. They knock on it, *knock knock.* From where he stands it makes no sound against the soft trickle of the fountain or the traffic seething along the avenue behind him but still he can imagine a dull bong with each strike, a kind of tedious Morse ringing out behind his ears.

Or it's his work phone vibrating in its compartment.

His boss' name is displayed there on the screen in LCD-white and he knows he's late for a meeting.

There was the time when he looked forward to his business meetings, when he would make her feel alone even when he was right next to her, receding into his work, the spreadsheets and particolored graphs. One night she told him—they were sitting side by side on the couch with the TV on and she told him that she missed him. He didn't look at her. He had his laptop open and positioned where it was designed to be and he told her that he was right here.

She just sat there staring at him for a while, watching his fingers clack over the keyboard and his eyes how they flitted across information so esoteric to her she wanted to take the fucking thing and chuck it across the room. She wanted to yell at him. She wanted to hit him. She wanted to lay her head in his lap and feel the weight of his hand.

But she had done none of that.

She said, But you're not.

It's fourteen months ago:

The intercom above the blackboard has clicked on with the morning announcements, blah blah blah, and now for the pledge. They still say the pledge here. It goes like this:

*I pledge allegiance to the flag . . .*

The door opens. The door closes. The class has gone silent, their small hands slowly falling from their hearts while the pledge continues over the loudspeaker flat and fringed with static, recited by rote.

They do not scream, the children, though already some have begun to cry. They are young but still they know what this is. They understand what is about to happen. A few remain still, stiff, paralyzed, while others have by now dropped to the floor, clambered beneath their desks where they wad themselves into little shivering balls and close their eyes. As if that will make the man go away. As if that will save them. Because this is what they have been trained to do.

The man has yet to speak. He doesn't need to. Standing there in front of the blackboard beneath the flag sagging red white and blue. One nation under God. Everything he's ever wanted to say will come flashing out from the barrel of that gun.

Of the children still standing some never take their eyes off the man. Others look to the teacher. But the teacher cannot help. She'd just that morning made a breakfast of eggs and toast and at the train station sent her husband off with a kiss and she'd parked the faded sedan in the lot beneath a budding oak and said hello to a colleague in the hall along with a small joke that solicited a smile and she'd made her coffee in the teachers' lounge and sat drinking it at her desk while she went over her planner and greeted her children as they entered the room by ones and twos to store their belongings in their cubbies and she'd written the day's agenda on the board before they'd begun the pledge and her fingers are still dusted with chalk. That is all. A dusty smudge against her blouse, lilac for the coming spring.

She is thinking that the last thing she will ever do is say please but instead she vomits.

The man with the gun stands there, as if waiting for her to finish, just the curdled splatter of it against the linoleum and the small voice still reciting the pledge in the wall and the whimpers of children.

He asks her, What are you?

He has the gun leveled at her and that is what she sees when she raises her head with the rank slaver on her lips and her hand on her stomach, so feeble a gesture.

What are you?

Please, she says.

She wanted to say please I'm pregnant but could not get all those words out and instead placed her hand upon the boy yet taking shape inside her and she doesn't hear the shot until she's on the floor. She collapses into her chair and sloughs down into her vomit clutching at her stomach, on her side and watching a dark spot bloom in the fabric of her blouse, trying with desperate fingers to claw the blood back into the neat red hole from which it's pumping steadily.

Then she hears the shot.

**S**he's in the garden now, something precious in a pot of unfired clay, there in the dappled light among other perennials and tarnished décor, the wrought-iron aphorisms stuck in the ground and things hewn from stone, small sculptures in allegorical poses. She is among these things. Only of course it's not her but a type of Hibiscus, *Hibiscus coccineus,* this is what the plastic label says, scarlet rose mallow. This is who she is now, what she is, with her petals fluttering in slightest breeze beneath a twilight sky scuffed with clouds.

Only of course it's not her.

But he talks to it as if it were. Never saying her name but just hey, or hey, and all the anecdotes he's pocketed between his morning commute and the evening, never becoming undone by this, just opening the sliding backdoor and walking out over the patchy lawn to say hey there, bad day, good day, perhaps just a shrug.

Just letting his work satchel slough to the floorboards and opening the fridge for a beer and something to microwave and cleaning his dish by hand before going out back and filling the galvanized watering can with the hose and walking out over the yard mottled with light and shadow to say hey, here you go.

Or, Hey, they put in some new art installation at Bryant Park. Jus' this giant sphere, glass sphere.

He had to order proprietary soil from a private company because the excessive sodium content of cremated remains prevents the release of nutrients within natural soil, so he was told, and he was never undone by any of this. This is therapy. Something a blog post told him might be helpful. Reading the instructions at the kitchen counter and mixing her ashes with the specially formulated dirt and setting the rose mallows in the pot and placing the pot on the bedroom windowsill, then the kitchen table. Finally the garden.

It's an interactive piece. He sees this now. Standing here before it with his satchel slung from his shoulder, just ten minutes off the train and already sweating in the borough humidity. There are people sticking photos to it. Photos of themselves. Photos of landscapes. Of buildings, company logos. But mostly it's photos of people, in all manner of poses and settings, or just faces, in whatever attitude you can imagine. These are photos taken from family albums, printed from social networking sites, there are even some freehand sketches here, a caricature of a child, a collage of time and demographics. He's walking around it. He will tell her about this. He will tell her it's been up only a day and yet perhaps a third of it is already covered. All the way around. The images overlapping, sort of panoplied, shingled, scaled, sequined, louvered. One of these words is right.

He finds a bare spot big enough for a fist his size and he makes one and raps against the glass and, no, not a dull bong but something that beckons the word sonorous into the mind. He knocks it twice more. It resonates all the way through, he can feel it in his chest. Then a man comes to say, Excuse me. He steps aside and watches the man cover the bare spot with a picture of a dog, it looks like a Border Collie. He asks the man if it is, gestures at the picture and says, What kind is it? The man shrugs, says he's not sure, was a rescue. Tells him it's some sort of mix. Then turns and walks away.

He watches him go, passing a group of people depositing photos into a bucket to be hoisted by the person standing in the boom lift perhaps some twenty, thirty feet above.

And the words up there, wrapped around the inner sphere. He glimpsed them before on his first trip around but forgot to read them, to register their meaning, and he circles the sphere again, reading the text as he goes, his lips moving mutely amid the stray voices and laughter and the electric whine of the boom lifts rising above the body heat gathered here on the lawn.

It reads:

*WHAT DOES AN AMERICAN LOOK LIKE?*

He keeps his picture in a notebook. Taped to the inside of the cover. The sonogram. This was his son, was and only was, was to be, who never was, future and present tense without. He looks at it every time, sometimes just a glance to make sure it's still there, the silhouette, the outline of life, then flips to the next blank space and transcribes a memory, a thought. This is another thing he learned from the blog post. Remember the good times. Record them. When he'd lay his ear against her stomach and imagine the nanopulse beating within, it conjures a sensation like a fingertip tapping away beneath your temple. It makes you smile. It makes you look up and kiss her, holding her face and kissing her and you cannot wait.

Or write about the pain, let the pain bleed out from the penpoint. Only lately they've been dreams, his writings, they've been fantasies. A father and his son catching fireflies in the dusk or walking through the snow with a thermos of hot cider and hacksaw in hand, looking for the perfect Christmas tree. Or sitting by the river with the mother just below them skipping stones across the surface, clear to the other side.

What does she look like?

What would he have looked like?

A week goes by and the sphere is nearly covered. Photos and drawings and a vast assortment of tchotchkes, memorabilia, there are even locks of hair, all colors, some beyond what is natural, these are things that seem to completely disregard the question posited by the inner sphere but perhaps that is the point.

There are records up there, old LPs and CDs and cassette tapes. There are menus and cooking recipes. There are so many items overlapping and jutting out at odd angles the thing is becoming shapeless. They're just putting things up there, beautiful and ugly all at once, grotesque is better, with tree bark and dust and withered flowers, spent cigarettes, boluses of gum, candy wrappers parrying the summer sun and national flags that ripple all likewise in the wind. Countries that are not this country.

Someone has put an old arm cast up there, signed with names, and book pages and dustjackets, magazine covers, newsprint clippings. He sees one with the shooter's name printed so formally in reportorial black, one more label among the ruck. But it brings it all back of course, that awful day and the weeks and months after, and he stands there staring at it until the letters resolve into a kind of ideogram.

The name of the shooter is not important. It means the myopic precepts found scrawled out on notebook pages among ethnocentric ravings. It means the interviews with family members and neighbors, former colleagues, the generic quotes stating that they never would have guessed, can't believe it, still in shock. Killed by a gunshot wound to the neck after exchanging fire with a SWAT team in the school hallway.

It means candlelight vigils and orange awareness ribbons pinned to shirts, hung in storefront windows, fluttering on car antennas.

It means the countless messages of condolence collected on an answering machine, with the light blinking red and red in a dark corner of the house.

It means the murder of seven children not including his unborn son, who died still in his mother's womb, the bullet that wrecked his prenatal skull.

The name means all the sick heartache and tension that loss presses on a marriage. You pay six thousand dollars to bury an empty casket and you need to select a reading and there are forms to sign and you fucking told her, didn't you? You told her you wanted her to stop going in, to take it easy. Because she was only three months away and you wanted her to take it easy.

The name means this:

Standing in a tiled room and watching a licensed crematory operator comb through your wife's ashes with a high-powered magnet to extract her fillings.

It's four months ago:

Their anniversary is a numbered square in a wall calendar showing a month from a bygone season but it is rather the long week's sundry disappointments and frustrations that make the ride so silent, heading across the Bear Mountain Bridge on their way back from Costco, the trunk crammed with bulk purchases and BOGO deals and the late sun glinting off the river below when she cuts the wheel just so, drifting into the shoulder, easing to a stop with the radio playing some garbled tune and the rear of the car jutting cockeyed into the eastbound lane and the traffic already mounting, horns blaring in irate staccato while the sedan's hazard lights blink a sound that goes *click click click.*

He says her name. He asks what is she doing. She doesn't answer. She's looking straight ahead with her hands gripping the wheel. She's put the car in park and hit the hazards but her hands are still gripping the wheel, gripping hard, blood fleeing from her knuckles.

She does not look at him. She closes her eyes for an extended moment, her breath whistling through her nostrils, punctuated by the odd muffled curse from the cars rubbernecking by. He says her name again and she's looking at him now but says nothing, her eyes betray nothing. Then she turns off the hazards and puts the car in drive.

One week later she goes back to the bridge. She parks in a scenic rest stop near the eastern approach and walks along the footpath in a serene daze of slurred colors and shadows and the backwash drag of traffic till a point perhaps midway where all of this recedes ever further as she climbs over the guardrail to freefall toward whatever comes next.

Before she left she stopped in the front door and said, I'm going. Not looking back but facing out at the weedy lawn and the street of faded asphalt, her hand on the tarnished brass knob. I'm going, she said, louder.

He never asked where or said bye or anything at all. He pretended he couldn't hear her and went up to his home office to see if cam girl Plum was online and it's not till hours after, sitting now amid the long shadows in the living room and a commercial for asthma medication listing breathlessly all possible side effects, that he begins to wonder where his wife is.

Then it's gone. He's standing there with the only photo ever taken of his boy and of course it's gone. There's nothing left of it save the pressed spot in the grass where it just yesterday had been, now pale of green and gleaming in the heat. This is its outline stamped here into the ground, its shadow, its silhouette. His phone is buzzing. The wind carries the slightest suggestion of dog piss. The photo in his hand is a photo of the original photo. He'd taken a picture of it with his phone and uploaded it to his computer and printed it out in grayscale, which it more or less already was.

There are people sitting at the tables beneath the trees, lounging on towels on the lawn, some even within the circle of flattened grass. Nothing has changed. His phone is buzzing in its compartment and he sends it to voicemail and he almost wants to enact some Hollywood moment where he sets the photo down in the grass and it means the perfect thing. But he knows how silly a gesture that would be. So he stows the photo away in his satchel and turns, makes his way toward the office.

But then he stops. He stops halfway across the lawn and doubles back and he does the thing regardless of how silly it is, how exceedingly romantic and ineffectual.

Taking out not the photo but the fortune slip and folding it, tucking it into the flattened grass, though perhaps interring is the better choice.

It's eight years from now:

He's on the couch with his ear to her stomach. There's a sitcom playing on the TV and there's a laugh track tapering away in the speakers but he hears none of this. He hears the little nanopulse beneath her skin. The word familiar makes a sound such as this. It makes him lift away his ear to replace it with his lips. It makes him whisper three words smaller yet than the thing its message has borne.

These are not words in a notebook. This is now, with the lights off and colors flashing palely against the walls, a flowerpot on the sill.

# Soliloquy of a Woman Silenced at the Foot of a Mango Tree

Nicole F Kimball

And there will be times our name sounds porous to them. Wrapped in the greensleeves of barren winter, where we go to undress our people; those ones that keep us up. In the night; the body asks for courage. Things we have done to get through man's clear eminence. Even the creatures unquiet in the forest do not wish for the great roots of the tree, or the just barely crawling plants. There will be times we come to reconcile the throbbing of the womb, the divine feminine we shed, sink, and recreate for. Recreate the way men say "god" or maybe how the stars cast spells on the numbness of our planet. We lose children as heavy clotting out of our mouths. Our legs spread like fall's evolving through to spring and then our breed slips out. Onto concrete and bright red sac, bundled pools of our body breaking her ribs, her heart, her almost human footprints. Now we are silenced as were the Queens. We must be hysterical for rolling sourly inside the intestine of lament. And what a feat it must be, to hear words like " reason, time, and purpose" and then still breathe on to recreate. The baby belonged elsewhere is only a metaphor to shush the irrevocable noise. That roaring satire they make for you may not be your time to unravel or even consider the place for mankind. For woman, for women who bury that red pool growing against the dirtiness of soil. There will be times they call that thing dead, that haven inside of us dead. That red is the color of the unborn and the shrivel. Aging of uterus, our orbits of lights within the body we rent. Birth becomes medicated & so ugly & so fowl. Pills conceal the huntress we spend a lifetime inventing. Humming of placenta and ripe mango trees; clay tail twisting, convulsing underneath begins the story of simmer broil knot to fissure wither mother-breast un-jeweled unearthly right of passage-hold this birth and every birth because there will be times we are told we are not women. Do not let them tell you about dirty aliens clumping at the feet of those mango trees. Do not let the sleeping be alone in your waking, or the fat sabbaths of June near those fat seeds you planted. Some kind of language it is, how belly buttons grow. Sublime intervention and how we say resurrection. Of this love, of another life. Watching-screeching dry their throats, watching fire burn.

PORTAL / LISA RIGGE

# THREE POEMS FROM *THE HORSE FAIR*

EDITOR'S PRIZE

*Three Poems from* The Horse Fair, *poems on the life and art of French animaliere Rosa Bonheur (1822-99). Part psycho-biography, part speculation and intuition, these linked dramatic monologues probe themes of gender, class, and artistic genius against the background of 19th Century Paris and environs.*

–Jana Harris

# HOW TO DRAW

*PARIS, 1843*

JANA HARRIS

*(Rosa Bonheur, b. 1822)*

The Hotel Lambert,
at the tip of the Ile Saint-Louis,
the Seine's inscrutable waters
like a moat around it.
Even in winter the walled

garden bloomed beneath
a palm tree as if
I'd stepped into French Algiers.

Inside the behemoth residence:
two schools, one for boys,
another for girls, conducted
only in Polish.

It was hoped that drawing lessons
would help Princess Iza with
her embroidery, her mother's famous
needlework auctioned to aid
emigres from the failed insurrection
flooding the streets of Paris.

In the grand hall
—The Gallery Hercules—
I positioned an easel,
the parquet floor lacquered
to luminance, the leaded
many-paned windows spilt
the light into rainbows thinning
to watercolor.

Above us,
in the ballroom, frenzied
piano chords vibrated down
through the ceiling.

From one end of the gallery,
the Cabinet des Muses,
soft tones of another piano;
at the other, the Polish library.

Walking between, a great migration
of exiled diplomats, their strange language

and an even more foreign tongue,
Russian, but uttered only as curse words.
Princess Iza spoke perfect French,
Polish, even Russian, so explained,
though she was forbidden
the language of the invaders.
In her homeland, her native tongue
was punishable by lashings
or worse—her brother Withold
forced to walk to Siberia in chains.

Iza's squirrel-paw hand
struggled with line quality, shading;
a new set of pencils sharpened
by her lady-in-waiting.
We moved on to variance
of line weight, practical textures,
shapes, realistic shadowing,
proportions, perspective.

Our progress inspected by her mother
who held up Iza's latest embroidery;
a disappointment, she said,
removing the stitches.

What a strange contraption:
a piece of canvas overlaid
by geometric patterns cross-stitched
and chain stitched in red wool and
metal fibers. Two little sails jutting
out at the top: *Que c'est?*
A fly mask for her brother Wladyslaw's horse—
we had a love of *les chevaux* in common.

When her mother, Princess Anna Zofia
was otherwise occupied,
when the ladies-in-waiting

were sharpening pencils;
when the diplomats congregated in the library
closed the vast double doors,
when Wladyslaw was away drilling
with the French cavalry,
when the warring Polish pianists
were composing in the Cabinet des Muses
and the grand ballroom upstairs, both
rehearsing for the annual Polish ball
attended by Balzac, Delacroix,
and that aristocratic lady author
who went about in masculine attire—
patron of the wan, pale-haired pianist...

When all were occupied,
when the coast was clear,
Princess Iza and I put down our pencils,
took off our slippers and slid
in white-stockinged feet, up
and down the Gallery Hercules,
attaining speed, careening, falling
or crashing into a wall
or over each other in a heap.
Stifling hysterical laughter,
we lay upended,
my white drawers, her white pantalettes,
Turkish trousers, white leglets with lace
trim buttoned on the bottom;
like two snow mounds,
our nethers immodestly presented
and, according to the Princess,
airing to prevent dampness.

Her undergarments
embroidered in bright silk thread
with the Czartoryski coat-of-arms.

A deterrent to some, she said; but
no impediment whatsoever
for the Imperial Russian plunderers.

Though Princess Izabella hadn't a gift
for embroidery, she had a genius
for the shades and variance of practical horseplay
that modesty—and language—disallowed.

# Mademoiselle Nathalie Micas Decides to Change Her Hat

*Paris, 1860*

Jana Harris

*(Rosa Bonheur, b. 1822)*

Optimistic or full-tilt harebrained?
*Le Chateau de By*; a country house
on the edge of Fontainebleau Forest
once bequeathed to the royal beekeeper:
chapel, garden plot, carriage port, barn
for the menagerie.

I'd won so many medals;
when I put them on,
they weighed more than armor.
My paintings—oxen plowing, sheep grazing,
imperial horses—hung on palace walls.
Still, the critics' venom
had a painful sting: Good brushwork
for a woman, but is it art?
Soot-heavy clouds pressed down on me,
the dingy Paris air seeped into my skin.

Looking into Nathalie's eyes,
all I saw was dead leaves.
She was like a horse, spooked
by sudden stirrings, loud noises,
being backed into a corner.

When she changed her hat,
I took it as a bad sign.
Hat after hat—fanchon bonnet to high-
brimmed spoon to straw boater—
until she came loose from her moorings.
I feared the tide would take her out.

Worse, in the kitchen,
when Mother Micas moved her lips,
nothing was heard, neither
cursing nor praying.

A heavy melancholy settled about us
like mist on the Seine.

When I signed the deed,
all my "what-if" terrors convened
like crouching cats to witness;
I wouldn't say there wasn't a smear
of indecisiveness in my hand.

I resigned the directorship
of the drawing school;
we sublet the Paris house.
A two hour train ride to meadow rue,
juniper, native geranium, thousands
of hectares of scots pine.
When we alighted, a breeze
toyed with loose tendrils of our hair
and the sun tricked us
into feeling warm.

I set up my studio
in the third floor billiard hall,
a fireplace large enough to stand in;

Nathalie claimed the sunniest room.
The glitter in her eyes awoke.
Medical bag in hand, she refused
to tend the menagerie hatless.
She donned flamboyant headgear,
a mousquetaire, with black and red
feathers atop an upturned brim.

In the kitchen, Mother Soup cooked
wild mushrooms and ceased breathing
through her teeth.

I smoked, wore trousers, tramped
through the forest: swirling leaves
clamored excitedly at my heels,
warblers dove from the sky. Before
a porcelain chip of moon came up,
a stag crept to the pond to drink.
As the grass whispered assuringly,
I made a mental sketch of his head;
I could feel him thinking, saw
a thought run through his mind.

As I watched, I was feral,
unfixed in time.

# Painting Lions:

## *Pierrette, Oil on Canvas, 1872*

Jana Harris

*(Rosa Bonheur, b. 1822)*

I owe it to Nathalie,
all these studies, sketches of
bone and sinew; the way
Pierrette's fur folds
into her mane, her abridged neck, the curl
then unfurl of her meter-long tail
and the flick of its end-tuft.
Pierrette is always in costume.

We had received an invitation,
—more of a summons—from her owner.

Churlish boars, volcanic bulls
a mercurial horse kicking at
its groom; calming them
is in my heartstrings.
But this African Lioness? The retired
cirque owner reassured us
she was bottle-fed as a cub.

I faltered at the snarl,
no matter how benign;

she of the rush and leap,
those elongated teeth
closing in a strangulation hold with
one black freckle dead center
in her broad, cherub-colored tongue.

Atop the acacia
she reclined beneath, a hawk
let out a warning cry.

Nathalie, tall as a tree,
strode directly toward her.
I hung back at the gate where
dry weeds leaned
through the iron fence
reaching out to anyone
who strayed too near.
Pierrette, do you think
I am Mlle. Micas's timid cub?

Natalie ran her hand
down the lion's spine.
I held my breath,
Pierrette preened
beneath her palm and
began kneading the ground.

I took a step closer.

But once I touched her fur,
got her flesh and skin between
my fingers, felt the magnificent muscles
of her shoulder, inhaled her
great cat aroma,

I could not get enough of her:

A curative for the Prussian war,
the siege—two-thousand slain
in the Paris streets—my age
( 50!), my knee injured
in a riding accident, my arm
injured in a riding accident;
my total lack of ferocious
predatorial might.

And there you lick and groom
your massive forearms,
extend, contract, extend
the black crooks of your claws,
always a ready assassin.

I began to feel your power in my brush:
your Tuscan eyes and amber face,
your soft paws, your ears
pricked, spaced on your crown
like a stallion's, but with rounded tips;
the hinge of a jaw that knows
no mortal equal.

Oh my Sun Goddess,
lend me your heart and cunning;
you are even more
glorious than Delacroix's horse.

I pencil you in.
I paint you. I paint you.

I become you.

# KONRAD'S BUKOVINA *KHOSIDL*

PETER NEWALL

QUARTERLY EDITOR'S PRIZE

The sky overhead was completely dark, a muffling darkness that did not admit the faintest white dot of a star. He stared into it until colored patterns began swirling in front of his eyes. He blinked; the patterns disappeared, the darkness remained. Turning cautiously, unsure what obstacle might be near him, he saw a faint pale streak stretched across the blackness.

Could that be the horizon, and the light be dawn? Was it that time already? He tugged back his coat sleeve, but even staring hard, he could not make out his watch. He touched the glass with his fingertips; the watch was there on his wrist, but invisible.

So the faint glow might be the first hint of dawn, or it might be the lights of a town, reflected on the cloud. He tried to guess what towns might be nearby. Zadowa? Strozhnitz? A string of places ran through his mind before he gave up. He might be anywhere; they'd gone through Czernowitz, and while he didn't remember seeing Stanyslaviv, he might have been asleep. Somewhere in the Bukovina, that's all he could say.

He'd been dozing in the darkness of a goods car when the train stopped for water, and they'd found him, the door slid open unexpectedly, a dazzling torch in his face, shouted orders, he'd had to scramble down to the tracks, dodging a half-hearted blow, then the train pulled away again. There was no station here, only a water tower and a crossing sign, nothing to tell him where he was. He'd seen flat fields stretching out towards the horizon in the light of the engine's yellow headlamp, but he wasn't prepared for how black it would be once the train rumbled away into the night. Its small ruby taillight glowed out there for a while, then vanished.

The Bukovina is named for its trees, but I can't see any trees, he thought, and I can't smell any trees, only coal dust and stale smoke, the smell of the railway, it's been absorbed into the earth here and it's soaked into my clothes, I can even taste it. I want to get moving, but I can't set out across country. I can't see my hand in front of my face, let alone see to walk across ploughed fields and climb over fences. If I am not to stay here for the rest of the night, I'll have to walk along the railway line. He looked hopefully at the distant streak at the bottom of the sky, but it was no brighter than before.

He tucked the violin case under his left arm, the familiar awkward shape of it nestling there, and set off, feeling the loose gravel between the soles of his boots and the broad wooden sleepers.

He had to walk carefully, like a slow dance, a hora, the *Moldavian Hora*, left, step, right, step, the melody revolves as the dancers' feet are picked up and set down. He could hear, as he walked, his violin part over the rhythm of his steps, then Artur's clarinet, weaving in and out like a wild rose climbing along an old wooden fence.

How often they had played it, he and Artur and Jerzy, the *Moldavian Hora*, in so many places, Poland and Hungary and the Banat, at weddings, in the taprooms of inns and village squares, at the garden-parties of the rich. And now they had been in Moldavia itself and they had not played it, had not played anything at all.

A heavy, hushed silence hung around him. The air seemed thick and stuffy. Now he had settled into a stride, awkward to match the spread of the sleepers but one he could sustain, he began to feel warm in his jacket and waistcoat. He was conscious of the beat of his footsteps, of the violin under his arm, of his shirt collar rubbing against his neck below his left ear.

Even after walking for perhaps twenty minutes, he could not see anything around him. Possibly the black of the sky was a lighter shade than the black of the trees alongside the track, but looking down he could not see his feet. Stretching his eyes wide open did not help; the night was just too dark. Crickets chirped occasionally, in and out of rhythm with his steps. On such a dark night they don't make much noise, and even if there is water nearby, the frogs too will stay quiet without moonlight or starlight.

A mess, the whole business back there in Moldavia had been a mess. Everything was difficult enough these days, but to get arrested in Suczawa was an unexpected extra problem. Usually a bribe will fix these things if you can only afford to pay it, but this time it was more serious, all of a sudden the police claimed Jews were not allowed in the hotel, even as musicians. They picked out Artur by his appearance, and because the others tried to stop him being taken away, they all three were arrested.

His first fear had been that their instruments would be stolen from them, or wantonly smashed, but that had not happened; once they had been marched down to the police station and pushed into a cell they'd been forgotten. The next evening, although it took all the German marks he had sewn into his coat and most of the dinars Jerzy had hidden in the shell of his accordion, the three of them had got out, with a warning from the fat sergeant, a threat mixed with garlic and stale brandy, that if they were still in town at morning there would be no such luck for them again.

There was not enough money now for their hotel bill, so without going back for their meagre luggage, they bought third-class seats on the night train to Vadul Siret, to get across the nearest border as soon as possible. They arrived just before sunrise. Artur wanted to stay there; Poland was safe for Jews and he had relatives in the town. Jerzy wanted to get further away from the border, so the three of them agreed to separate. Standing on the steps in front of the small white railway station, they shook hands. Artur walked off down a street lined with dusty plane trees, disappearing into the soft early morning light. Jerzy, who had papers that would stand almost any scrutiny, took the slow train on to Lwow, reckoning he had a good enough chance of avoiding ticket inspectors.

He himself had passable papers naming him as Konrad, Wojciek Konrad. It was not the name he was given at birth, nor the name printed on the posters and handbills when the trio played at cafés and theatres throughout Galizia, but it was a name that did not attract trouble, and there was no point in making matters more complicated for himself than need be.

So he waited, sitting on a bench at the back of the station with his violin beside him, looking out over a yellow sunflower field until the late afternoon sun had turned it a dusty orange-gold, then jumped the local train heading west through Czernowitz, riding in a goods wagon because even the few groschen for a third-class ticket were precious; he would need to eat sometime that day or the next.

The train had got to Czernowitz just after dark, the high arched doorways of the station lit up from within like giant keyholes, in front of it shiny black cars and horse-drawn carts weaving in and out of each other's way in the light of flaring streetlamps. After the train had pulled out again, heading toward Stanyslaviv and then Lwow, he'd allowed his chin to drop to his chest and dozed, aware as he slept of the rhythmic rattle of the wheels and the smell of the sacks of grain piled halfway up the wagon's sides.

He was walking automatically now along the sleepers, his legs sore from the foreshortened stride, but he was wide awake, he could walk all night like this if he had to. He moved the violin case from under his left arm to under his right. His collar stopped rubbing his neck. That was simple; if only he'd done it half an hour ago.

Without this violin I am nothing in this world, merely a man with bad papers, without a job, who speaks every language, even my own, with an accent, a foreigner everywhere except in the valley round my home village, and I am not going back there.

But with the violin I can at least get a welcome, a suspicious guarded welcome in many places, but a foot in the door, a place near the fire, a drink of slivovitz or beer or wine, maybe a meal, a bed, sometimes better even than that. And there is the music itself, the tunes run deep in the blood and playing them is a joy. With Artur and Jerzy it's best, but even by myself a pleasure, the soft sweet sound of the bowed strings, more human than the voice, the sound that makes listeners fall silent, even in rowdy inns. The old remember their youth, the young feel theirs. And I too feel entirely alive when I play. Sad tunes, the old doinas, or happy, a freilach learned from the manuscript books or from another player, but all of them make me feel alive.

Konrad smelled the dark earth in the fields around him; the railway stink had left his nostrils. Heavy soil, recently moistened by rain, a bitter reek from the tall rank weeds growing beside the track, somewhere beneath that, a faint scent of damp pines or firs, coming across the fields with a slight breeze. Ah, the air is moving, dawn must he not far away.

It is strange how little we know of what is to befall us, and how our feelings are straws on the wind, blown about in any direction by circumstance. Three days ago I was tolerably happy, about to start a week of playing for weddings in Suczawa. I had money in my pocket and was about to come into more, for we were certain to profit from the generosity of bridegrooms and brides' fathers, made liberal by the occasion and wanting to show their standing in the world. And from guests, warmed by wine and moved to tears or to dance by the music, pushing banknotes, blue, purple and very occasionally a red one hundred note, into our pockets as we walk around, or tossing them into my open violin case, making a lovely multicolored heap on the rusty green silk lining.

Then two days ago, because the local police captain had a whim, or received an order from Bucuresti, there was no happiness and no music ringing in our ears, just the hollow sound of our voices echoing in the stinking cells as we talked to each other trying to dispel the fear, the fear that we would be left there for months, that we would be beaten by the bored guards, or worse, if our papers were looked at too closely, sent back to a jail in the capital.

And then yesterday that fear gone, but our money gone too. So back to the start again, like playing a *nign*, you get nearly to the end and the tune goes round on itself again. Same with us; three men once again at a railway station, carrying our instruments under our arms, dividing between ourselves, once again, a pitifully small bundle of dinars and lei, no future apparent except whatever God might grant us.

And now, as a consequence of all those apparently unrelated actions, I am walking along a railway line in the Bukovina in the middle of the night, when I thought I'd be sleeping in a hotel bed, the sleep of the pleasantly drunk, the night's music echoing in my head, the violin resting in its case but still with a faint vibration in its strings from the last song, *Kolomekyes*, probably, one of the old tunes. When I play it well, I can see flames dancing along the bow. And now I'm here under a black sky, neither happy nor sad nor fearful, but once again poor in the world.

A dog barked, off to his right in the darkness, out there is a habitation, maybe a village, or even the edge of a town.

Konrad stopped, carefully put the violin case down on the railway cinders, stretched his cramped arms and flexed his fingers, and looked around him. There was a dirty cream-colored smear low in the sky, which this time had to be dawn. As he looked at it the breeze freshened. Another day, and an end to the darkness, God be thanked. Now what am I to do with it, this day I might not have seen as a free man, how am I to get the first necessary things, food, coffee, a place to sit, that come before thinking about money and a clean shirt and the future.

The sky was lightening enough to make out something of what lay around him. The countryside was flat. A little way off the dark shadow of a pine forest, the resinous smell coming to him as the dawn-wind got up. On the other side of the railway line, fields stretched away toward an uncertain horizon.

In front of him a road crossed the railway, a good road, wide and straight and level, very different to the rutted, muddy Romanian roads curving round rocks and tree stumps nobody could be bothered to remove. You can see where the Austrians have been, he thought wryly; roads and bridges. But a road like this must lead to a substantial town, and from a town he might go one way or another, but he would surely find food and rest. He walked to the crossing and took the road to the right, to the north.

It took him another fifteen minutes' walking, and the day had really begun, a soft autumn day with a pale blue sky mostly covered with thin cloud, before he saw anything more than ploughed fields and distant trees. He came up to a small crossroad, with a sign pointing in three directions. Kolomyja ahead, said one arm, Kosmach, back the way he had come, said another; the third, pointing down a small side road, was blank.

Ridiculous, Konrad thought, they have gone to the trouble of nailing up a sign, complete with its pointed end, on this signpost, they've even painted it white, but they didn't know what name to carve on it.

Kolomyja, that was a big enough place, with three or four hotels, some lively restaurants, and a whole street of tailors. There was a theatre, an officers' club, women in nice clothes, plenty of people, and there he could, once he had played a bit, get the money for a new suit and a second-class railway ticket on. And from there he could get to Lwow, meet Jerzy there, or even on to Krakow, where there were friends, even relations, and many places hiring musicians, restaurants and inns and dance houses.

But the small side road and the blank signpost bothered him. What does it mean, a blank signpost? How am I to understand a sign that points somewhere but does not tell me what that somewhere is called, or how far away it is? That is contrary to sense. There must be something down that narrow road, roads lead to places, that's in their nature, so where does this one lead that they do not want to tell me?

Just go to Kolomyja, he told himself; straighten your hat, put your violin under your arm and set off. At least one cafe will be open by the time you get there, and there is enough money in your pocket for coffee and rolls. Considering food made Konrad's stomach cramp slightly, he had not allowed himself to think how hungry he was until that moment. When you have eaten you should be able to get a cigar, too, he thought, and suddenly he wanted tobacco very badly, even more than food.

But he was used, over the years, to having to wait to eat, sometimes for a day or more, and to going without cigars when he did not have cigars, and he knew unless things went very badly he would eat sometime that day, some way or other, even if he had to beg at a farmhouse. And the blank sign still bothered him.

It struck him it was intended only for the initiated, not written in ordinary letters for the ordinary traveler, but set there for the particular person who would understand its meaning. And having thought that, he did not like to admit that the secret unwritten language was meant for another, not for him. He turned onto the narrow side road and walked down it without looking again at the broad level one leading to Kolomyja.

It was now full daylight, the sun was up behind him, and the plain stretched away into the distance. Mingled with the grass beside the road were scattered banks of buttercups, the small yellow flowers looking at him inquisitively. Closer to him, in the damper soil at the road's edge, purple mallows sat among their dark green leaves.

Some young birch trees came into view, two or three standing alone, and then a small grove. There were more ahead, along both sides of the narrow earthen road. Their slender trunks, at first glance straight but actually curving slightly, reminded him of violin bows, the long thin branches resembled strings, and the white bark with its delicate black markings looked like musical scores rolled up tightly and changed into trees.

Looking up at the birches as he walked among them, a melody began to create itself in his mind, a melody based on the arrangement of these trees, their simplicity and grace. The melody wound on as he walked, and he heard it in the form of a *khosidl*, played over a slow rhythm.

The tune he heard was lovely, it moved him almost to tears as it unfolded in his head. He had no part in shaping it, it simply emerged, drawing on all the tunes he had ever played, all the tunes he had ever heard, *chocheks* and *doinas* and *bulgars*, Polish songs and Russian songs and Gypsy songs and even Hungarian czardas with their dancing cimbalom decoration.

And as the *khosidl* developed, he heard it sounding on the violin in the sweet clear morning air, even though the violin was shut in its case under his arm. He could hear the strings vibrating with the lovely melody, the birch tree *khosidl*, the Bukovina *khosidl*, as it came into being in his head and his heart.

As he walked on under the blue sky, between the birches, the tune went back to the beginning, replayed itself, went through the same changes, imprinted itself in his mind, his fingers knew already how to shape it on the violin's neck, a sweet smooth slender white tune, sad but happy, like all tunes that stay in your heart.

He had it now, he could hear every bar of it, this tune which had never yet vibrated in the air, never yet danced its way through the smoke and shouting of a taproom, never yet entered the ears of lovers at a village dance, never yet drifted and hung in the evening sky after the twilight had ended, never yet been accompanied with clarinet or accordion or bass fiddle, a pure tune, just as it had come from God, this tune given to him, his *khosidl*, his Bukovina *khosidl*.

And he knew he would never, however often and well he might play it, hear it again so fresh and perfect as he heard it now in his head as the graceful birch trees danced around him, swaying as they made their circuits, dancing to his *khosidl*. No man will ever be able to render it like this, he thought. I could not, even the great Avram Makonovetsky could not, play this tune like this. Once you play it on a real violin, wood and gut and glue, once you put clumsy human hands on it, it will be imperfect, like all human things, a flawed mirror to God's perfection.

Even so, to play it on the violin will be wonderful, it will give pleasure to me, to those who hear it, to the air, to the heavens. God will look down on me playing it and will smile, and say, ah! I gave that tune to the right fellow; listen how sweetly he brings it out for the world to hear.

He smelled woodsmoke, and dragging his eyes down from the dancing birches he saw a house near the road, a small place with dark walls and a low roof, and at exactly that moment two or three dogs behind the house burst into furious barking. Thank you for waiting until my tune had finished coming to me, he thought, now you can bark all you want. He heard a man's voice shouting at the dogs and they retreated into sullen growling, but he was past the house now.

Another bigger house stood just down the road on the other side, and further on he could see more dwellings, and further on beyond the houses a spire and a dome showing where a church and a synagogue stood.

This must be the place without a name. The blank signpost sent me here, Konrad told himself, feeling a surprising happiness swell inside him. I understood I was to come here, and I came. And because I walked down that narrow road, I am not the same man who stood at the signpost. Because I took that road, I am, on this autumn morning, transformed, I am the one with the Bukovina *khosidl* in my head, in my hands, in my violin, God's gift to me, which I will pass on as my gift to all those who hear it. Konrad smiled into the morning sunlight.

## II

**H**e was walking down a paved street now, with rows of houses flanking it. The church spire above their rooftops showed he was approaching the center, the town square.

Turning into the square he saw half a dozen people, the first he had seen in the town. One looked over at him, then began walking directly towards him, a short, bearded man who strode across the open space with the confidence of one who had an official purpose there.

They met in the middle of the square. The bearded man looked him up and down, and Konrad was aware he was unshaven and dusty, and carried nothing but a worn violin case.

"Well, stranger, what is your name?"

"Konrad, Wojciek Konrad, at your service."

"All right, Konrad," said the bearded man, "I am Weisser, and I am the mayor. What do you want here?"

"I play the violin for a living, and I came here thinking you would have a wedding or a funeral, a christening, a bar mitzvah, or a dance."

The man looked him directly in the face, in the country way that in the city would he rude. Konrad knew he was assessing him, weighing up his odd accent, his clothes, his eyes.

"You have no money?"

"No," he agreed. Beyond a few groschen coins he had perhaps two hundred lei, but that was not money here in Poland.

"Come with me," said Weisser. They walked together across the square to what Konrad saw was a tavern, a two-story building in brick with an awning over the front door.

Inside it was dark, except where crooked rectangles of bright morning sunlight fell through the windows and broke over tables and chairs and onto a wooden floor. The mayor spoke with the innkeeper; to his surprise Konrad understood he would be served breakfast, and given a room to rest for a time.

"You will not have to pay for this," the mayor told him. "It is our custom to give a meal to a musician who visits here, and if you wish you can go on your way this afternoon, when you have rested. But if you stay, I want you to play at a party tonight in my house. I will come back at evening to see if you are still here."

Konrad nodded to convey both thank you and yes, not so many words needed here in the country, no need for the explanations and repetitions filling up city conversations.

He was suddenly tired now that he could stop walking, his legs ached, and he ate the food and drank the bowl of coffee mechanically. Then, directed by the landlord, he climbed a short flight of stairs to a small room, one of several along a corridor, and, taking off his coat and boots and laying the violin case on a bedside table, fell asleep on the narrow bed.

**H**e had been watching the tall white shape moving to and fro for some time when he realized it was a curtain, a long curtain of thin white cloth, languidly swelling and retreating on a slight breeze. He was lying in a room with white plastered walls and a low dark wooden door. There was light behind the fabric of the curtain, a full even daylight, departing afternoon daylight or growing morning daylight he was not sure. And the particular smell of this room, a mixture of paint and drying herbs and beeswax, was new to him; he had not been here before.

Turning his head, he saw the violin case near him, on a small table. Then he remembered, he was in a country tavern, somewhere in eastern Poland, he had walked here. In another moment he had it all back, he'd come here after getting out of the police cells over the border and jumping the night train, and here they had given him breakfast and a bed. The light suffusing the window curtain must be afternoon light, and now he heard pigeons cooing outside the window. He swung his legs over the edge of the bed and held the curtain aside.

Below him he saw the town square. It was late afternoon. Sunlight, surprisingly warm and strong for autumn, slanted in over the edge of the roof above him and fell onto the flagstones.

Directly beneath his window two or three small tables were set out in front of the tavern. At one, two men sat with small glasses before them. Across the square was a restaurant, its name in faded letters on the plaster above its arched doorway, ***Królewskie Jadło***. As he watched, a cook in a white apron came through the double wooden doors and stood outside, caught in the golden light from the westering sun, his sharp shadow falling onto the mustard-yellow wall behind him. He looked up and down the square and went back inside.

There was still a sound of pigeons cooing. Looking up Konrad saw them circling overhead, caught in the sun's rays while they were above the roofs of the square, then fluttering down into the shadow to settle on the windowsills to either side of him.

He heard a soft knocking. As he turned toward the door it opened, and a maid came in carrying a steaming ewer and a towel, and put them on a washstand in the corner of the room, a wooden washstand with a stained mirror set into its frame. She went out without speaking, treading silently in felt shoes.

With pleasure Konrad saw that with the towel he had been given soap and a razor. Stripping off his shirt, he bent over the porcelain basin, delighting in the hot cleansing water, feeling a younger, stronger man as he washed the railway smoke and dust out of his hair and shaved the stubble from his face.

He stood at the window drying himself on the coarse grey towel. Even while he had been washing, the afternoon shadow had taken a great stride across the square, and was climbing the walls opposite. A low door in the building next to the restaurant opened and his acquaintance of that morning, Weisser, emerged. He turned and locked the door behind him slightly fussily, with a key from a large bunch which he returned to his coat pocket. Without looking up at the man standing in the window he walked directly across the square toward the tavern.

Konrad reached for his shirt and put it back on. As he did, he noticed his wristwatch and, after a moment's thought, unbuckled the strap and slipped the watch into his coat pocket. Shortly there was another, firmer knock on the door; he opened it to the bearded mayor.

They exchanged greetings, slightly awkwardly, then Weisser told him that as Konrad had stayed in the town, he wished him to play at his house that evening, a party for his daughter who had become engaged, that he would pay him ten zloty for this, and that if he were hungry the restaurant across the square would give him a meal on account until he was paid. Konrad said he would certainly play, and could he also get a couple of cigars on account? The mayor smiled slightly and fished a thin black cigar out of his coat pocket.

"It is six now," he said, "and I will send someone here at eight to bring you to my house." Konrad nodded, and Weisser departed, his boots stumping down the bare wooden stairs.

When he didn't have a cigar, Konrad was able to do without. Now he had one, he had a problem; he wanted to smoke it straight away, but he knew he would want it even more after he had eaten. He agreed with himself to smoke just less than half of it now, and finding matches on the night table he lit up, and stood at the window, smoking and watching the light outside fade.

It's odd, Konrad thought, this fellow is treating me as if he knew me, or has recognized me, why does he want me to come to his party, when there must be violin players, musicians anyway, already in this town? He stood at the window for a little longer without finding an answer. Shrugging, he stubbed the cigar out regretfully and put it in a twist of paper in his shirt pocket.

Pulling on his coat he left the room, taking the violin with him. He came out onto the square to see a pale violet evening sky above the roofs. Lights were on in most of the buildings, their windows glowing dull yellow. Konrad strolled around, looking with interest at the shopfronts.

He walked around the whole square, then returned to the restaurant door. ***Królewskie Jadło***, he thought, *king's feast*, there were restaurants called that all over the country, but not too many kings have eaten in this one. Inside were wooden walls and small tables crammed together, and a pleasing smell of cooking meat. He told the waiter the mayor had sent him to have a meal, and he was shown to a table without comment.

From the list of dishes chalked on the wall he ordered veal and potatoes and a liter of beer, which came newly brewed, cloudy and smelling of fresh hops.

He ate and drank slowly, enjoying the meal. He listened to the conversations around him to see if he could at least discover the name of this place, but all he learned was the state of the weather and the price of pigs.

Finished, he walked out into the now-dark square and lit the remaining half of his cigar. It still tasted sweet, and with the first lungful of smoke he felt straight away content; calmer, happier, wiser. The night was soft and pleasant and the food in his stomach sat well with him. When he'd finished his cigar he walked back to the tavern and, nodding to the landlord as he entered, went upstairs to his room to wait.

He sat in a straight-backed wooden chair near the window, picked up the violin from its case, bowed a few chords from it, then began to play, a slow tune, a *bulgar*, the "*Kishinever Bulgar.*" The old song drifted out the window into the night, floated around the chimneypots on the tavern roof, hovered above the still-warm paving stones of the square. For five minutes Konrad played the melody, embellished it, then stripped it back to the basic tune, brought it back in through the open window, back into the violin, brought it to an end. He laid the instrument down. Then he sat for a time in the darkened room in silence, his hands resting unmoving on his knees.

## III

When the mayor'Ss man came for him Konrad was ready, and they walked out of the tavern together. For three or four blocks they walked in silence past shops, storehouses, a fire station, its big wooden doors barred, then past the fences and gardens of private homes. This is a bigger place than I had realized, Konrad thought, and this is the better part of town, the houses are large, the roadway is level and the footpaths are paved. They came to a house set back from the street, a substantial two-story villa with lights shining from every downstairs window, and an avenue of what looked like walnut trees leading to the main doors.

Turning into a small gate in the fence, Konrad's escort led him along a brick path to a side door, showed him into an anteroom, and told him he could have a drink if he wished before he began to play. Konrad nodded, slipped among the hurrying waiters to a table on which bottles and decanters stood, and poured himself half a tumbler of slivovitz.

The spirit cleared his head and warmed his stomach; he breathed more deeply and easily. Looking around, he saw an accordion sitting on a table; ah, so he was not to be the only musician. He saw coming through another doorway a short, dark man with heavy bags under glittering black eyes. A *zigeuner*, a Gypsy, thought Konrad, he will be the accordion player.

The Gypsy picked up his accordion by its worn leather straps. "Will we play together, fiddler?" he asked, in thickly accented Polish. "Why not?" said Konrad, and putting down the case, took out his violin and tucked it under his chin, holding it there while he tautened the bow. He bowed two chords to test the tuning, then the opening phrase of the old song "*Swiodeshka.*" Before he had got four bars into it the accordion player had picked it up, and they ran through it together. This fellow is good, thought Konrad, he has a lighter touch than most accordionists, not too many notes, he gives me some room to breathe. He grinned at the Gypsy, who shrugged, smiling faintly, as if he had read Konrad's thoughts.

They left the anteroom and entered the main salon, a spacious room with a high ceiling, lit by a chandelier with electric light bulbs. People stood around talking, some holding glasses of wine. They walked through the room as they played. Konrad, warmed by the slivovitz and the music, smiled at people who caught his eye as they wove through the crowd.

As always, the music filled him, filled his heart and mind and blood. He didn't think of anything while he played, he was absorbed in the swoop of the bow on the strings, the sobbing of the violin. He was happy to have the accordionist with him. He hadn't even asked the fellow's name, but names didn't matter, they were playing, they made the music come out and live, breathe. They played the "*Moskva Chochek,*" then they played "*Bei Mir Bistu Shayn*" especially to the mayor's daughter, a short plain girl, who giggled and held on to her fiancée as the two musicians circled round her, making eyes at her. They played the sad Romanian song "*Ben Avrameni,*" then a polka they made up as they went along, then a czardas the accordion player started but Konrad took over, playing in the hot style, enjoying it so much that he finished the tune sweating into his shirt and with horsehair trailing from his bow.

To have a rest, he started "*Lyuba,*" a Gypsy song, and let the accordion player take it. A sentimental tune, Konrad thought, even though Gypsies are the most unsentimental people in the world.

When that was done, he played the first bars of "*Erdelezi,*" but the Gypsy put his finger to his lips. "Not here," he said. Konrad didn't understand why, but he let it go and started "*Beygele*" instead, which they played for many choruses, walking round the rooms of the mayor's house, rooms full of drinking, talking, laughing people.

At the end of that they stopped for a drink in the small anteroom. The accordion player produced a pack of cigarettes and they each lit one. They exchanged names, but didn't shake hands; it was unnecessary, they had played music together, an acceptance far closer than a handshake.

Konrad was leaning against the wall, smoking, allowing the fingers of his left hand to hang loosely, nervelessly, a discipline he had learned as a student at the Academy. He wanted nothing more than to stand there, drawing in the blue cigarette smoke, knowing soon he would play again, that later tonight he would get some money, not much but a start, and later still would sleep in a clean bed.

It was then he saw the girl. She came into the room with a man, a tall pale fellow in a blue chalk-striped suit with padded shoulders, but Konrad ignored him after a glance and stared at her. Her hair was the first thing; reaching down past her shoulders, heavy black ringlets framing her face and cascading, there was no other word for it, down to her breast. Her eyebrows were black too, a soft black as if they were marked in charcoal, and only after seeing them did you realize her eyes were also black, a shiny black like olives or bitter aloes.

Her skin was soft pink, flushed with the warmth of the night and with youth and happiness, and she wore a blouse that showed her throat and the same warm pink skin there. Her hands were white and slightly chubby, her forearms, bare, shadowed with a faint dark down.

But it was not the detail of her appearance that entranced Konrad, but the whole of her, her presence, the liveliness that made her seem illuminated by a different light to everyone else there, and within all that, a mystery behind her eyes, an unguessable unique self that Konrad did not know, but in the moment of looking at her wanted to know very much.

She looked round the room. Her eyes passed over him then returned, perhaps noticing his intent stare. Embarrassed, he looked down at his cigarette as he drew on it. When he looked up again, she was turning to leave the room, the long black hair waving even more thickly down her back.

He caught the accordion player's eye and took up the violin again, wanting to play straight away. He played "*Gaspars Freilach*," fast and sweet, walking through the main room toward the high doorway at the far end, the accordionist behind him. A blonde woman in a long dark blue dress swayed toward him and smiled as he passed her, but he kept walking through the rooms, looking for the dark-haired one.

This time he played no longer just for the pleasure of playing, to hear within himself the music he created, but to reach out to someone else, the black-haired woman, to tell her he recognized her worth. And to tell her in turn who and what he really was; his playing would convey that. She was somewhere ahead of them in the crowd, but Konrad was sure she could hear the music.

He played quickly and lightly, stepping deftly around guests in his way. Someone pushed a banknote into his top pocket. He didn't even look at the fellow, but kept his eyes fixed ahead. Then he caught sight of the girl's glossy black hair, and slowed his steps. He wanted her to hear him, to give her time to take in his message.

The *freilach* was too simple for his purpose, so he ended it and began the "*Stoliner Sher*," playing with emotion, bringing out the sadness and nobility of the tune.

She had turned back toward him, watching, listening. He played another chorus; her companion in the suit leant over and spoke into her ear, but she shook her head slightly and put her hand on his sleeve to silence him. Konrad knew the music was working, his playing was working, she wanted to hear it, and with the next tune she would realize he was playing only to her. A scent of night-blossoming jasmine came into the room through the tall open windows.

Without breaking off he moved into the *"Odessa Bulgar,"* the slow beginning decorated with elaborate flourishes, an announcement, something is coming, watch out, the Gypsy picked up his intention and played that way too, it became a contest between them in melodrama. Konrad drew out his last note as far as it could go, until it was stretched in the air as thin and high as a spiderweb, then, grinning, swung into the fast break. Someone behind him cheered, *oy oy oy,* and she laughed and clapped her white round hands together. Konrad smiled at her, and she smiled back, openly, and didn't look away from him, he kept looking at her as he played, he brought the tune back to its slow part and took a pace toward her as he did. He was beyond pretending now. He wanted to play for her, to woo her, to steal her, and he wanted her to know it.

Then it came to him; he would win her if he played the birch-tree *khosidl*, his new Bukovina *khosidl*. The beauty and purity of the melody would announce his good heart. The newness of it, sounding in the air for the first time, would be as sweet and sad and melting as it would ever be. A perfect gift, it would warm her soul, it would sweep away any reservations, any thoughts of others, it would be the theme tune of their romance, for however long that lasted.

In the moment he thought of it, he knew he should not do it. He had been a musician all his life, and now he had been marked out for this high gift, this melody, he had been found worthy to receive it. It was a gift from God. He could not use it selfishly, for profit, to steal. When he played it, he had to give it to the world open-handedly, openheartedly.

Then he looked again at the girl, flushed, smiling, caught up in the music. And is she not one of God's creatures, too? And if God gave me this beautiful tune, He has also placed this woman here on this earth, given her this particular richness of hair, whiteness of skin, given her her time as a small girl in the village, her coming of age, friends, a sweetheart, rides in automobiles, walks in the forest picking mushrooms; made her choose this dress and these shoes, placed her here tonight and then brought me here with this tune in my head and heart, the tune that came to me as I walked down the nameless sandy road to this town.

The tune is a gift, a gift for her. A gift to youth and beauty, a gift to the loveliness of all women at parties on autumn evenings, a tribute to the fleeting sweetness of being alive.

He played a long slow chord to end *"Odessa,"* and glancing at the accordion player made a quick flat gesture with his bow-hand, stay out of this next one. The fellow nodded slightly with his chin. Konrad took a deep breath, held the bow over the strings for a moment, and began to play.

The first long note, a simple low G, swelled out of the heart of the violin, out of the dark space within the old curved wood he had handled so much that he knew it better than his hands or his face, and wound into the air, and Konrad felt it was not like any note he had ever played before, it had a strength and richness he had never heard under his own hands. Wondering, he shaped the next notes of the melody, hearing for the first time from the strings the tune given to him there amongst the birches. It flowed out of his violin, flowed outward and upward.

The room had fallen into a hush. Conversation had stopped. Only the notes of the violin filled the warm autumn evening air. The melody flowed and swooped and climbed, and it was tears and laughter and regret and hope all in one, it was joyful and melancholy, it carried every emotion with it as it surged out into the room, curved round under the ceiling, stretched itself out through the windows into the warm night, so the birch trees outside in the garden resonated with it. And it blended so much with the scent of the night-jasmine that for everyone who heard Konrad play that night, the two could never again be separated, the scent of jasmine and the melody of the *khosidl*, the birch-tree *khosidl*, Konrad's Bukovina *khosidl.*

Konrad had been playing with his eyes closed. He opened them; the light from the chandelier was too bright at first, but he could see a circle of faces around him, and another circle behind those, all looking at him. And he smelled the rich smells of tobacco smoke, of perfume on warm bodies, of brandy, of jasmine, all in a rush together.

He was bringing the tune towards its end, moving toward the last chorus, when he realized he was looking directly at the black-haired girl and she was looking at him. He could smell her perfume alone amongst all the others, he could feel the warmth from her over the several paces between them and he could see the light shining on her blue-black hair as it tumbled down over her shoulders. Her eyes, black and shining, held his, and he stared back into them as he played, as if each dared the other to look away, and neither did.

But the skill of his playing did not desert him and the tune did not falter but flowed through the repeat of the last chorus and came to an end, resolving from the minor third to a major chord, so the hearer was satisfied, and the tune ended.

He stopped, and there was silence; that moment seemed to last a very long time, then all at once someone said, “Bravo, fiddler,” and several others laughed delightedly, and some others clapped, and Konrad took the violin from under his chin and looked down at his hands; he offered a silent prayer of thanks. Then the accordion player started up a Gypsy tune on his own, fast and rhythmic and cheerful, and people's voices all burst out at once, talking of whatever they had before, and the room moved again and the night moved on.

Konrad stood looking down in wonderment at his hands, at the violin. But when he looked up again, she had not moved but was standing front of him. The fellow in the padded suit was not there, and the girl looked at Konrad now in the same frank way she had when he was playing, only now he was not playing, he had no violin between himself and her. If he wanted to speak to her now it had to be with words, however poor they would be after the music.

He inclined his head in a small bow, and said to her, “Konrad, Wojciek Konrad, at your service.”

“Rebekah Hannewitz,” she said. Her voice was low, dark, husky, surprising. And Konrad wanted badly to tell her his real name, names generally did not matter to him much, but now he wanted this woman to know who he was, why she should take him seriously. But his caution had been earned dearly over many years and even now he did not abandon it.

Instead he told her he’d arrived today, and he asked her the name of the town. She smiled and said, “Did my uncle not tell you where you are?” and he realised this was the mayor’s niece, someone with money and importance in the town. He hesitated, because here he was no more than a wandering musician, but then he remembered how she'd looked at him when he was playing, so he brought out his best card, and told her he had just written that tune, and he wished to name it after her if she would allow him, and she said it was a lovely melody and she would be happy if he used her name, so he told her the tune was now called "Rebekah's *Khosidl,*" and she smiled, and dear God her teeth were so white in her flushed face and Konrad, who could hear the accordion playing in the next room amongst the voices of the partygoers, reached out and took hold of her plump white hand and brought it to his lips and kissed it, and she smiled still, and Konrad put down the violin and stepped close to her, and she looked up at him, and he put his hands on her shoulders, feeling the heat of her skin through the black silk of her dress, and kissed her, and she kissed him.

Then he took her arm, and leaving his violin there on the table, which he had never done before in his life, he walked with her across the room and out the French windows into the night garden, where the scent of jasmine was all around them.

And when they had been out there a little while, she said she had to go back inside, and she stepped carefully across the wet leaf-strewn lawn and through the double doors into the lighted rooms. He waited a minute and then went in himself. He picked up his violin, untouched where he had left it, and walked through the house looking for the accordion player.

He found him standing at a table eating. There were baskets of rolls, plates of cheese and pickled cucumbers, a bowl of potatoes and a ham, but Konrad was not hungry. "*Ach, manus,* what was that song you played before?" the Gypsy asked. Konrad shrugged. "I made it up," he said, "today." The other looked long at him.

"Well, if you say so, Pan Konrad," he said at last. He picked up his accordion, slipped the straps over his shoulders, and played a couple of runs to loosen his fingers. "But it didn't sound like a song anyone just made up, it sounded like one of the old songs I heard as a child, one of the songs my grandfather learned from his grandfather, yet I know I have never heard it before." Konrad said nothing.

"If it's your tune, what do you call it?" The Gypsy played a few notes which, to Konrad's surprise, resolved into the melody of the *khosidl.* He was amazed to hear it played by another's hands on another instrument. Was it even still his song, or did it have its own life now he had brought it out of the magic lamp?

"I call it 'Rebekah's *Khosidl,*'" said Konrad.

"If I had made that tune," said the Gypsy, "I would not call it after any woman. I would name it after myself, so I would be remembered forever when I am gone from here." He shivered slightly, then smiled. "Anyway, Pan Konrad, shall we play some more to earn our ten zloty?"

So they struck up another tune, Konrad didn't think about what they played, the songs came easily to him, but all the time he was thinking of the embrace of the dark-haired woman in the garden, her perfume mingled with the jasmine, and his blood was hot in his face as he thought of seeing her again at the end of the night; they had not spoken of that, but he knew he would look for her and find her.

They passed through the downstairs rooms of the big house often enough that Konrad recognized each guest there, the men by their suits and the women by their faces. About the third time through the main room Weisser stepped over as a song finished and gave each of them ten zloty. Konrad had already been given nearly thirty zloty, in ones, twos and fives, by guests as they played. Weisser told them they could stop if they wished, and told Konrad he would owe nothing if he wanted to sleep in the room at the tavern tonight, but that he owed two zloty at the restaurant, and Konrad thanked him and said he would pay tomorrow.

Konrad had no desire to stop playing, even though he had been paid and the crowd of guests was thinning. By midnight, though, many more guests had left, and Konrad and the accordionist, by unspoken consent, put down their instruments, dragged two wooden chairs out through the French doors into the cool night air, sat and smoked. After a bit the Gypsy cleared his throat, spat into the darkness, and stood. "I will go now, Pan," he said, and Konrad said "Another time, then," and the accordion player said yes, and then, in his awkward Polish, "I have to tell you, some men in there looked very ill at you as you passed by them in this last hour, and then spoke among themselves. I was behind you and saw it. Do you want to walk away from here with me, so there are two of us and you do not remain here alone?"

Konrad was surprised; he hadn't noticed anything. But there was no question of him leaving, he was staying to find the black-haired woman, and so he told the Gypsy he could look after himself, and the man shrugged, and asked him if he had a knife, and Konrad said yes, and laughed, thinking the fellow was making too much of it, and the Gypsy said very well, and took up his accordion and, hanging it over one shoulder, walked away across the garden. Watching him go Konrad remembered that his knife had been taken from him in the lockup back in Suczawa, but it could hardly matter, what mattered was to find the woman, Rebekah. The feeling of her warm, firm shoulders under his hands returned to him, and he drew in his breath sharply. She is waiting for me, and every minute I sit here and do not find her is a minute wasted.

He dropped his cigarette on the ground and put his foot on it, then rose and stepped back through the open French doors into the house.

## IV

The next summer was unseasonably hot, with drawn-out sunny days and long warm evenings. It was still twilight at ten at night at the end of June, and people were in good spirits as they strove to enjoy all there was to enjoy. The restaurants and theatres were full every night, and there were parties and weddings in every city and town and village. Officers and soldiers garrisoned across Bukovina and Galizia and Ruthenia seemed feverishly anxious to have a good time, and landlords sold more champagne and beer and slivovitz than they had in memory.

And in the dance halls and house parties, at wedding receptions and engagement parties and in restaurants, in Czernowitz and Wittwitz and Stanyslaviv, and further east and west, in Tarnow and Premsyl and even Lwow, there was a tune all the bands played that last hot summer, dance bands and klezmer bands and Gypsy orchestras and violin trios, a haunting, slow dance, sweet and sad and elegant and romantic all at once, a lovely tune, a masterpiece. No one knew where it had come from, although Henryk Wars, who led the Odeon dance orchestra in Lwow, said he had learned it from a Gypsy accordionist from Czernowitz.

Everybody knew the song as "Konrad's Bukovina *Khosidl*," but nobody knew who Konrad was, except with that name he was a Pole, and everyone agreed he was a master fiddle player. Some said he had given up playing in despair after writing this perfect melody, knowing he could never write another as good, others said he had gone to America and become a millionaire leading a band in New York; another story was that he had been killed in a knife fight over a woman. The Gypsies said, spitting on the ground, that the devil had given him this melody in exchange for his soul, and had taken him.

And that summer, just for that summer, the custom developed everywhere that it was the last song of the night, this slow, sad but joyful melody, this melody everyone stopped talking and drinking to listen to, which ran through their heads as they took their way home, groups of tipsy officers humming it as they walked arm in arm back to barracks down dusty streets in wretched villages or through busy garrison towns, in a state of melancholy rapture.

And it was so on one moonlit night in September, after an autumn day almost as warm as high summer. At restaurants and music theatres and dance halls and parties, the last tune played that night, the last night before everything changed, before the guns began, was the final chorus of that lovely, sad and sweet tune, "Konrad's Bukovina *Khosidl.*"

# A MASCU-POEM

MALICK CEESAY

DIGITAL EDITOR'S PRIZE

*This play, this body of movement, is a self-exploration of the body of a Black man. In all of the Black man's complexity, agility, and boldness, comes many features that are kept trapped. That being weakness, feeling sorrow/grief, and playing with the femininity that co-exists with the testosterone inside ourselves.*

*This is dedicated to my mother. I love you beyond the universe.*

**a mascu- poem.**
*an original screenplay*

| | |
|---|---|
| **Created by** | Malick Ceesay |
| **Choreography by** | Rayna Howard |
| **Sound by** | Saberina Calle |
| **Music Score by** | Malick Ceesay |
| | Jahi Davis |

**CHARACTERS**

WAKE
SANE
NEED
SIDE A
SIDE B

**EXTRAS**
DATES
FATHER
YOUNG SANE
CROWN BOY
BULLIES

**ACKNOWLEDGEMENTS**

*A special thank you to Red Eye Theater, Ambiance Theatre Company, Studio Gradient, and for your gracious support, feedback, and essential resource that played a role in both this writing and performance process. I am forever grateful.*

## ACT I

*Burying the feeling**

### SCENE I: HORIZON

**EXT. MAILBOX - EVENING**

**Sound: Outside noise**

*There a truck shot of WAKE walking to a mailbox. He reaches the mailbox and pulls out all the loose mail, until he reaches a small packaged item.*

**WAKE**

(*walking with sadness.*) What the...?

WAKE takes all of the mail and examines the package as he leaves out of frame.

**INT. LIVING/BEDROOM - EVENING**

**Sound: Inside noise**

WAKE opens the package. He pulls out a phone and a letter conjoined by a rubber band. WAKE opens the letter. After taking a moment to read, WAKE places the tape inside a player and presses play.

**SIDE A**

(*from cassette.*) Son ... I know it seems odd receiving this after all this time. I made a promise with a friend to not send until you turned a certain age. Hopefully they listened, as this was a dying wish... I wasn't there— for you. Wasn't there enough to show you the proper way to be a man. This tape is the answer to all. If you don't think you need it, change your mind. We come from a history of strong Black men ... not no sissies. Ignoring what's on this tape is like removing your manhood—

During this letter, there is a montage of WAKE putting on a durag and taking pills, but hesitant. (INT. BATHROOM). WAKE begins part of the voicemail and then suddenly turns it off. WAKE goes to sleep.

**EXT. LAKE - DAY**

**Sound: water washing on a shore.**

**Music: "Calling" (Crescendo into the scene)**

WAKE is woken by the sound of his father's voice echoing the words, "removing your manhood ..." WAKE wakes to a body of water in front of him. He wears a mask. He slowly takes it off and dreams of a dance, dreamlike sequence. SANE and NEED join him. In that dream, WAKE is reciting:

**WAKE (voiceover)**

*I wake*
*Sleep away my demons*
*Quantify the word relax*
*and sink into a head of satin*
*my breaths beg for change*
*but I'm too tired to listen*
*crazy... I wake*
*each inhale*

**breaths*
*feels like my freedoms*
*are getting handed back to me*
*but its fantasy.*

*I fantasize a freedom.*
*bury a time-capsule called, "feeling"*
*And put my insincerities deep*
*Deep*
*Deep*

*I want to climb out*
*I prayed air*
**breaths*
*Where I, be I and nothing else*
**breaths*

**ALL (Voiceover)**

**calm*
*where I, be I and nothing else*

SLOW MOTION ON:

There is a shot of SANE coming up from underwater.

BACK TO DANCE:

**WAKE**

*yet the systemic is the very thing*
*keeping me from being ... me.*
*From being free*
*I bleed a Black waving goodbye*
*A boat load leaving on*
*An ocean of man keeping me*
*From me ...*
*I check the horizon for depth,*

*But my mother ...*
*Told me a long time ago ...*
*That this depth is the step into*
*A dreadful learning curve,*
*And I didn't listen ...*
*I slapped dread in the face*
*And said ...*

SHOT CHANGE TO:

A shot of the sky and clouds moving.

**ALL**

*Give me man.*
*Give me man.*

**WAKE**

*a boy is a waste of time.*
*A boy takes too long to grow,*
*But I know a man is pivotal to mold*
*And the waters in the horizon*
*Beg for my love ...*

**ALL**

*I walk forward ...*
*touch the water ...*
*open my arms ...*
*fall forward and ...*
**beep*

The ensemble shakes, studders, and murmurs as though a voice is interrupting their movement.

**SIDE A (voiceover)**

Hello? ... hello? Are you there, son?
**beat.*
Yeah ... I can feel you breathing. I get it.
I know she's no longer with us, but
be strong!
To be a man ...

**WAKE**

*(running to the edge of the water.)*
*is as though the water is concrete.*
*never falling through ...*
*But ...*
*I lay there and wait for*
*my Black to liquefy ...*

*Sleeping away my demons*
*Quantify the word relax*
*and sink into a head of satin*
*my breaths beg for change*
*but I'm too tired to listen.*
**mask back on*

**SIDE A**

You wanna be a man? Ha ... well. Here's the first step ...
**beat*
Stop being a sissy.
**beep*

WAKE is woken by his dreams in the early hours of the night.

**Scene II: REFLECTION**

**Music: "No Need Baby, I Got This"**

**INT. COFFEE SHOP**

NEED is sitting, staring into the camera visibly upset.

**NEED**

(*to his date.*) Calm down? Huh ...
You don't know who you're talkin' too ...

NEED takes a sip of water.

You know what a sissy really is?
sissies, are people who are dishonest
with part of themselves.
And *I am* 100% real ...
*beat
with 100% of my feelings.
You know why?
'Cause I'm a man.
A real man will tell ya how he feels ...
No hesitation.

Another sip of water.

Is you confused?
I'm not ...
*beat
Is a REAL man, a "sissy?"
*beat. to self.
Listen, I'm uhh ...

There's a shot of NEED's date, staring at him weird. NEED makes a clinching face.

This shot rewinds into a black screen. The music shifts.

**Music: "Second Choice"**

**SIDE A**

*beep

See youngin ... you just gotta ... *ease* a woman into your world. Don't rush. This the second step, son. The wrong story, the wrong body language ... shit ... the wrong breath will end your chances in milliseconds ... *milliseconds* youngin ...

**EXT. Sidewalk** - NEED is walking, prepping for his date. He stops and checks a window with his reflection. In the reflection is NEED with a mask on. As the reflection turns back, all three of the men are together, ready to begin another dance.

If you respectful, polite, looking deep in her eyes, so she knows you there, you'll get her hooked. That's just level one though ... don't think it is easy sailing from there ... this just mean she cares long enough to continue the conversation ...

**beep*

BLACK SCREEN

**INT. COFFEE SHOP/RESTAURANT**

NEED is on a date with a black woman. On this date, the is a series of back-and-forth closeup shots between NEED and his date. However, on occasion, each time it returns back to the shot of NEED's date, the woman changes. There's at least three to four different women in this seat with NEED to signify the amount of times he has started, continued, and ended his dates the same way.

**NEED (Voiceover)**

*She sat right there.*
*Staring at me ...*
*It seems the conversation faded*
*Now we only talking with our thoughts.*

*It was a staring contest ...*
*I stare at her, she stares at me*
*I stare at her, she stares at me*
*I stare at her, she stares at me*

*We both stubborn to converse ...*
*She sat right there.*
*Staring at me ...*

*Sipping her drink ... all careless like ...*
*As though her cares are not in this room ...*
*Her thoughts on any stressor is insignificant ...*
*She mediates in pride ...*

**ALL**

*Greedy for some voice ...*
*I ask ...*

**NEED**

*(to the date.) Well ... this is ... hmm ... a nice spot, yeah?*
**shakes head*

**ALL**

*She stares differently ...*
*She won the game.*
*I look down in defeat.*

*A headshake ...*
*A ...*

The date smacks her *lips.*

**NEED**

*Her lips bring me closer to what I want, but ...*

**ALL**

*Intensifies the silence.*

**NEED**

*But then ... as though the motion shifts ...*
*She looks at me ...*
*And says ...*

**ALL (speaking as the date)**

*(giggling.) Hmmm ...*

**NEED (Voiceover)**

*I've had trouble with ... love.*

**EXT. SIDEWALK/ INT. COFFEE SHOP**

This shot returns to the three men on the sidewalk. They begin a dance. Much like the back-and-forth shots with NEED and his date(s), this sidewalk dance will be added to that back-and-forth, moving from NEED, to his dates, to the sidewalk dance, and returning.

*So troubled, that it feels as though God*
*Says, it's never meant for me ...*
*So troubled, that I be Thinking,*
*But, I be ready at every turn ...*

*Moment I can embrace a heart.*
*Shower in the gift of intimacy*
*Hold hands down the park of requited hugs ...*

*Kisses weaving through the branches*
*As though quarter notes building a harmony*
*A measurement of this faith in us*
*A testament of all the*
*carnations, the chocolate, the cards ...*
*the "cares"*

*I thought this time ...*
*I found that heart,*
*Those quarter notes,*
*The cares that could*
*Baptize a true relationship*
        **beat*
*between us ...*
*but ... I just had to say that ...*
*"impatient ass" they call me ...*
*that you are magic to me ...*

*You are extraordinary ...*
*Like no one else ...*
*I just ...*
*Love everything about you I say ...*

**INT. COFFEE SHOP**

**ALL**

*I think I can be with you forever.*
        **beat.*
*She says ...*
        **a record scratches.*

**NEED (as the date)**

*I only known you for a week.*
*Calm down.*
**Shakes head*

**NEED**

(*to his date.*) Calm *down?* Huh ...
You don't know who you're--
*(he wants to respond, but is tired of explaining.)*

**SIDE A**

**beep.*
You just gotta ... *ease ... ease.*

**EXT. SIDEWALK**

NEED is still looking at his reflection in the window.

**SCENE III: A JUNGLE AHEAD**

**Music: silence.**

**INT. LIVING ROOM – EVENING/NIGHT**

SANE enters the living room. In front of his eyes is his father, sitting on a recliner, watching something on the television. He is deeply distracted, while SANE is deeply in need to open himself up.

**SANE**

*Father ...*

FATHER turns his head slightly, to show his side profile silhouetted in the television lights. In addition, there is a closeup shot of SANE going back and forth.

**SANE (voiceover)**

*If only a conversation*
*Separated the feeling ...*
*of hesitation.*
*potential pain ...*
*predicted neglect.*

*If only this conversation ...*
*Could separate the negative*
*Could bring proudness*
*Bring contentment*
*To the seed*
*That you birthed ...*
*Father. If only--*

**SANE**

*(spoken aloud.) Father?*

FATHER turns again. We see more of his face. This time the glare remains.

*Listen, I want you*
*To know that--*
**beep*

**EXT. PARK - DAY**

**Music: "New song" - not created yet.**

There is a shot of a young boy, a younger SANE, hanging upside down from a monkey bar. This a rotating shot, starting as though he is right side up. The rotation happens throughout the voicemail.

**SIDE A**

*Listen boy ... you want to be a man? Second step, you need to show yo confidence. Everybody wanna be real until the real hits you in the jaw with fear itself. Realness does this to see if people hide who they, really, are. Be confident in front of everybody. Whether it's that new girl, yo best friend, boss, me. Yo daddy. Always show you got the confidence to do what you do. NEVER display weakness. If you do ... people will take advantage of you instantly. Instantly! I promise you, at that point, yr strength to them is no longer relevant. They will take and control. Question is: when you gon' push back? Show yourself what you are capable of? How do you challenge the perspective in front of you? Even if it's been there for a long time?*

**beep*

In the same rotating shot, at the end of the voicemail, YOUNG SANE turns his head in a direction.

**EXT. GRASS HILLS - DAY**

There is a closeup shot of SANE in a mask, slowly taking it off. The camera zooms out to the three men, again, preparing another dance on some grass hills.

**SANE (voiceover)**

*It was the jungle gym.*

**EXT. PARK - DAY**

Returning to the park, there is a shot of a different young boy, hanging on top of a jungle gym or playground. He fusses with a crown and eventually puts it on. He then, after a moment, looks at YOUNG SANE, hanging from a monkey bar. During this shot, the dialogue below continues.

**SANE (Voiceover)**

*I felt it for the first time*
*That feeling ...*

*My friends kept telling me*
*how they had that feeling*
*for a girl*

*Almost a spontaneous*
*Jump into doing anything for them ...*
*Yeah, I never felt that ...*
*At least ...*
*Not for a girl, per say.*
*Honestly not for anyone ...*

*Until ... well.*
*The jungle gym ...*

*There he was*
*Upside down*
*Much like how grade school felt*

During this sequence (much like the coffee shop/sidewalk scenes) there is a back-and-forth between the PARK and GREEN HILLS where the three men are dancing.

*My heart felt the same.*
*But my barrier*
*Was girls like boys*
*And boys like girls*

*There's never an in between*
*No alternative*
*No other option*

**EXT. PARK** – a group of different boys, some bullies, are playing catch until one notices YOUNG SANE on the monkey bar ready to jump down.

*The boys in the field*
*Saw it before me*
*They saw my intensity for*

*A boy, before a girl*
*Was even thought of ...*

**EXT. PARK** – YOUNG SANE on the monkey bar jumps down and stares back up at crown boy.

*I tried to lie using my*
*Body*

YOUNG SANE tries to walk "like a man."

**ALL (voiceover)**

*walk with a heavy heel*
*shoulders closer to my ears*
*chest as though a rope is pulling*
*me into a masculinity*

**SANE (voiceover)**

*I've always hated ...*

*Before I could*
*Reach the jungle gym*
*I felt a hand on my shoulder*

YOUNG SANE tries to approach crown boy, but is stopped by the bullies.

*They turned me around*
*And ask ...*

**ALL**

*"You fruity, huh?"*

There is a menacing shot of two to three bullies staring down at YOUNG SANE.

**SANE (voiceover)**

*If only a conversation*
*Separated the feeling.*
*of hesitation.*
*potential pain ...*
*predicted neglect.*

*I feel it come*
*Before it even approaches*

**ALL**

*The beating*
*Of feminine out of me.*

**SANE**

*I never understood*
*Why I always had*
*An issue*
*How is it INSANE*
*to be this ...?*
*Why couldn't I be I and nothing else?*

**ALL**

*I, be I and nothing else ...*

**SANE**

*But before the*
*Jungle gym*
*I get taught a lesson*

The bullies, as though the POV is YOUNG SANE, grab toward the camera as though they are grabbing him.

*About my existence*

*Who I soon will become*
*A dagger to the heart*
*Of my father.*
**sounds of fighting*
*A waste of time.*

The bullies, in a similar POV, are punching, kicking, harming YOUNG SANE from the view of the camera looking up at them.

*Yet wasted*
*Blood*
*Scrapes*
*Torn shirt*

*I stare at the jungle gym*
*I see it personifies me*
*A boy*
*In an upside-down world*

There is a shot of YOUNG SANE sitting up from the beating. The rotating shot returns, but in reverse, so that it ends with YOUNG SANE upside down.

*Surrounded by chain and metal*
*That represent a masculine frame*
*I will soon leave after recess.*

*Every day I come home to myself…*
*But my father won't see*
*Until the gym comes home*
*In hopes to fill a voided room*

**EXT. LIVING ROOM – EVENING/NIGHT**

**Music: silence again**

Music is cut out. A closeup shot of SANE staring at his father.

**SANE (Voiceover)**

*For my father's son.*
*Me.*

*Yet, I--*
*(spoken aloud.) Father ...?*

**FATHER**

*BOY! What you want?*

His father stands and steps to him. SANE runs away, out of frame.

**SANE (Voiceover)**

*I--*
*I forgot*
*How cold jungle gyms are ...*

There's the slam of a door that transitions into a ...

**INTERLUDE: "AHHHHH"**

**Music/Sound: This scene has a crescendo of breathing throughout the entire interlude.**

**EXT. WATERS - DAY**

There is a zoom shot of a body of water, slowly zooming in to show more detail of the waves (most likely from a bridge). As this shot is zooming in, we hear the voicemail return.

**SIDE A**

This is the last thing I'm gonna say before you flip the tape. Another thing you got to learn is reserving your emotions. Releasing too much causes a man to become nothing ... but a shrimp.

**EXT. BEDROOM - MORNING**

WAKE is staring across the room.

**SIDE A**

Save it for when loved ones die. Or when you need that anger, that *drive* to beat the competition. Don't make them about yourself. Emotions lead you to a softer shell.

**EXT. SIDEWALK - NIGHT**

NEED is sitting by a bus stop, looking both ways of the street.

**SIDE A**

Softer shell smells danger. Mm, hmm. It's a perilous decision. You'd reek a burden that many people would absolutely hate. And worse: what nobody wants anything to do with.

**EXT. PARKING LOT/DRIVEWAY - NIGHT**

SANE is outside of his home, head in his lap.

**SIDE A**

I say this, not to hurt you, I say this because that is a part of growing up. It's a way of life for a Black man. You have to have a hard shell. You need to be tougher so that they never assume you aren't. One of the leaders of the sea, not just one that inhabits it. Not a shrimp, but a whale.

There is a sudden weird cut, a *skip* in the cassette player.

Not a shrimp, but a whale ...

Not a shrimp, but a whale ...

Not a shrimp, but a whale ...

This line is repeated over and over as the breaths have reached a high volume. WAKE doesn't notice as though it is a line in his head and not an error in the tape. It escalates into the three men doing a collective:

**ALL**

AHHHHHHHHHH!!!!

As the men yell, there is a sudden sound from the tape, almost a mechanical sound, as though a ghost tampered with it. As it happens, you hear:

**SIDE A**

(*a different voice.*) Baby ...

**INT. BEDROOM**

WAKE, feeling confused, he walks to the recording. He takes a moment to wait for a voice, but the tape cuts off. We see a shot of WAKE flipping the tape and placing it back in.

*Click**

**EXT. WATERS**

We zoom away fast from the waters into a black screen. The three men let out a large exhale.

## ACT II

*Dig it back up**

### SCENE IV: SIDE B

**Music: "Avenue Eatery"**

SANE is standing by the waters. SANE begins to dive into a spiritual/freeform dance with the mask on from previous sequences. WAKE and NEED are on opposite sides. During this moment, there is a back-and-forth with all of the following:

**INT. LIVING ROOM (WAKE) - MORNING**

A quick shot of the tape recorder with the new voice. There is a shot of WAKE pressing play, tearing up in the process. As he presses play, you hear:

**SIDE B**

(*with a soothing mezzo-soprano voice.*) Baby, it's me. You know who it is. I just want you, first to know, that I love you. Second, I tried to save this before the fragile masculinity that is your father came to give you false thought ... false *hope*. I listened to it all and was appalled he'd give you this, so I wanted to stop him before.

**EXT. PARKING LOT/DRIVEWAY (SANE) - NIGHT**

SANE is looking out and hears someone coming from the door behind him. It's his father. They sit together.

**SIDE B**

But ... even if you did listen, I'm glad you did. Because you may know every *wrong* way to approach life. At least, before I can get a chance to tell you myself. Baby ... I want you to write this down for me. Promise me you'll keep this with you everywhere you go.

**INT. LIVING ROOM - MORNING**

WAKE grabs a piece a paper (or his phone) and begins to write.

**SIDE B**

You do come from a history of strong men. But those men were once boys too. They were once fragile and small and weak. Many grew to men still carrying those same traits, but, that did not make them any less of a man.

**EXT. OUTSIDE (NEED) - NIGHT**

NEED has gone on an exploration somewhere. At this moment, he is on a bench staring out at water. As this is taking place, there is a car that pulls up behind him. He looks back almost instantly.

**SIDE B**

It is okay to be weak. Just teach yourself how to be strong at your pace. No need to prove anything. Next, I'd say, ummm .... Your father was right, you should take your time with a woman, but—also give her a voice in the same space. Don't make it all about you, otherwise by the end of the first date, she is certain she won't want to explore you as you didn't make time for her.

**INT. LIVING ROOM - MORNING**

WAKE takes a moment to stop and begins to get prepped to go outside. He leaves as SIDE B continues to speak over.

**SIDE B**

You can be awkward. This is a way of life. We can't ever move it, therefore, embrace it. One more thing is—be unconditionally emotional. For a young man ... at one point a young boy ... you need to release in order to grow, release in order to learn, release in order to *heal*. You are young, but even if you're old, don't rest in the uncertainty of how you *should* feel because masculinity has told you not to.

**EXT. PARKING LOT/DRIVEWAY - NIGHT**

SANE and his father are talking, it seems as though they have been for a while. Suddenly, SANE's father embraces him and they share that moment. The camera slowly zooms in on them.

**SIDE B**

Baby, the sea ... *the waters* ... is one large ecosystem in itself. Every species, one way or another, need each other to survive and live the cyclical process that helps every invertebrate grow. Maybe you are a shrimp, but you are also eating a bacterium that could possibly save an entire coral reef army. You just don't know ... but, look at how God can work.

**EXT. OUTSIDE - DAY**

WAKE is on his way to the waters.

**SIDE B**

I want you do this for me. I want you to walk outside and find ... the waters. Then look into that ecosystem.

**EXT. BENCH/CAR - NIGHT**

NEED looks by the car. It is a previous date; she waves him over. There is a shot of NEED walking toward her; he walks out of frame.

**SIDE B**

Stare real close. And when you get to a moment, you see something interesting ... do you see it yet? Yeah ... isn't it beautiful? You know what makes it beautiful? It's because of imperfection, mixed with confusion, with a lot of things that still need to be figured out.

**EXT. WATERS - MORNING**

WAKE is by the waters. Similar to the one in his dreams. He stares hard and sees ...

**SIDE B**

You know what is in common with this? You. It is enough to say that you are NEEDED. To say you are loved. To say you are a SANE human being. But you must WAKE up to who you are: A Black man in a society that pushes an agenda on you. It's time to be free from that.

*To be a man ...*
*to be a BLACK man ...*
*can feel like ... like ...*
*a weird nightmare.*
*Like yr mind is soiled with antagonism.*

**EXT. PARKING LOT/DRIVEWAY - NIGHT**

SANE leaves inside with his father. As they go inside, SANE remains slightly behind and looks around. After a moment, he leaves inside as well.

*That the moment we see yr true selves,*
*yr true revelation,*
*We beat them up before yu get a chance to ...*
**breath*
*Breath.*
*And smell the fresh water.*
*glaze at all that is beautiful in the oxygen.*
*Hmmm ...*

VOLUME 3, ISSUE 4

**EXT. CAR - NIGHT**

NEED is driving in the passenger. There is a shot of his arm flowing out of the window to the wind.

*The Black men yu idolize,*
*WE idolize,*
*Push so hard to bury the feeling.*
*That, it feels like we*
*Should be stoned to death*
*To ever want that in our lifetimes.*

**EXT. WATERS - MORNING**

There is a shot zooming in on WAKE with his body facing the waters. We see a silhouette of his body and you can tell he is weeping.

*To ever get a bite of love.*
*Feel full from the appetite for flowers.*
*Just to say that*
*beauty, herself, can love a MAN too.*

There is a quick shot of each of the men's faces, before the ending ...

*Can love you.*
*Yes, you baby.*

BLACK SCREEN.

**END OF FILM.**

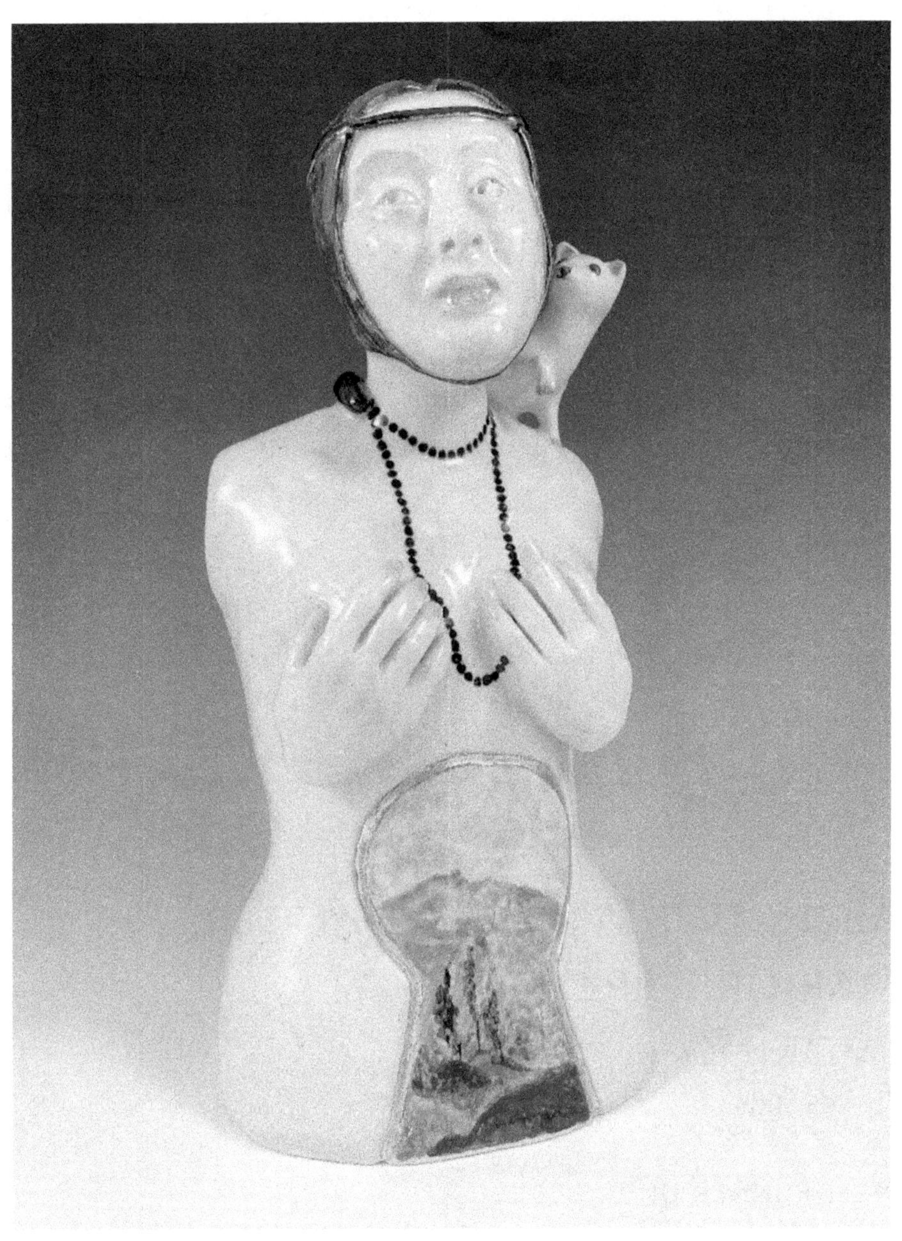

## Girl With an Ermine / Lilianne Milgrom

Geminga Finalist

Annual Editor's Prize

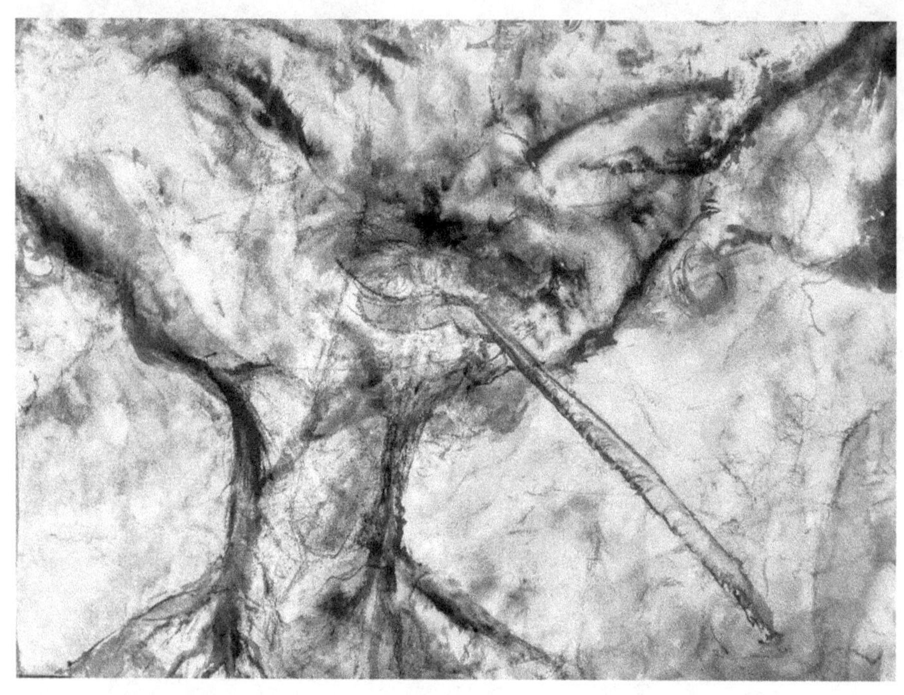

# Although a Superb Dancer, Marjorie Preferred Smoking

/ Dave Sims

Rigel Runner-up

# Learning to Make Fire After the Meteor Strikes / Dave Sims

# Out of the Mojave

Drew Smith

Inception Contest Finalist

In the emptiness of Pinto Basin I sense the gods. Not the austere jealous gods of the Book. Nor the jolly gluttonous fornicating gods of Olympus. Not even the Piute man-eater Tse'nahaha. I'm talking about the gods that came before. The ones that never speak to humans, never notice us at all. The ones that devour their own children in blind eruptions of rage and lust. The ones that lie mute and formless beneath the sand and rock. Wholly beyond human comprehension, we ignore them in hope that ignorance will save us from a humbling.

I have entered the Basin and Range country of the Mojave Desert, following a route called the Desert Trail. It is not actually a trail, just a set of directions for walking through the deserts of California and Nevada, should one wish to do so. Aside from a few abandoned jeep tracks, the travel is cross-country. It is a full immersion into the desert.

I walked some 50 miles to get here, starting at the Mecca Hills north of the Salton Sea. I intend to walk another hundred miles north to the Marble Mountains and the highway that twists around them. There I will return to society and a world which believes it controls nature.

# PASH / Christie A. Cruise

Inception Contest Finalist

# Blood Creek

Andy Carpenter

Inception Contest Finalist

Indian Summer fades—Same as us—Even if we ain't ready.

Come late November, the sun walks herself out backwards to wherever she lays low. This land gives way to the early reaches of winter. All around us the water drops. Cricks thin out. What was for most of the year, deep pools, usually too deep to wade, narrow down to resemble the closing eye of some old serpent with scales made of stones and polished threads of exposed minerals. Brittle leaves shuffle along the sediment, catch in runs, and swirl across the top of the water akin to caddisflies. Some springs run unbothered by events occurring outside their purpose.

Late Fall has always been my favorite turn of season—a final appearance of regal autumn corn stalks standing erect—a faithful and contemplative congregation. Knuckled leaves fold like hands clasping just-closed hymnals, waiting for the last soft echoes of a beautiful hymn to fade away. The stalks wait patient as their tough summer limbs get whispery and hollow and bow under the weight of the heavy husks. A hush will settle before the preacher's harsh words warn of what might befall us if we ain't careful in the ways we account for ourselves.

# Matrilineal Cubes / Aylah Ireland

Inception Contest Finalist

# Character Fragments

Francxs Gufan Nan

Inception Contest Finalist

Tell me the textures you were made to forget:

soot      musk  oil     camphor     black ink brush
  a sea   of wet strands     thick bound
        horsehair waltzing

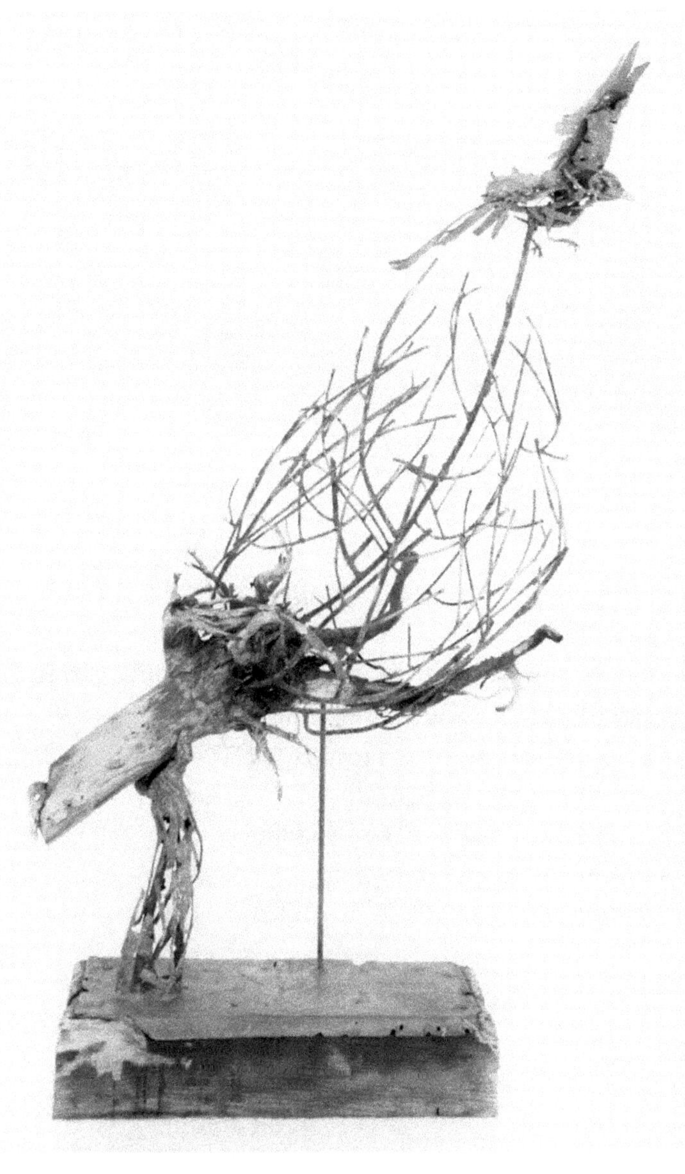

# Pica Nuttalli—Yellow-Billed Magpie / Dallas Frederick

Photographer: William Bazargani

Inception Contest Runner-up

# Our Beloved

Melisa Casumbal-Salazar

Inception Contest Winner

The Descendants

The Nanays hadn't yet decided on us, so we were still only perfect in form. Do you remember that time, *kapatid?* The time before body?

It was here, right here, by the water. This is where it all went down.

You don't remember, do you?

Listen, when the Nanays tell the wedding story, it's all *ube* and ocean and ancestors. It's messy as fuck, so you have to pay attention.

But if anyone asks, you didn't hear it from me. I'm no *tsismosa.*

## OUMUAMUA / MARIEKEN COCHIUS

CULMINATION CONTEST FINALIST

# LACQUER

A. J. BERMUDEZ

CULMINATION CONTEST FINALIST

When the bottle of polish spills, a lagoon of Peach Side Babe No. 909 on hardwood, it is not only the shade of her toes but now the soles of her feet, carving rivulets in the skin of her heels and the pads beneath the toes, leaving ghosts of pink footprints en route to the kitchen. There, amid a junkyard of ceramics and utensils, beneath a spiral of light from the overhead bulb, she locates a towel. She has not consulted the literature, does not know whether the bar soap in the half shell on the edge of the sink will do the trick. She will clean through the night, not because of the polish but because now, on her knees, she sees it is already a disaster--flecks of plaster and hair, crumbs and dust and detritus of unspecified origin. She will see herself in the mirror, amid the half loaf of bread and the candlesticks from Spain and the cup with the chip and the towels that should really be replaced, the needles and thread and waffle iron and flat iron and from her vantage on the floor, it looks as though she is holding all these things aloft, a caryatid of unwelcome history. She will finish her work, extinguish the bulb, and tread back to the bedroom, slick with error, over a floor that has never been so clean.

# TUCKAMORE / LEAH DOCKRILL

CULMINATION CONTEST FINALIST

# WET PAVEMENT

JASMINE KAPADIA

CULMINATION CONTEST FINALIST

bury me. bury me & be gentle but *tian ah*, bury me bury me bury me.

here: the angel is pulling at his leash.

## Droplets / Barbara Ayala Rugg Diehl

Culmination Contest Runner-up

# OUTLAW

CHRISTINA RAUH FISHBURNE

CULMINATION CONTEST WINNER

The refrigerator buzzes like the giant bees that terrify the woman's children. Giant bees hold no power over Robin Hood Bunnykins. Something fills with water. Or drains. A hose is involved somewhere near the refrigerator. Birds call to each other in the garden. The clock ticks. The clock face has a wrong Roman numeral. The "four" is incorrect. Robin Hood Bunnykins cannot tell the time without first telling the clock it is wrongly made. He hears *mistake* with every tick. But he makes due. As he must. As the woman does when there is no half and half and she must make it with heavy cream and milk like some sort of peasant.

Robin Hood Bunnykins watches the woman swallow ghosts of composed coffee in her soft ugly chair beneath him. Everything is beneath him. The spirit world is awake at this hour when undisturbed floorboards pop. The monitor in the child's unseen room is silent, becomes more silent the harder anyone listens for him. No books fall from his bed. No words fall from his sleeping mouth. Prince John, his hands on his hips, his tail puffing proud behind him so that it casts a shadow, surveys the shelf with pointless self-importance. Will Scarlet sits stupid and still, his bag of gold coins between his legs. Everyone is behind glass now, poised for assault but with no reason to move. Robin Hood Bunnykins can smell yesterday. Yesterday is still here. Yesterday is the same as today.

# Voilà

Margot Douaihy

Geminga Finalist

There it is: there you are, *voilà*, she thought, I've been waiting for you, moon, but she did not think, the thought thought her, the floating rock brought her to the firmament—that's it, *voilà!* here she is—here we are—nodes in the rhizome, embers glowing in the furnace of the heart of the breathing planet, hovering slowly, *voilà*, the us-ness, the you of me & the me of you, the id, ego, supermoon, *voilà!*, a true fact, even when it's not, like the orb of eye always awake & always asleep—the brightest light under the darkest lid.

# You Arrived

Morgan English

Geminga Finalist

like a boot in my trawl, craving myth.
A forest of figs. Scuppernongs.
The iron forged dinner bell.
Going to a dance, eucalyptus in my hair.

# First Light Puerto Vallarta

Alfredo Quarto

Geminga Finalist

Soft skin of morning
Bright-plumed birds sing hosannas
To harbor dawn.
Ripples define where
Fish have tempted water bounds
Sea reflecting clouds.

# Terra Incognita

Julie Noble

Geminga Finalist

When the arid winter is coming, leaves the color of pumpkin flesh fall late from trees in the isolated walled patios of unassuming adobe houses camouflaged against the earth they came from. Shy homes among the pervasive spiky *ichu ichu* show pride in their sheep and llamas, the rows of potatoes nearly ready to harvest and make *chuño*. On *Ruta Nacional* 1, beyond Machacamarca, the city has not yet leached into the *altiplano*, swallowing or squeezing as it urbanises with brash metal roofed cubes on tiny crop and animal-free plots; for now, this is still terra incognita on Google Maps.

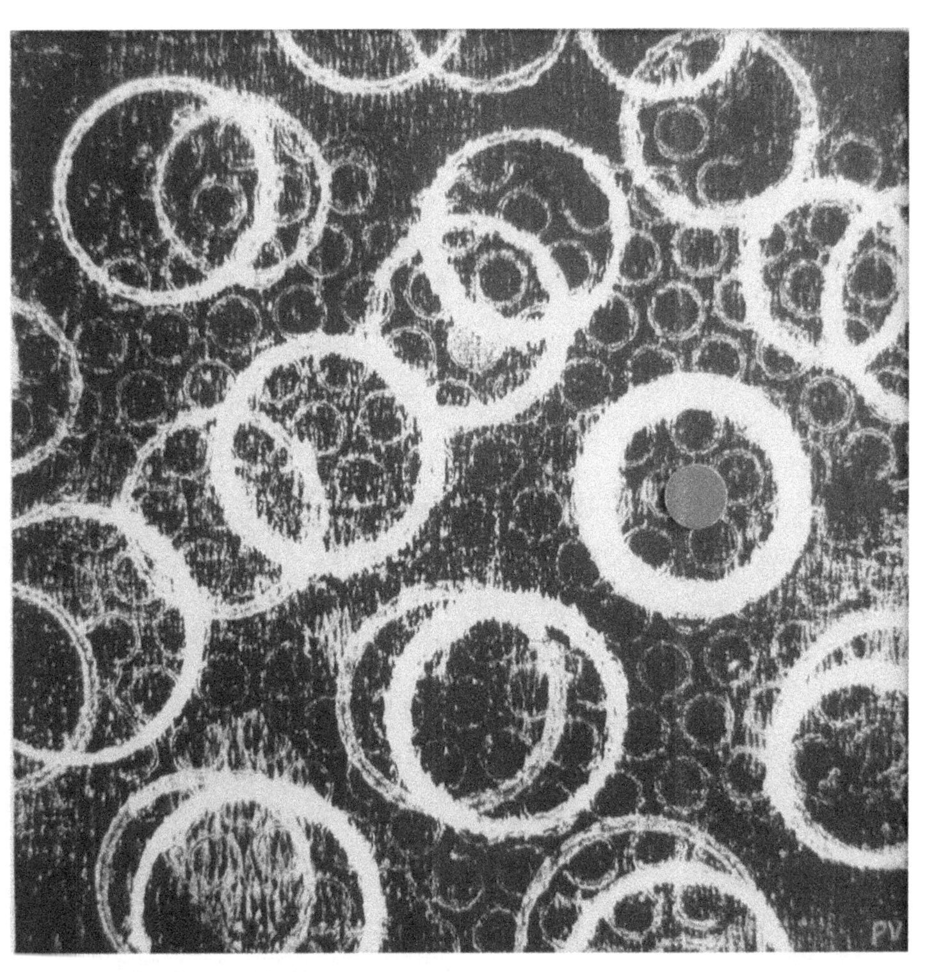

# Running Around in Circles

/ Pamela Viggiani

Geminga Finalist

# And What of Love?

Daragh Byrne

Geminga Runner-up

And what of love, that vast and splendid thing
That eats her young, while teaching them to sing?

# Of Being / Jackie Ta

Geminga Winner

# THE CITY OF DREAMS

AINHOA PALACIOS

RIGEL 2021 FINALIST

The only thing I could think of that morning was the way my mother told me things written in red were bad luck. A omen of something dark. *Corre pal otro lado*, she'd say.

## 1.

From what I can remember about the summer of 1980, it had only been two months since Tati's departure. Still, I could not—despite my best efforts—recognize my dear friend planted in the entryway of our village train station. There was the empty platform and lack of disembarking bodies, both typical of our station (if that's what someone chose to call that dilapidated metal shed), and yet I squinted and strained and still found her outline inconceivable. Maybe it was her newly upright posture. Her chin tilted skyward. Her jet-black hair let loose instead of in a pristine bun. Maybe, it was her smile that seemed to have grown larger in a way unrelated to size. Showier like it was waiting to be approached, waiting to spill forth with stories of her adventures.

That night I boiled the kettle while my dear best friend unpacked her suitcase right on the kitchen floor. *It's the future Mari!* She'd relentlessly dragged on with the same enthusiasm since our walk back from the station. *You just won't understand it until you go, you simply can't.* She was nearly shouting at me as if I'd tried to dispute her when in fact, I did believe her and needed no convincing. *It's like a whole city has just sprouted up from beneath the ground. Like it has been there all along and it's just now being dusted off. Overnight I'm telling you. Overnight!*

Over the next two hours, Tati would describe ad nauseam her two months living away. She would explain the intricacies of one's home city, or rather lack thereof, and its irrelevance. How nobody was a native, and 'transplants' was the word they used for one another even if one was only there for a short time for soon they'd undoubtedly make their return again. Why would anyone stay away? How could they? For once, a city flush with jobs. Anglers, phone assemblers, construction workers. A legion of construction workers because how could there not be if on every block something splendid and towering was being built.

Months later and before the first snow fell, Ms. Lupe's son returned to our same dilapidated metal shed of a train station. Wide-eyed and with a cheerfully spooked expression that was beginning to seem to be a side effect of The City of Dreams. That's what people were calling it. Ms. Lupe's son, if memory serves me right, was a pompous lad of 25 who could not help from spouting off about the new high rises appearing every three days. Once again, we had to see it to believe it. What I never did understand, even all these years later, was this incessant need to convince, as if we, their listeners, were set on disbelieving.

## 2.

It was over dinner that I finally collected and mobilized what little courage I may have carried inside, sucking my belly close to my spine and withholding my exhale, reciting to myself *wait, wait*. Wait until mother was ladling arroz con leche onto father's bowl. I must've hoped the purple potatoes and choclo lulled them a bit, left them with the same sleepy docile haze of the village cows after they'd grazed.

I must explain to you that I, Mari, at twenty, was meek and small-framed and knew no other way to assert myself than let the unrehearsed words barge out of my mouth. *I want to go*, I said like a child lacking vocabulary. As if the location of my sentence was a given.

I expected gasps from mother and aggressive frowning from father's eyebrows, the way they both did when they did not agree. I expected a disregarding of my foolish ideas yet none of this could've stopped me for I was convinced this was my fate.

**3.**

My entire life, all pitiful twenty years of it, I'd accepted, even welcomed the idea of a struggle. My mother's lessons—*You are given what you are given,* and *Ese es el mundo Mariana*— reverberated inside me anytime a less than grateful thought arose in me.

I spent my childhood listening to stories of my grandparents who'd struggled yet still gave thanks for their small room which provided *no relief on mosquito-ridden nights*. And I knew mother and father's story as if I'd been there myself. Born into a generation whose land was abruptly and unjustly no longer their own. Working tirelessly for hacienda owners who gave them little to feed themselves. Members of a village burying starved infants every other month, and when the protests began the only thing gained was the fear to sleep at night. But still, they gave thanks.

So why would my life be any different?

It was on that train ride, hidden in a back corner of the cart and compressing myself against the fogging window, that meek Mari finally dared to indulge that little girl who'd been aching to dream. Dare to dream in The City of Dreams. Cliche I know.

It wasn't that I dreamt of peasant turned millionaire. The word millionaire had little meaning for me. I didn't even dream of being an owner, a boss. No silly title allured. Not yet anyway. What I wanted was rather uncomplicated and unassuming— a life I'd decided on with something to strive for. Whatever that turned out to be.

The train ride was ten hours long, all which flew by for a young and fascinated woman like myself. I, who'd never been outside my village and once tried to measure its length using only my 6-year-old feet, didn't fight collapsing eyelids like the man sat beside me. I was pleased, no, thrilled to witness each sight. I wanted to absorb every river and lake and patch of open land my memory could hold.

The train was headed south, the direction my father told me I'd be traveling. He said mountains would begin popping up. Lush green mountains, jagged and uniform like a tiger's mouth. I decided then that was my favorite part and it remained so until the light blue billboard appeared, glimmering and sparkling:

**"Everyone who comes to The City of Dreams belongs here."**

**4.**

The City of Dreams turned out to be the city of magic, the city of hope with air so crisp it tickled your nose. It was grandiose and frightening, something like the thunderstorms back in the village with lightning bolts drawing you near, beckoning you closer than what father said was a safe distance, prompting you to ignore your racing heart.

I meandered through the streets— streets three times, four times, five times bigger than the ones in the village— with a slacked jaw. I inspected the shade of each edifice as if I were shopping for paint. My favorite was a cobalt gray like my mother's only winter coat. Others had no real shade but rather a shiny metal that reflected my image more times than I'd ever wished for and yet I didn't mind. I came across bamboo stems threaded together, magically tied at their meeting points only to pause and watch the men sat like schoolgirls on the beams. Feet dangling naively. How confidently they hammered and drilled, shirtless, unprotected, and unafraid of the falling debris. I could see the pride in their eyes, up mounted so high on their altars. Their orange hard hats serving as lanterns to the daytime sky.

Tati had given me one name: Ayacucho. This is where you'll find housing. An urban village, she called it. What I came upon was a stone wall so statuesque and smooth and magnetic, I entered without hesitation, and when I crossed the stone archway, what I found was a future full of possibilities.

Just beyond the cobblestone view were hundreds of buildings the color of weathered works of art. Light pinks, and yellows, lilacs, blues, patches of missing concrete. The only path veered right and down an alleyway so thin, I could spot neighbors exchanging gossip through the metal safety bars outside their windows. Later, I'd learn the jargon of the locals. Handshake houses and kissing buildings.

Outside a fruit shop where papayas ripened beneath the city's sun and *platanos* wafted their sweet tang through the air, I met a sturdy old woman whose smile outdid her size, one whose name would become so entangled with The City of Dreams, I would never dare to imagine one without the other. A lifelong friend, a second mother, who on this day must've taken note of my timid smile and my sunken eager gaze because she proceeded to reach out with a tray of cherries.

*Try one*, she smiled.

I hesitated but she cut my pause short. *They were just delivered this morning, go on.*

Thanking her for the single cherry, I plucked it from its stem with my teeth and held it in my mouth for as long as the pit yielded any hint of sweetness. Even the fruit tasted sweeter in this city!

*I don't recognize you. What are you looking for here?* she asked. Before I could get further than the word apartment, the woman was reaching for her purse from behind the counter. Follow me she commanded leading the way down the bends and loops of corridors. She explained the manager of some of these buildings didn't live far off. Just a few blocks down, plus she was certain there was room in her building. She was sprightly for someone with a hobble, speaking at the similar speed of one of those sports announcers. *How old are you? Do you have a husband? Are you also following the great migration?* It was a rapid-fire of questions requiring no response because finally, she settled on, *Oh yes, everyone is welcome in Ayacucho,* and the questions stopped.

Her name was Adelita.

## 5.

To my delightful surprise, both my dear friend and Ms. Lupe's son hadn't exaggerated when they said the city was brimful of factories.

My days began at four a.m.

Four a.m. was the only way to squeeze in the hour bus ride to a factory sitting in the outskirts of the city where I would begin twelve hours of sewing and stitching, and unstitching, and trimming lace fabric. Me and the fifty other women who did so with glee. Under fluorescent lighting, and sat with our sewing machine, scissors, knives, tape measures, pins and pincushions, tools I'd yet not learned the name of. Surrounded by circular padding meant for women's brasiers. Lace and satin. Pink fabric one week. Black another. Who would have imagined it? Me! A seamstress!

## 6.

Besides Adelita's fruit shop was Mr. Camilo's everything shop bursting with so many everythings a person could only fit inside if they walked laterally. He himself called it a junk shop. Plungers, pots, notebooks, mirrors, kettles, pens, hairbrushes. No one item ever displayed a price tag yet Mr. Camilo knew the price of each item through memory alone. It was never a made-up-on-the-spot number, something I'd first assumed until I began to test him. Asking the price of something in particular, writing it down, and waiting one month before asking again. His answers were always consistent.

Across from Mr. Camilo's everything shop was Sofi's flower shop. She and Mr. Camilo often sat playing rummy late into the night when surely nobody would visit either of their shops. I always did love to stop by Sofi's after work just to scout out any new flowers. I'd ask their name and write them down in my notebook, but mostly, I stopped by to see the brightest smile in the neighborhood, Mario. A shaggy-haired big-brown-eyed boy of four who, every morning, stood inside a red bucket bathing himself and splashing water on the stray dogs napping nearby.

## 7.

Every other Tuesday was my day off, and on those days, I purchased two *licuados* and a bag of *picarones* which I carried to Mr. Camilo's door, where I knocked, in the same manner, every time—two consecutive and delicate taps, a pause, and then a calling out of his name. Mr. Camilo always shouted back, *it's open*. Once inside, I'd slip my sneakers off and he'd offer me a cup of coffee which I never accepted because I knew he never kept milk around.

Without exchanging any more words, I left one *licuado* on the door-side table, carried the other to his blue-stained rocking chair, nestled down, and tucked my knees tight into my chest. The phone always rang six times before Flor from our village's post office answered. *One second Mari, they're right here.*

*Hi father. Hola Mari. Your mother is right here. Hi mother, cómo están?*

Our conversations were like a script we'd committed to rehearsing every week. Seldom did anyone forget their lines, much less miss the pauses indicating we were about to move on to the next question.

*How's your job mija?*

*It's good. Tiring, pero estoy contenta.*

*And when will you return?*

'Soon' was always my answer. Though soon was in fact not soon, and we all (father, mother, and I) understood it to mean never which must be why father always followed with *apúrate niña, that city is not your home.*

I always did agree, nodded my head as if father could not only hear me but see me. As if by agreeing with him I could convince myself against my own truth, a truth I decided the day I dashed past the light blue glimmering billboard.

The City of Dreams was my home, and I don't think I would have ever given that up.

**8.**

When I first told Adelita of my idea she was unboxing grapes and picking out the battered ones.

An underwear shop! I declared.

Adelita stopped her search for bruised grapes and looked at me with luminous eyes. The corners of her lips expanded to let a joyous laughter out.

For the last ten years, I'd watched as Ayacucho grew to become a small city of its own with its fruit shops, massage parlors, fortune tellers, flower shops, nail salons, shoe repairs. Everything one needed sat inside our fortress walls and finally, it occurred to me, it was my turn to join the story.

Plus, after all the cutting and stitching and sewing, and years of gazing onto cardboard boxes and their logos, I knew who could provide the fabric. If they were any good for business. If they were cheap enough. I'd grown to be an expert at manufacturing brasiers. How thick a strap should be, how many clasps, the cut of a cup for the cut of a woman.

At first, my shop had no sign, no way of differentiating itself from the others but slowly it came together. I hung a fluorescent pink sign reading Mari's Collections. I painted the rolling garage door a peachy pink, and its inside a bright white. There was a small changing room behind a satin black curtain and an even smaller room where I could take measurements in private if someone wanted a custom order. And boy, were there custom orders. All of the women in Ayacucho came to me!

**9.**

The only thing I could think of that morning was the way my mother told me things written in red were bad luck. An omen of something dark, *corre pal otro lado*, she'd say. And there was the word demolish written on the garage doors of my eight-by-six shop.

The letters dripped like blood. Casually. Leisurely as if demolish was a slow process and not as swift as a 13,000-pound wrecking ball. Adelita stood silently, head bowed the way she did when she visited her church and prayed to her saints.

*When did they write this?* I asked and she shrugged. Her shop hadn't been marked yet, but we knew it would be soon for The City of Dreams hadn't stopped. Not in forty years. In fact, in that time it had grown to be 38 million people's City of Dreams.

The term the world used now was Dream speed. Birthed from the quickness with which buildings were demolished and rebuilt, built to be demolished, planned, and executed in this city, people in those days liked to use phrases like: I'll be there in dream speed.

**10.**

*I am now standing in front of Ayacucho Village.* I hated that reporter. *One of the original villages in The City of Dreams. Here live the modest workers who some call the heart of the city. Today, the most historic parts of this city face being demolished as the city's mayor announced new plans for these notorious handshake houses.*

I remember those sentences like I do Hail Marys.

She was lean. Wore a sleek tidy bun, a pencil skirt, and patent leather pumps. Her steps were the length of a toddler's because I could only assume she feared stepping in the cracks between cobblestones. She'd marched right into our home a few weeks after the construction company came to hand us our notice. She pried and snooped, insisting on interviews with a stiff smile painted on. Insensitive bitch she was. She probably lived in one of those towering buildings beside us, one of the ones that would be built atop our shops to house more people like her. More insensitive bitches.

Adelita was kind to her from the start and she pushed me to do the same. *It may be our only chance at surviving*, she said. If people knew, if they cared, maybe the government would listen.

They wouldn't.

Since The City of Dreams had begun its rise, the number of suburban villages in the city had decreased from 2,000 to us. We were the last standing and so we knew well, from hearsay, there would be no reparations. At least not for the renters. For the lucky landlords, to be demolished was to hit the jackpot. They would be paid millions of dollars for their run-down roach-infested buildings with which they could easily purchase any number of extravagant apartments in one of the thousands of new skyscrapers The City of Dreams had erected in its short history.

We, however, were given two months to evacuate. When we asked where should we go, the landlords said, home.

## 11.

Soon it will be The City of Dream's fortieth anniversary. The whole city will celebrate. Families of all ranks—the rich in uppity restaurants, the poor in the unadorned and simple. Every bar will be bursting, swarmed with people, shots of Pisco passed around.

The city's most beloved park will be the place to go for the display of lights against the tallest skyscrapers. I will stand bearing witness to the bursting pixels of ruby red and fiery orange on the towers. Images of families skipping through hills, the outline of kites—pictures that rang truer to me many years ago. Patriotic pan flutes will resonate down streets whilst fathers hoist their children on their shoulders and mothers sob with pride. Our city.

On this day, I will no longer be a meek 20-year-old, but rather a decaying 66-year-old woman who has made her last trip into The City of Dreams. I will be carrying Adelita inside a golden locket and thinking of Mr. Camilo, and wondering where Sofi and Mario are these days and if I'll ever see them again. I will, for the last time, look upon that glimmering blue billboard which will no longer glimmer the way it once did for me for I know it will soon be taken down. Replaced with one that's sleeker, bigger, shinier. What will this one say?

And I will feel the pang of longing for a past I cannot recover. For a city that once wrapped me in acceptance, welcomed me like a mother does her newborn child. A city that once stood so beautifully, yet on this day, monstrously. For a city that won't forget who built it. A city I once belonged in.

THE COAST / VERNON SHIPWAY

RIGEL 2021 FINALIST

# THE HERMIT OF ILSWHER

RIGEL 2021 FINALIST

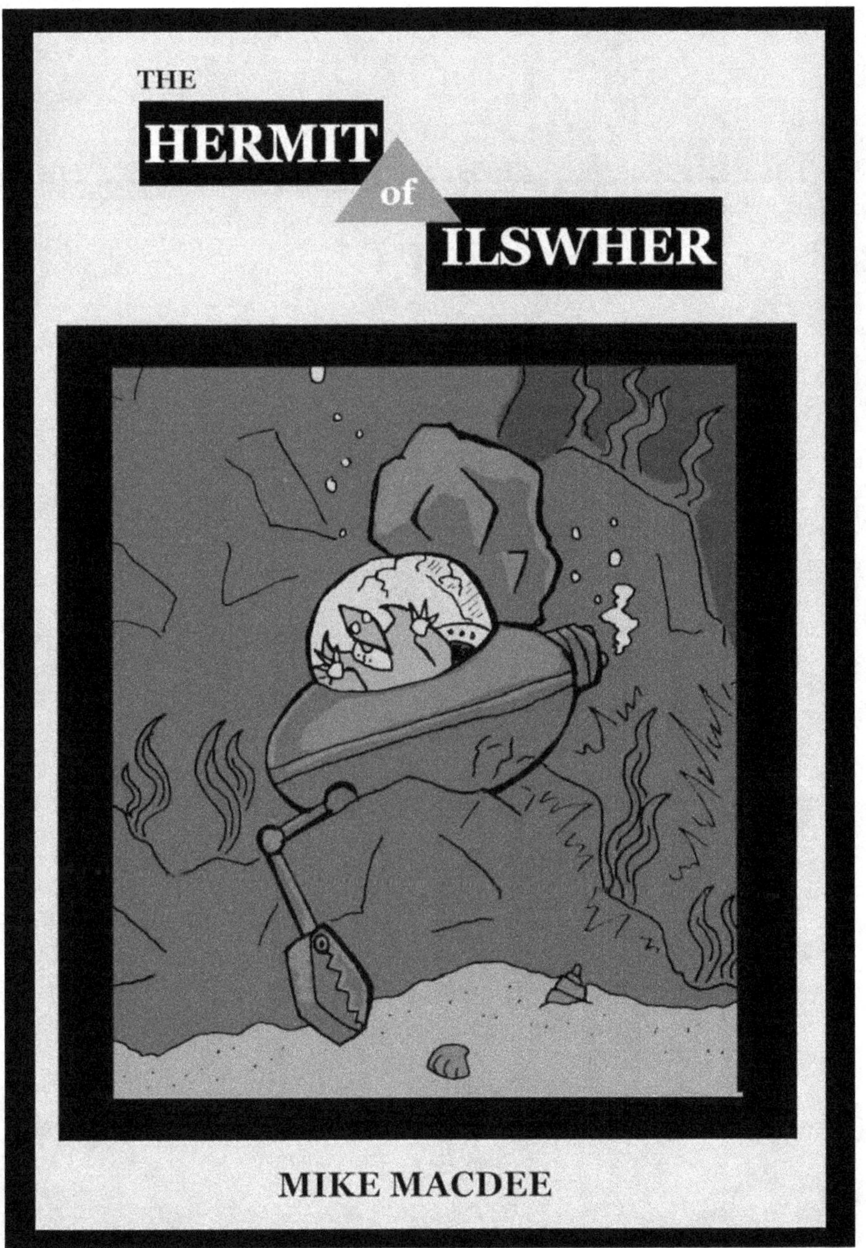

CHILDHOOD
DOCTOR!
MY SON IS DEFECTIVE.
AND THERE'S NOT A DOC IN TOWN WHO KNOWS WHY!
HMM...
HE CAN'T SOCIALIZE, AND CAN'T MAKE FRIENDS.
COMES HOME FROM SCHOOL CRYING EVERY DAY.
FASCINATING...
ALL TESTS COME BACK INCONCLUSIVE.
HOWEVER, HE'S EXCEPTIONAL WITH MACHINES.
HE MIGHT BE HAPPIER AT THE ENGINEERING COLONY ON RELL 7.
HIGH SCHOOL
DON'T INVITE HIM OVER HERE!
WHY?
HE'S WEIRD.
WROONCH WROONCH
HEH. YEAH.
HE ASKED ME OUT YESTERDAY.
HE'S SO CREEPY.
WHO'S HE THINK HE IS, ANYWAY?
TWEAK TWEAK
FWEEEE

RECLUSE
VVVT! VVVT!
VVVT VVVT!
VVVT!
BLAT
SPLOOSH
WHRRRRRR

NEIGHBOR
DRIP
DRIP
DRIP
DRIP
?
DRIP
DRIP
DRIP
FLIK FLIK
DRIP
DRIP
WUPPAWUPPAWUPPA
DRIP
?
DRIP
PUSH
K-KRAK
PSSSHH
BLOOSSSHH

ASSISTANT
WROONCH
EJECT
POP
POP
POP
POP
POP
POP
GKK
GKK
GKK
TINK
TINK
TINK
TINK
??
POP

BOFF
WROONCH
PRICELESS PEARL.

FRIEND

# First Image from "Facing It Together" Series / Jack Bordnick

Rigel 2021 Runner-up

# Bean Soup, or A Lesson in Time

C. Adán Cabrera

Rigel 2021 Winner

for R.E.C.

You're seventeen years old and you're having a bad day. Well, it's actually another bad day, in a string of rotten months, in what is turning out to be a terrible year. But you don't want to talk about it. You never want to talk about it. Not anymore, at least.

Your mother doesn't take long to notice. She motions for you to sit and scoops out some uncooked pinto beans from the reserve she keeps in a white plastic tub with red handles, the same one from your childhood that once contained a gallon of Neapolitan ice cream. The plastic is still stained pink and chocolate brown.

She announces that she's going to make bean soup and pours the hard *frijoles* onto the kitchen table. Some scuttle across the chipped wood, others lodge themselves in the webbed and yellowed doily. She then grabs one of the cast-iron pots that she keeps beneath the sink, next to all the knotted up plastic Walmart bags, brand new pink sponges, and half-empty bottles of cleaning liquid. (Twenty years later, when you have your own mortgage and a little girl and a husband, the area under your kitchen sink will be almost identical.) After rinsing and dabbing the pot with a paper towel, she sits down across from you.

She puts on her glasses—the pair she'd reluctantly bought after several fights with your father; *aún no soy vieja*, she complains—and lets them rest on the tip of her nose. And though the process is something familiar to you, your mother explains it anyway.

*Before you cook them, you have to examine the beans,* she says to you in Spanish. *Pick out the pebbles and any beans you can't eat. Take only what is useful.*

She grabs a handful of the uncooked beans and places them in front of her. You watch silently as she uses her ring finger to separate one from the rest. She examines it for a moment before she places it in the pot. She does the same with three or four beans, and turns to the rest of the pile. They each clang in the pot when she deposits them.

Your mother picks up speed as she works. In fact, she's been practicing all her life, ever since she was a little girl in El Salvador. She sees a jagged, rust-colored pebble and separates it from the rest of the beans, continuing for a moment before speaking again.

*No rush,* your mother says in English. She pauses to remove another pebble. This one is bigger than the rest she's pulled out so far. She switches back to Spanish. *Otherwise, you might lose a tooth.*

Though you know the story about how your *abuelo*, the one you've never met, lost his right molar—one day, one of your *tías* in San Salvador made bean soup without checking the beans first and, while eating it, your grandfather suddenly stood up from the table, clutched his jaw, and spit a bloodied pebble onto the kitchen floor along with part of his tooth—your mother tells it again anyway. Right then, you couldn't possibly know that in less than ten years he would be dead, his funeral in a hot and crowded church becoming the first and the last time you would ever physically see him. But you feel something shift inside of you this time.

Your grandfather's memory will forever be tied to a dental deformity. Similar to when he suddenly cracked his tooth—you imagine—the feeling catches you off guard.

You listen quietly and grab a small pile of beans. You start sorting through them as well. Out of the twelve beans you've picked up, nine are fine, which you deposit into the pot, but three are discolored, almost rotten. You hold them tenderly in your palm and inspect them in the fading light of the weak December sun. What happened to these? you wonder silently. Where there should be dark brown speckles, there are what look like burn marks instead; one has a hole the size your pinky nail. You cast them aside.

*No rocks,* your mother says. She has been watching you. *Imperfect, but still good.* She motions for you to put them in the pot.

You grab another handful. Another twelve. There are two rocks this time, and nearly four of the beans are inedible. You pick out the rocks and the misshapen beans and toss them in the pile with the rejected ones. You hear your older brother's hatchback pull up in the driveway. After getting fired from yet another job, he is living at home again. He's twenty-one, four years older than you. In two years, he will be locked up in the county jail for robbery, and though you know it wasn't entirely his fault, that he was so fucked up on meth that he couldn't tell his right foot from his left, much less *right* from *wrong*, he will stare at you and your mother from behind the plate-glass shield, telephone cradled against his ear, and say nothing when she asks him to explain himself. He will just stare down at his orange jumpsuit, tracing the seams with his free hand, not making eye contact once. Your father will disown him and refuse to speak to his namesake for years after he's released from jail. So deep will be the shame. But your father will eventually come around, after your brother gives him his first grandchild.

You will swear to yourself and to your parents that you will never touch drugs, that you will never take a single puff of weed or feel your nostrils burn in anticipation of that high. You will, of course, not keep this promise, and a year after your brother is locked up, you will find yourself trudging up his old dealer's stairs in Pico-Union to get your next fix. You will fall for a junkie then, some white boy a decade older than you. He will call you beautiful and you will believe him and he will kiss you between hits of ice, blowing clouds into your mouth, crystallizing your fantasies of a life with him. All of which will break all too easily. The time you spend together will be a rite of passage. You will learn by being cast into the fire and learning how to crawl out one step at a time.

But right now, you're still seventeen and you're still sitting in your mother's kitchen. Right now, it's just bean soup and those punk asses calling you a faggot that have you all worked up. You and your mother work in silence, each of you taking a handful of beans and separating what is useful from what must be discarded—what will nourish you from what will only destroy you. You're on the brink of adulthood, learning that some days and years will be better than others—that some disrupt the flow of time and remain lodged forever in your memory, while others will allow time to pass, peacefully, on its mad rush to oblivion.

# Contributors

**A. J. Bermudez** is an award-winning writer and director based in Los Angeles, California. Her work has been featured at the Yale Center for British Art, the LGBT Toronto Film Festival, Sundance Film Festival, and in a number of literary publications, including *McSweeney's*, *The Masters Review*, *Hobart*, *Columbia Journal*, *The Offing*, and more. She is a former boxer and EMT, a recipient of the Diverse Voices Award, and currently serves as Artistic Director of The American Playbook.

**Jack Bordnick**'s sculptures and photography incorporate surrealistic, mythological and magical imagery—often with whimsical overtones—aimed at provoking our experiences and self-reflections. The predominant imagery deals with facial expressions of both living and "non-living" beings, and things that speak to us in their own languages. They are mixed media assemblages that have been assembled, disassembled and reassembled, becoming abstractions unto themselves. Jack has been a designer and design director for the past twenty years, including for numerous companies and projects.

**Michael Brosnan**'s most recent poetry book is *The Sovereignty of the Accidental* (Harbor Mountain Press, 2018). He's also the author of *Against the Current*, a book on inner-city education, and serves as the editor for the website Teaching While White.

**Daragh Byrne** is an Irish poet writing in Sydney, Australia. He has had work published in *The Blue Nib* and *The Honest Ulsterman,* amongst others. His poems have been commended or placed in a number of competitions in Ireland and Australia. He runs The Sydney Poetry Lounge, a long-running open mic night.

**C. Adán Cabrera** is a Salvadoran-American writer, translator and editor based in Barcelona, Spain. Among other publication credits, Carlos' writing has appeared in *Switchback*, *The Acentos Review*, *From Macho to Mariposa: New Gay Latino Fiction*, *BorderSenses*, *parentheses*, *fresh.ink* and *Kweli*. His debut book of short stories, *Books Can Only Take You So Far*, explores the complex intersections of race, class and sexuality, and the way these shaped his writing and worldview. A 2011 Lambda Literary Fellow, Carlos is hard at work on his second collection of short stories called *The Last Day of Summer*. Visit Carlos online at www.cadancabrera.net.

**Garrett Candrea** grew up in Eastchester, New York and currently lives in Astoria, Queens. In college he elected the wrong major and now holds a bachelor's degree in computer science from Fordham University.

After **Andy Carpenter's** high school run-ins with the law, a couple visits to juvie, foster care, rehab, etc., he pursued a career in substance abuse counseling, child protection and suicide prevention. Those work experiences, and the rural and urban places he invested himself in, left lasting impressions about the hardships and triumphs of the human experience. He sustains a deep love for the land and people he met along the way. Andy is a member of the Atlanta Writers Club, the Columbus Writers Guild, facilitator of the Strong Land Writers Group, and has a website, strongland.live.

In 2019, **Melisa Casumbal-Salazar** resigned an academic appointment as an assistant professor of politics to enter the writing MFA program at the University of California San Diego. She is the daughter of post-1965 Philippine migrants, and has been active in Filipinx and queer people of color community arts and organizing since the 1980s.

**Malick Ceesay** is a playwright and music producer from the Twin Cities. His play, *Waiting in Vain*, was workshopped and produced at Augsburg University with Ambiance Theatre Company. He was a finalist for the Many Voices Mentorship through the Playwrights' Center (Minneapolis, MN) in 2018. His work has been featured in the digital anthology *Black MN Voices* (published in 2020), and he has written for The Plugged App. He currently resides in Los Angeles where he is pursuing his MFA in Playwriting at UCLA as a Graduate Opportunities Fellow. Synopses and samples of his plays can be viewed on New Play Exchange.

**Mandy Clark** graduated in 2012 from Pacific Lutheran University with an MFA in Creative Writing. Her fiction, nonfiction, flash fiction, and poetry have appeared in *Whitefish Review Literary Journal, RWW Soundings, 100 Word Story, High Shelf Press,* and *Third Point Press,* and are forthcoming in *Sad Girls Club*. She lives in Corvallis, Oregon, and loves pizza and rain in no particular order.

**Marieken Cochius** is a Dutch-born artist whose meditative and intuitive work often explores growth forms, movement of light and wind, root systems, and animal architecture. In 2017 Cochius completed a public sculpture commission for the Village of Wappingers Falls, NY with a grant from the Hudson River Foundation. She is a 2020 recipient of a Foundation for Contemporary Arts (FCA), as well as others. Cochius' work has been exhibited in numerous national and international galleries and institutions. Her work was recently featured in *Willard and Maple Magazine, Sunspot, Columbia Journal, Superstition Review, High Shelf Press, Tule Review 2020, Cold Mountain Review, Mud Season Review, Art for a New Earth, DeLuge Journal, Alluvian Environmental Journal,* and *Raw Art Review.*

**Christie A. Cruise,** PhD is an author, educator, and social justice advocate with a passion for empowering Black girls and women to speak their truths boldly and unapologetically. In January 2019, Dr. Cruise released her first book of prose and poetry, *It Don't Hurt Now: My Journey of Self-Love & Self-Acceptance*. She has contributed to blogs for the Black Mental Wellness Corporation and The Healing Collective Global. In February 2020, her thoughts on colorism were published in the inaugural *Gumbo Magazine Black Edition*. Dr. Cruise writes a monthly blog that discusses a variety of issues and includes some of her self-portrait photographs.

**Ayshe Dengtash** was born to immigrant parents from North Cyprus. She spent the formative years of her childhood on a council estate in Southeast London, in the

United Kingdom, and her teenage years in North Cyprus. Her first novel *The Grieving Mothers of the Departed Children* was published by Alden, Allegory Ridge in November 2020. Her short stories have been published in *Cleaning Up Glitter*, *Newfound*, and *The Journal*. She currently prose reads for *The Walled City Journal* and Black Lawrence Press. She lives in Hong Kong with her partner and her two cats.

**Leah Dockrill** has been a visual artist for over thirty years. She has exhibited her work in Canada and the US, and has earned many awards. Her art has been published in art and literature journals including *Sunspot* (2019), *Split Rock Review*, *Unlimited Literature*, *Mud Season Review*, *The Esthetic Apostle*, *The Scriblerus*, *Glassworks*, *Marvellous Art*, *ArtAscent*, and *Beyond Words*. Leah is a featured artist on Camelback Gallery's roster. Leah is represented by Tag Art Gallery, St. Catharines, Ontario, Canada, and nowords Gallery, Cambridge, Ontario. She is an elected member of the Society of Canadian Artists and the Colour and Form Society, (Canada).

**Margot Douaihy**, PhD, is the author of *Scranton Lace* and *Girls Like You* (Clemson University Press). Her work has been featured in *PBS NewsHour*, *North American Review*, *Colorado Review*, *The Florida Review*, *The South Carolina Review*, *The Wisconsin Review*, *Tahoma Literary Review*, and elsewhere. She is a member of the Radius of Arab-American Writers and Creative Writing Studies Organization.

**Morgan English** is a Vermont poet and textile/garment maker. Her poetry has appeared in *St. Petersburg Review*, *Literary North* and she has been nominated for Best New Poets (2012).

**Christina Rauh Fishburne** has an MFA from the University of Alabama and is at work on her third novel. Find her at www.christinarauhfishburne.com.

**Dallas Frederick** studied Visual Arts at a small liberal arts school in the Pacific Northwest and has shown in various exhibitions and group shows. The sculpture in this edition is a statement on how global warming will negatively impact the habitat of endemic species. He hopes this work provides the space for further dialogue on climate change, its causes or solutions, and its impact on our environment and people (particularly for communities of color). Find him on Instagram: @dallasgriffinfrederick.

**GJ Gillespie** is a collage artist living on Whidbey Island north of Seattle. Winner of seventeen awards, his art has appeared in dozens of regional shows. The artists he admires tap unconscious feelings of longing for existential meaning that emerge from cultural icons. In his view, abstraction should be more than pleasing design. Art should evoke connotations that permit the viewer to experience a sense of wonder, awe and new perspectives of being.

**Summer Hammond** has traversed every state in the continental USA in a fuchsia eighteen-wheeler. This is her go-to "surprising and unusual" fact. She and her husband Aly earned bachelor's degrees online while long-haul trucking. Summer went on to teach ninth-grade reading in Austin, TX. Her most recent back-road adventure was moving cross country with Aly and achieving her MFA in Fiction from the University of North Carolina Wilmington at the tender age of forty.

**Jana Harris** teaches creative writing at the University of Washington and at the Writer's Workshop in Seattle. She is editor and founder of *Switched-on Gutenberg*. Her most recent publications are *You Haven't Asked About My Wedding or What I Wore; Poems of Courtship on the American Frontier* (University of Alaska Press) and the memoir, *Horses Never Lie About Love* (Simon & Schuster). Other poetry books include *Oh How Can I Keep on Singing, Voices of Pioneer Women* (Ontario), *The Dust of Everyday Life, An Epic Poem of the Northwest* (Sasquatch), and *We Never Speak of It, Idaho-Wyoming Poems 1889-90* (Ontario). Her two novels are *Alaska* (Harper & Row) and *The Pearl of Ruby City* (St. Martin's). She lives with her husband on a farm in the Cascades.

In a past century, **Heikki Huotari** attended a one-room school and spent summers on a forest-fire lookout tower. He's a retired math professor and has published poems in numerous literary journals, including *Crazyhorse*, *Pleiades*, and the *American Journal of Poetry*, and in three collections. A fourth collection is forthcoming.

**Aylah Ireland** is a conceptual artist, photographer, and curator. She received her MFA from the University of Maine in 2020 and a BA in Art from UMA in 2017. Aylah was awarded the 2020-2021 Dick Higgins Fellowship to aid in her Ph.D. research. She has received several intermedia grants from the University of Maine, and curated the UMA Alumni Art Exhibition in 2019 at the Harlow Gallery in Hallowell, Maine. Aylah has exhibited in solo shows and group art shows throughout central Maine and has been a guest speaker and artist mentor at UMA.

**Brian L. Jacobs** resides with his husband in California, has been teaching English thirty years, and is working on his PhD. Brian was the assistant to Poet Allen Ginsberg while earning his MFA. During that time he walked halfway around the world while on a peace pilgrimage. Brian is also a three-time Fulbright Scholar, a NEH grant recipient, and renewed poet.

**Jasmine Kapadia** is an Asian-American teen from the Bay Area. She has work featured or forthcoming in *Same Faces, The Daphne Review, Malala Fund's Assembly, Cathartic Youth Lit, Potted Purple Mag*, and *The Rising Phoenix Review*, among others. Find her on Instagram: @jazzymoons.

**Nicole F Kimball** is a twenty-three-year-old Jewish mother, poet, and musician from SLC, UT. She holds an A.S. in Writing Studies, and loves to express herself through words. Her works have most recently been accepted into *Bear Creek Gazette, Trouvaille Review, Book of Matches*, and *The Hearth*, as well as being a featured writer in *THE POET Magazine*.

**Kate Koenig** is a queer writer and photographer living in Houston, TX. She is a current Creative Writing MFA candidate at The New School and earned her BA in English and History at the University of Pittsburgh. Her work has previously been published in *Gulf Stream Literary Magazine, Three Rivers Review, La Piccioletta Barca*, and *Vita Brevis Press*. On most days, you can find her watching dog videos online when she's supposed to be writing. Find her on Twitter here: twitter.com/KateK_Writing.

**Susan Landgraf** was awarded an Academy of American Poets Laureate award in 2020. Books include *The Inspired Poet* from Two Sylvias Press (2019), *What We Bury*

*Changes the Ground,* and *Other Voices*. More than 400 poems have appeared in *Prairie Schooner, Poet Lore, Margie, Nimrod, Sunspot, The Meadow, Calyx*, and others.

**Mike MacDee** is a veterinary technician and an author of comics, books, and games, who can't seem to find time to sleep. He is always eager to pet a dog, smoke a good cigar, or share amusing stories with likeminded weirdos.

**Tracy Mann** is a contributor to the John F. Kennedy, Jr. anthology *250 Ways to Make America Better*. She has written lyrics for Grammy Award-winning albums by the Manhattan Transfer and Sarah Vaughan, and has been a scriptwriter for the children's television series *My Little Pony*. Her writing has appeared in *Adelaide Magazine, Earth Island,* and the *Sarah Lawrence Writing Institute Journal*. She is currently at work on a memoir about Brazil.

**Alan P. Marks** received his MA in Creative Writing from the University of Maine (Stephen King's alma mater) in 1998, and then never left. He has spent the last twenty-three years there as an instructor of writing and literature (teaching a course on Stephen King among other unusual topics such as vampires, monsters, and the apocalypse). A later-in-life emerging writer, he had his first short story publication earlier this year in *Carcosa Magazine.*

Born in Paris, **Lilianne Milgrom** grew up in Australia and now resides in the United States. She is an multimedia artist, author and published writer on the arts. She is the recipient of multiple awards and residencies. Her artwork can be found in both private and institutional collections around the world.

**Taylor Moon**, Class of 22, is a junior from South Korea who attends the Chapin School in New York. Taylor has studied art at TASIS International School in Switzerland, studied with Sheery Camhy at the Arts Student League of New York and the Ashcan Studio in New York.

**francxs gufan nan** is thirty and an emerging poet currently living in Sunnyvale, CA. Recently, Ada Limón selected their *balding haibun* as the winner of the inaugural Pigeon Pages NYC 2020 Poetry Contest. They also won second place in Artblog's 2019 Music Writing Challenge. Their favorite of their five tattoos is a red topographic map of a mountain across their left acromion, or shoulder top.

**Peter Newall** was born in Sydney, Australia, where he worked as a road-mender, in a navy dockyard and as a lawyer, but later lived in Kyoto, Japan, where he sang for a popular local blues band, and now in Odessa, Ukraine. He has been published in England, Hong Kong, and the USA; his story "The Chinese General" won the 2021 New Millennium Writings Fiction Award.

**Julie Noble** is from the northwest of England but has lived in Bolivia for over twenty years, where she works with young offenders. She writes regularly about the challenges and delights of life in Bolivia. She is currently studying for an MA in Creative Writing and, apart from reading and writing, loves cycling.

**Sarah O. Oso** is a Nigerian-American writer, poet, and storyteller. A first-generation immigrant and proud Atlanta young person, she commits to honoring the human experience through highlighting the importance of spoken and written expression. Numerous local readings and art events, including the annual AJC Decatur Book Festival, Poetry at Tech, and 2019 Agnes Scott Writers' Festival have featured Oso's work, and her poetry has been Pushcart Prize nominated. Currently her work is appearing in *New Ohio Review*, *Rigorous*, and *Helen Literary Magazine*, among others.

**Ainhoa Palacios** was born in Lima, Peru, and moved to the US at the age of six. She grew up in Florida with her mother and sister, as well as her grandmother, who occasionally visited during summers. She graduated from the University of South Florida with a B.A. in journalism, but soon after remembered it was a different kind of storytelling she loved. Since then, she has completed a novel and countless short stories, one of which was recently long-listed in Fish Publishing's Short Memoir contest. Ainhoa lives in Shenzhen, China with her dog Mambo.

**KC Pedersen**'s writing appears in *Sou'wester, Emry's Journal, Hunger Mountain, Weber Journal, Superstition Review, Eclectica, Under the Sun, Juked, Still Point Arts Journal, PANK, Cleaver, New World Writing, Mslexia Magazine* and elsewhere, and includes nominations for Pushcarts, Best American Essays, and other awards. *Getting a Life-Coming of Age with Killers* was selected as Notable for Best American Essays 2018. Additional writing can be found at www.kiriepedersen.com.

**Claudia Putnam** has prose in *Confrontation, phoebe, Cimarron Review*, and elsewhere. She has received residency support from Phillips Exeter Academy, Kimmel Harding Nelson, and Ragdale. Her poems appear in dozens of journals, including *Rattle, Spillway, Literary Accents, Tar River*, and *Poetry East*. She lives in Western Colorado, where she is a craniosacral therapist. More info: claudiaputnam.com.

**Alfredo Quarto** is an environmental activist and poet. He's been published in numerous poetry publications including: *Poetry Seattle, Catalyst, Raindance Journal, Piedmont Review, Haiku Zashi Zo, Paperbag Poems, Seattle Arts, Spindrift, Arts Focus, Arnazella, Dan River Anthology, Amelia, Americas Review, Vox, Middle House Review, The Closed Eye Open*, and *Tidepools*. He has also had articles published in *The Guardian, Cultural Survival Quarterly, Earth Island Journal, E-Magazine, Wild Earth, Bird Conservation, Tokyo Journal* and *Biodiversity Magazine*.

Australian by birth and Montenegrin origin, **Pavle Radonic's** eight years of living in southeast Asia provided unexpected stimulus. Previous work has appeared in a range of literary journals and magazines, including *Ambit, Panoply, Citron Review, The Blue Nib, Ginosko,* and *New World Writing*.

**Lisa Rigge** has been involved with photography since the early 1980s. Her schooling includes two years at the MIT B & W Photography Lab in Cambridge, MA, courses at Chabot Community College in Hayward, CA, and workshops through the University of California, Santa Cruz and Santa Fe Photographic Workshops, New Mexico. She has studied with many nationally known photographers, including Kate Jordahl, Al Weber, Holly Roberts, Kathleen Carr, Mark Citret, and Debra Fleming Caffrey.

**Jessica Ripka** is a writer, audio producer and musician based in Los Angeles. A Tin House Fellow and graduate of the Transom Story Workshop, her writing has appeared in *Hippocampus*, *Pithead Chapel*, *Pidgeonholes* and *Eclectica Magazine*.

**Paul Rousseau** is a semiretired physician and writer published or forthcoming in *The Healing Muse, Blood and Thunder, Intima, The Human Touch, Please See Me, Months To Years, Sleet, The Examined Life, Burningword, Cleaning Up Glitter, The Centifictionist, Dr. T. J. Eckleburg Review, Another Chicago Magazine, Tendon*, and others. Lover of dogs.

Originally from Nevada, BARD (**Barbara Ayala Rugg Diehl**) currently works and lives in Massachusetts. She brings her diverse backgrounds into her art subject matter and processes. She received her BA in Theater and English from Brandeis University and her MA in Sustainable International Development from the Heller School for Social Policy and Management. Her art has been featured in solo and group exhibits in seven states. BARD most recently completed a residency with the Cordial Eye Gallery, exploring how joy is formed and shaped by the senses.

Beyond kindness, being queer, and reserved by nature, **Muhammad Saleem** possesses an obsession for recording his experiences and dreams, and a predilection for stories that incorporate elements of romance, slice of life, and fantasy. Currently, he is doing a Masters in Women and Gender Studies.

**Mary Senter** writes in a cabin in the woods on the shores of Puget Sound. She earned certificates in literary fiction writing from the University of Washington and an MA in strategic communication from WSU. Her work can be found in *Ponder Review, Cleaver, SHARK REEF*, and elsewhere. She is the graphic designer for *Crab Creek Review*. Visit her at www.marysenter.com.

**Vernon Shipway** is an illustrator and writer based in New England, with interests in printmaking, bookmaking, and storytelling.

**Dave Sims** makes art and music in the old mountains of Pennsylvania. His traditional and digital paintings and comix appear in dozens of tangible and virtual publications and exhibits, while his totem carvings continue to catch the eyes of many strangers and his songs still leave listeners shaking their heads in disbelief. Experience more at www.tincansims.com.

**Drew Smith** is a PhD molecular biologist and long-distance hiker. As a scientist, he developed first-in-class rapid tests for diagnosing infectious diseases. As a hiker, he completed the Colorado Trail, the Arizona Trail, and most of the Pacific Crest Trail. He has been published in *Aeon, Undark, New Scientist, Trail Groove* and *BackpackingLight*.

**Jackie Ta** is a twenty-three-year-old Vietnamese artist working in the US. Ta is currently pursuing an MFA degree in Painting at Clemson University. She has been exhibiting throughout the United States, and took an internship at Josephine Sculpture Park in Frankfort, Kentucky. Having a chance to stay inside more, she created a series of mini paintings of mundane still lives to act as memory-keepers.

They keep her calm and help her react to the beautiful surroundings that have always been there, but which can be difficult to notice.

**Reg Taylor** is a South Australian writer whose stories, often based in the River Murray area, published in a number of print and online venues within Australia and overseas.

**Charisse J. Tubianosa** was born in Manila, Philippines where she started an MA in creative writing, but ended up getting degrees in economics instead. She currently resides in Barcelona, Spain. Her stories tackle themes related to identity, race and the immigrant experience. She's completing a collection of stories on being a Filipina woman in her country and beyond its borders. She was selected to join the 2021 Voices of Our Nation (VONA) Summer Workshop, has a story published with *Spanglishvoces,* and another forthcoming with *Litbreak Magazine.*

**Pamela Viggiani** is a mixed-media artist and art educator living in Canandaigua, NY. Her art has been featured in *Small Works, Light Space & Time Online Art Gallery, Another Chicago Magazine*, and *Press Pause Press.* Her works are manifestations of ambiguity. She produces visual interpretations of particular ideas or concepts in order to explore the relationship between word and meaning. While reflecting the world back to the viewer, Pamela gives room for alternative reactions to each piece of artwork, revealing hidden realities and challenging our own entrenched ways of thinking.

**Lyndsey Kelly Weiner** is a graduate of Stonecoast MFA and teaches writing at Syracuse University. She blogs at haikuveg.com.

**Jeanne Wilkinson** is a writer, artist, and art professor sharing time between Brooklyn, NY, and Madison, WI. Her essays have been featured on WNYC's Leonard Lopate Show and NPR's *Living on Earth.* Her fiction has appeared in *Columbia Journal* and *Digging Through the Fat*, and chapters from her memoir *1969: My Year with a San Francisco Drug Dealer* have been published by *Raven's Perch, New Millennium Writings, The Write Launch*, and *Metafore.* Her short experimental films have been screened at BAM and the Greenpoint and NYC Indie Film Festivals, and a video installation was shown at the 13th St. Repertory Theater in Manhattan.

**Amanda Woodard** is a freelance poet, essayist and ghostwriter, and an MFA candidate at Antioch University. She studied social science and journalism at the University of North Texas and attended writing workshops at the Mayborn Literary Nonfiction Conference and Writing Workshops Dallas. Her work has been performed in Oral Fixation and published in *Ten Spurs, eris & eros, Cathexis Northwest Press* and *Button Eye Review.*

# WRITING A NEW WORLD

*Sunspot Literary Journal* believes in the power of the written word. Fiction, nonfiction, poetry and art speak truth to power with the power inherent in all human beings. Our mission is to amplify every voice. Four digital quarterly editions are produced per year, along with one print volume.

## SUPPORT *SUNSPOT LIT*

Today more than ever, literary journals are forces of change in the world. *Sunspot Lit* is funded entirely through private means. Every donation, even ones as small as a dollar, makes a difference. Please take a moment to drop a few bucks into the *Sunspot* magnetic field flux.

A PayPal link on the website makes it easy to send a tip, donate enough to publish the next digital edition, or go supernova and fund the next print edition. Please visit https://sunspotlit.com/support for details.

## ADVERTISE IN *SUNSPOT*

Classified ads are available in quarterly digital editions and special editions. Spread the word about your writing and arts contests, residency programs, awards, workshops, and more. All classified ads are also posted on the website's classified page. Ad rate: $150 for up to 25 words; $5 for each additional word.

Print ads are available for the annual edition. All ads are black and white. A full page is $850, a half page is $450, and a quarter page is $295. Buy two ads of the same size for the same issue or for two sequential issues to receive a 10% discount. Set up three or more ads and receive a 15% discount.

*Sunspot's* groovy graphic designer can set up your ad to your specifications. Flat rate of $325, and the design is yours to use multiple times in *Sunspot* or any other magazine.

SUNSPOT LITERARY JOURNAL

WRITING A NEW WORLD

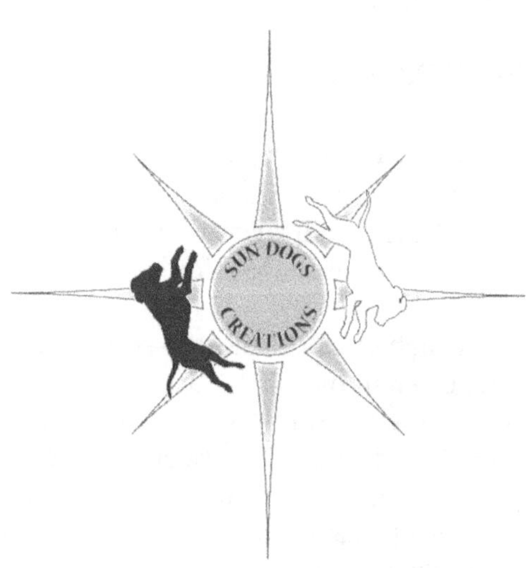


SUN DOGS CREATIONS

CHANGING THE WORLD ONE BOOK AT A TIME

www.ingramcontent.com/pod-product-compliance
Lightning Source LLC
Chambersburg PA
CBHW071240190726
48292CB00007B/2367

* 9 7 8 1 9 5 1 3 8 9 1 3 0 *